Memoir of Mariposa Avenue

Bix B. Whitcomb

Memoir of Mariposa Avenue

Twenty-Three-Oh-Seven Publishing
Pebble Beach, CA

This is a work of creative nonfiction. While memory can be selective, inaccurate, or revisionist, the events and persons described, and the conversations that have been reconstructed herein, are true and faithful to the best of my recollection. Some names have been changed to protect the privacy of those still living. Others have given their permission for their names to be used.

This story is based on reality,
but some events and characters
have been fictionalized.

First trade paperback edition December 2009
Cover and text design by Patricia Hamilton
Manufactured in the United States of America

ISBN: 978-0-615-31045-9

Printed in U.S.A.

For James Howard Beattie

CONTENTS

Photo by Mike Stempe

"A home is not a mere transient shelter: its essence lies in the personalities of the people who live in it."
H. L. Mencken

1
A Long-Lost Friend

Jim and I flopped down onto the rain-wet soil and laughed at the sky.

We'd come looking for our old house, only to find it gone. First we drove up and down the street, bewildered. We even parked the car, got out and scanned the street for signs to remind us how life had been those two years we lived together back when love was free and gas was twenty-five cents a gallon. Soon we spotted something familiar—the two big redwoods that guarded our front porch like the portals to Narnia—but behind the trees, only open space where the house had been. In a way, we weren't too surprised. The place had always been like that. It had a quality of invisibility that made visitors miss the driveway more often than not.

Passing between the trees, we stepped onto the property. Only a scattering of cinders remained to mark the footprint of our old home that had been the scene of so many magical encounters. Had someone torched the house for sport? Or maybe the fire department burned it to the ground as a training exercise to remove a public blight? We could only speculate.

We walked the floor plan from room to imaginary room, remembering: Here, the back porch that served as our front entrance; there, the Wedgwood stove we sat beside with friends, warming our mitts and telling tall tales; next to the kitchen, the hammock room; then, the orange and gold bathroom with its claw foot tub where Jim once took a bubble bath with my girlfriend, Janie; now, the bedroom where we could almost hear the moans of passion; and the living room where we set up the amps and played music, the same room where Jim and Sue got it on one night, and blue sparks of static electricity flew between their nipples and lit up the room.

After some minutes of reminiscing, Jim and I got quiet and breathed in the cool moist air while raindrops plopped on our heads, just as they had dropped on my long blond mane on the solitary night of Tomatoes in the Dark so long ago.

As we lay there I was sure we were both thinking the same thoughts: Who in their right mind would ever believe, let alone imagine, all the scenes that played out behind our doors? All the angst of old was gone. In its place, only gratitude flowing from my core to my extremities like warmth from a mug of hot cocoa on a winter's day; only memories of laughter, bliss and passion among friends and lovers, times that seemed timeless and therefore eternal even as I lay in the mud with Jim that New Year's Day, 1991.

A flood of sensory memories came to me wordlessly at first; then, the words started to flow like a tone poem, the one that I knew would begin my story:

> *Twenty-three-oh-seven Mariposa Avenue is a scent of bay leaf tea simmering in a pot, a perfume of sandalwood and frangipani, the smell of newly tilled soil, the crunch of almonds and brown rice cooked al dente. She is the sound of love being made at all hours of the day, of massage oil being smoothed on, of Moody Blues singing "Tuesday Afternoon" on a Tuesday afternoon. At 2307 Mariposa Avenue, I greeted myself coming in the back door like a long lost friend.*

2
Finding Mariposa

On a midday Monday in early August, the streets and sidewalks of downtown Chico were deserted. Heat shimmered above the asphalt in wiggly mirage lines, giving the illusion that I was pedaling my bicycle through a lagoon of boiling water.

I had to be out of my mind to be out in this heat. But I had my urgent reasons. I was badly in need of a place to live, cheap, and soon. Living in my Step Van had been a failed experiment. Cops hassled me daily. (That's why I was riding my bike on this particular day.) Then came the interlude in Carol's apartment, but that lasted only two weeks, and now I was on the street again. I missed the camaraderie of the apartments where Jim and I lived before the university razed the building for a parking lot. I was lonely and bored and horny, and I needed a hot shower.

Living in the van did have one important advantage: As long as I had no address, the Selective Service System couldn't catch up with me; but, even more important than my immediate problems, I was seeking a long-needed sanctuary.

NO WAY WAS I GOING to let anyone get the jump on me in Chico's annual housing war. With students returning to town, the classified ads hot off the press were my best offense. Whoever got to the newspaper office first had the edge in house-hunting.

Rounding the corner of First Street onto Broadway, I glanced up at the newfangled dot matrix display on top of the bank at Second and Broadway. It read a hundred and thirteen degrees at one o'clock. Despite the heat, I was feeling tolerably cool in my white undershirt and paisley drawstring pants. The trick in this heat was to slow down. I was running late, but I wasn't about to pour on the coals to get to the office of the Enterprise Record in time to get the newspaper as it came off the press.

Having arrived late on this day in August, I was resigned to the dregs, but the weather was in my favor. Everyone must have been indoors, hanging out by their swamp coolers.

When I walked into the office, Susan, the receptionist, looked up from her typing. Recognizing me, she picked up a newspaper from her desk and set it on the counter to her right. "You're late, but you're the first one here," she said, and went back to work.

"Heat slowed me down." I picked up the paper, still warm from the press. I held the paper to my cheek and moaned with pleasure. "This reminds me of the scene in Our Town when Emily talks about all the good things in life; clean, warm sheets being one of the good things."

I thought Susan would be impressed with my literary savvy as well as my sensuality, but Susan kept typing.

"Thank you, beautiful Susan," I crooned. On the way to the door, I ditched all but the classified ads in a bin.

One more try with Susan, and then I'd better start dialing. On the way out the door, I spun on a heel. "Do let me know if you ever leave your husband, or you need a little diversion, will you?"

Susan concentrated a little harder on her typing.

Out on the blazing sidewalk, the sun, at perpendicular, offered no shade. I took up my battle station at the freestanding pay phone and started to peruse the ads. Cradling the receiver on my shoulder, I pretended to be having a conversation while looking through the ads, deciding which one to call first. Still, I shouldn't waste time. While I'm perusing the ads, papers are being delivered; dimes are coming out of pockets, phone receivers being lifted.

The first several housing ads rang busy. Damn.

Then a guy came out of the E-R office and stood on the sidewalk, ads in hand, staring at me. At some point, cradling the phone on my shoulder and reading the ads at the same time had become too awkward, so I gave up the pretense of talking on the phone, and let the receiver dangle while I searched the ads. Soon the young man approached, asking, "Are you going to use the phone?"

"Yes," I said, and went back to perusing the ads. "Do you think I could use the phone while you'rereading?" he enquired.

"No," I said.

We stared at each other.

"I need to use the phone," he pleaded.

"Are you looking for a place to live?" I asked.

"Yes."

"Well, tough shit then. So am I."

"Are you using the phone?"

"Not right now, but I will be as soon as you get out of my face and leave me in peace to read the want ads."

"How about letting me use it while you check the ads?"

"Are you kidding, pal? The way things are in this town in August?"

We stared at each other some more. I didn't have time for this shit.

I sized him up: Wimpy looking. Assuming a martial posture, and moving within an inch of his face, I said, "Look, College Boy, you have exactly two choices: Physically remove me from this booth, or go find another phone somewhere else."

He looked up and down my athletic frame. (Eight years of competitive swimming hadn't been for nothing.) He must have decided caution was the better part of valor, because he went and stood by the wall and waited. Before long, to my relief, he disappeared.

At 1:10, I started dialing from where I'd left off, and got more busy signals. Okay, I bet no one else was starting from the bottom, so that's what I did. "House on acreage" and a phone number was all the third ad from the bottom said.

A single dwelling and good soil to grow a garden: That was my dream: I was gonna "live off the fat o' the lan' " like the Joads in Steinbeck's *Grapes of Wrath*.

The number rang fourteen times with no answer, so I hung up and tried the next two ads up the list. Busy. Damn, I'm thinking, I hope no one calls about the house with acreage, so I called again several times to hear a busy signal. I kept dialing, hanging up, and dialing again until the phone started ringing, but no one answered, so I hung on, deciding not to risk letting someone else's call go through.

I started counting rings. Twenty-six rings reminded me of how many rings it had taken, eight years before, for my father to answer the phone in the middle of the night. Our old neighbor in Van Nuys was calling to tell my father that his eldest son and my eldest brother, Jon, had been murdered. He was twenty years old. She had seen it on the news that evening.

Before the phone had started ringing on that December night

in 1962, I had a prescient dream in which I witnessed my brother Jon being murdered with his own gun. Startled awake, I knew something terribly wrong had happened. Then the phone started ringing.

I lay in my room, eyes on wide alert, pulse pounding, counting rings and wondering what was wrong. After 26 times, the ringing stopped. Then it started up again. After another twenty rings, I could hear the muffled voice of my father, but I couldn't make out the words. The next day, I asked what the call was about but I was stonewalled.

Another image from that time flickered across my memory screen. I am in the living room in Lafayette. My father and stepmother are in the kitchen on New Year's Eve, dressed for a party. From muffled snippets, I can overhear my father asking his wife, "Is it appropriate for us to go to a party at a time like this?"

She raised her voice. "Dead is dead! He's going to stay dead, so what difference does it make?" At that point, I still didn't know for sure who "he" was, but I had my suspicions. The next day, when I was home alone, Western Union called and dictated the message from a Marine officer in San Diego. I didn't dare confront my father with the facts, so I waited. Several days after the phone call in the middle of the night, and some days after the call from Western Union, my father got around to telling me my older brother Jon had died.

When I asked my father why he had taken so long to tell me, he said, "I was in shock." These memories passed through my mind like a hot August breeze as I continued letting the phone ring in front of the newspaper office. While I was standing there, a scruffy looking guy in a faded red and white '56 De Soto parked at the curb and got out. Doubtless, he would be looking for a place to live, too. He looked familiar, but I couldn't place him. He went into the E.R. office, presumably to pick up the classifieds.

I put down the phone, waited thirty seconds, and dialed again. Busy. Damn!

Just then, the guy came back out. He was about to get into his car, but I couldn't let him get away without finding out how I knew him. I was reluctant to leave my post, but College Boy was nowhere in sight, so I hung up and dashed over to the car before the driver got in. Approaching him, I still couldn't place him, but I felt an inexplicable rush of love toward him. I got his attention with a "Hey you!" I wrapped my arms around him, and gave him the kind of full body hug that was popular in the free love era.

Mike S. had been my college roommate in our sophomore year at Chico State. I hadn't seen him in four years. Just back from Vietnam, his body language said he wasn't ready for a longhaired hippie stranger on the street to walk up and put the wraps on him. It took a few minutes of conversation for us to sort out how we knew each other. He said he was looking for a place to live with his girlfriend.

"I hope you don't get the house I'm looking for, or we'll be roommates again!" I chided. He said it was okay; he thought he had found a place already. He was just picking up the ads in case that deal fell through. He told me where to find him, and that was the beginning, or continuation, of a friendship that continues to this day.

Our friendship wasn't the only thing that was fateful about running into Mike again. Back at the phone booth, after several rings, I got an answer. If it hadn't been for Mike's interruption, the timing of the call might not have gone off as well as it did.

When Mrs. Whitlow answered, she sounded irritated. Nonetheless, in my best phone manner, I said, “Hello, my name is Bix Whitcomb, and I’m responding to the ad in the paper about a house with acreage. I’d very much like to rent such a place because I want to grow a garden. Is the place still available?”

“The phone has been ringing off the hook ever since I put the ad in the paper yesterday!”

“Well, you’ve had a good response then. Has the place been rented?”

“No. Everyone who calls, as soon as I answer the phone, they shout, ‘I’ll take it!’ without even giving their name. Finally, I quit answering the phone. Then I took it off the hook for a while. Just when I put it back on the hook, it rang again, and it was you. You are the first one to give your name and ask politely about the place. You can have it, but you’d better go take a look first, and call me back.”

“Why is that?”

“You’ll see what I mean. Just go take a look, and call me back. The place is yours if you want it.”

It couldn’t be this easy. There had to be a catch. A house with acreage? I couldn’t possibly afford it.

“How much is the rent, please, Mrs. Whitlow?”

“Don’t worry about that. Just go take a look, and get back to me.”

“Pardon me, I heard you say to go take a look, and I’ll do that gladly, but are we at least in the same ballpark as far as rent’s concerned?”

“I was going to ask $125.00, but the place needs some work. Just go take a look, and we’ll talk about it.”

“Does it have hot and cold running water?”

“Yes.”

"And a flush toilet?'

"Yes."

"Gas and electricity?"

"Yes."

"And acreage for a garden?"

"Yes."

"And it's a house, not an apartment?"

"Yes, but it only has one bedroom."

This was too good to be true. "Please hold! Don't go away!" I said, and ran in the E-R office to borrow a pen from Susan, but she was too busy to find me some notepaper. Back at the phone, I cradled the phone on one shoulder and took down the address, 2307 Mariposa Avenue, on the back of my hand, hoping I wouldn't sweat it off before I could write it down somewhere.

"What if someone else calls in the meantime?" I asked.

"Don't worry. The place is yours if you want it, but go look first."

That phone call to Mrs. Whitlow was to change my life forever, but I didn't know that as I pedaled back to my home-on-wheels parked on Laburnum next to Bidwell Park.

Later in the afternoon, when the temperature dropped below 95, I would check out the property.

Meanwhile, I pedaled slowly to conserve energy, and tried not to get my hopes too high.

Having a house with land would mean a lot to me. Inviting Janie to live with me was a dearly held hope. I hardly knew her, really, other than our one encounter a week earlier, but she was fetching, and I could dream at least.

Was I fooling myself? Why, with a college degree in my hip pocket, had I cast adrift since graduating a year earlier? Prior to graduation, my life had been all about goals and structure: Getting the grades to go to college, improving my times in swimming, setting records, studying for a year in Europe, graduating with honors. Then I turned down two offers of full-ride assistantships to work on my doctorate. I was fed up with the Ivory Tower. My present course was into uncharted waters.

Pedaling past the flagpole in the town plaza, I wondered, *what am I going to do with my life?* I pictured myself as a flagpole sitter, a popular gimmick of the day, something people did to try to get into the Guinness Book of Records. From my lofty point of view, I could see into the future. I could see myself balancing one-footed on the ball atop the flagpole, ready to do an intentional off-balance maneuver. Then with a sudden burst of insight, I exclaimed out loud, "I'm stepping off the 100 foot pole!"

Perhaps I would crash and burn, but not before knowing the freedom and sensation of flying. And what if I did crash? Part of me didn't want to live anyway. "Or maybe," I thought, "I'll land softly with my feet on the ground and walk away."

What if I don't get the house? Fear seized my solar plexus, and it went into spasm. Negative thoughts of failure, loneliness, and jail or being drafted flooded my imagination. Some lines from a Bob Dylan song came to mind, and I sang aloud:

How does it feel,
to be on your own,
with no direction home,
a complete unknown?

Negative thoughts be damned, I thought. Don't worry. What the hell, you're twenty-four years old and you've got the world by the balls! Gonna get me a house, make a lotta love, smoke a bunch of dope, drop acid, grow a garden. Ain't gonna worry 'bout nothin'!

Back at the van around 2:00, the heat had me thinking maybe I'd forget about looking at the house that day, but when I thought over the events of the past month, getting situated in a house jumped back to first priority. I wanted to drive out to the house right away, but once again fearing John Law, I figured I'd better ride my bike once the day started to cool down.

WITH A COUPLE OF HOURS to kill before the temperature dropped into the nineties, I lay on the foam mattress in the van and thought about the events of the past month leading up to the phone call to Mrs. Whitlow.

What an intensely messy, chaotic, delightful and scary month it had been!

First came the forced move out of the apartment. Jim decided to buy a van to live in until winter, and I followed suit. While Jim flew under the radar in his little white '65 Dodge van, my big old bread truck shouted, "Hippie!" Cops were stopping me daily. John Law and I were actually getting acquainted on a first name basis, and I had to hide my stash under a rock in Bidwell Park.

The novelty of the van had worn off quickly. By night, Jim and I worked in the nut processing plant. By day, we camped out at various locations along the creek that ran out of the foothills, through Bidwell Park and town and the college campus, and on out to the Sacramento River; but, Jim and I hardly ever saw each other, and I missed his company. I wasn't meeting any women because most weekdays the skinny dipping holes were unpopulated. Bored and lonely, I missed the camaraderie of the Captain America house, so called because the downstairs residents had painted their several windows in a red, white and blue theme and printed "Captain America Lives Here!" in huge letters for all passersby to see. In adjacent apartments in the beautiful old Victorian on the corner of Second and Ivy, Jim and I began some of the traditions that carried over to the Mariposa house, such as an open door policy, shared meals and mutual friends visiting at all hours. Some of them later became an integral part of the Mariposa scene, including the indelibly handsome and charismatic Eugene who lived in a series of caves.

Then came the frustrating encounter with Earlene the Camper Queen and the chain of events that followed. If it hadn't been for missing Susan and meeting Earlene and Carol and the Blue Hash Pipe Incident and falling in love with Janie, the necessity of finding a place wouldn't be so urgent.

SUSAN

Susan was a bright and beautiful former cheerleader from New Jersey. I met her in the natural foods store. When I lived in the Captain America house, we had a loose arrangement. I didn't know where she lived, and neither of us had a phone or a car. Whenever she showed up, it was beautiful. We ate, listened to music, talked for hours, and sometimes we made love and snuggled together all night. Then she'd be gone. When I moved into the van, we lost contact. I missed her sweetness. Being with her brought welcome though temporary relief from the often intense loneliness I'd felt since my college sweetheart Em (not her real name) had jilted me a year and a half before.

Well, if there weren't any women around, at least I could hook up with Jim for a swim. One day he agreed to meet me at the end of the Upper Park road.

EARLENE THE CAMPER QUEEN

I waited, and he didn't show up. Thinking maybe he'd gone ahead, I started up the trail. Parked just past the end of the road was a pickup with a camper on it. The back end was open, and inside sat a pretty young blonde who invited me to climb in with her. Like a fool, I told her I was supposed to meet a friend at the swimming hole, and I proceeded along the trail. Not finding Jim, I swam anyway. By the time I went back, hotly anticipating a tryst with the flirtatious camper queen, the back of the camper was shut and lovemaking noises were coming from inside.

That night at work, Jim told me he'd come along behind me and met Earlene.

Damn.

PLAN B

That episode got me pretty revved up. I was fair game for any huntress on safari! Walking the student housing area on First Street near campus, I met a nice young coed named Carol on the sidewalk. She invited me upstairs, and I stayed for two weeks. I told her it wasn't love, and she was okay with that, at least at first. Not only were certain obvious needs met, but this arrangement got me off the street (and off the radar of the local police).

THE BLUE HASH PIPE INCIDENT

At Carol's, I thought I was safe from the cops, but not quite.

We decided to have a party one night. I invited Jim and the aforementioned Eugene, aka Gene or Geno, whom I had met in Modern Dance class. In turn Gene invited his girlfriend, Tina, and Jim invited Earlene. During the party, I decided to go out to the Step Van to change into warmer clothing. Fearing cops, I hid an ounce of marijuana in a baggie in my underwear, figuring a cop wouldn't frisk me there. Unfortunately, a blue glass hash pipe rested on the dash. Just as I was thinking about what I'd do if a cop arrived, one did.

In the blinding lights of the cop car I rocked nervously from one foot to the other as the cop questioned me. "Are you sure you haven't been drinking?" he asked. "You seem a little woozy."

I took the hint. It was okay to be drunk but not stoned. "Oh, yesssh, offisher, I did have shum wine at zzzhe party there in Carol'ssh housh, but I'm going right back inshide. I'm not driving anywhere. I'm shtaying here tonight. [Hiccup.] Would you care to come in for a drink, offisher?"

He let me off with that explanation, but I panicked. In the dark back yard of Carol's house, I buried the beautiful blue hash pipe handcrafted by Billy B. in Vacaville State Correctional Facility. (Imagine smuggling a hash pipe out of prison, but that's what a prison groupie named Laura did! Upon my brother's release from prison, he lived with her; she gave him the pipe, and he passed it on to me. That pipe had an outlaw aura that appealed to the rebel in me.)

Thanks to Earlene

After almost getting busted and burying the blue hash pipe, I went inside and found Earlene and told her what had happened. I held out my hand to show her I was still trembling. "Look. I'm so shaky! I need to take the edge off my nerves." I admit I exaggerated the tremor, for sympathy.

"Let's get you calmed down," she said. That's when Earlene took me out to her camper.

It was sweet and friendly, nurturing and matter of fact. Earlene got me nice and calmed down. The way things were going, I couldn't stay with Carol much longer; yet, I didn't want to be back on the street either, so I hung with Carol a while longer.

The next day I met Janie.

Janie

Janie and I first met at the bottom of the stairs leading up to Carol's place. (The house was divided into two apartments, upstairs and basement.) I had seen Janie coming and going a few times. She was petite and exotic, almost aboriginal in the way that extremely good looking brown-skinned, black-haired women can be, with high cheekbones, slightly flat nose, luscious lips, and a trim figure. Her thick lustrous black hair flowed down her back to her thighs. Her olive eyes had a sort of lavender halo around the irises. She had a fetching way of tilting her head back with her mouth slightly open and a look of wonder in her eyes when I spoke to her.

Later I found out she had been getting it on with the guy downstairs. That's why, on the day we met, she declined my invitation to come up and see me sometime, but one day he wasn't home and she knocked on Carol's door. Carol was at work, but Jim and Gene, Gene's Tina, and I were hanging out when Janie knocked. When Janie came in, Jim and Gene and I all tried to act nonchalant, but we couldn't keep our eyes off her, and she knew it. She always recognized and enjoyed the attention of men.

Jim and Gene and I were all jockeying for attention but trying to be cool about it. Gene invited her to sit on the floor next to him, but I said, "Wouldn't you prefer a seat?"

There were no empty chairs. She looked around doubtfully, and asked, "Where?"

"Right here," I said, patting my lap. I was sitting in Carol's rocking chair.

"Well, I don't know…." Looking back and forth at her choice of handsome young men, she bit one half of her lower lip the way she always did when she was making a decision. "….I guess I *would* like a chair better," she said in a playful tone.

This was only the second time we'd met. She came over, sat in my lap, and draped an arm around my neck. She sat and I rocked. She squirmed a little, getting cozy, but not being too obvious about it. Breathing in her delicious scent, my nostrils flared. My scalp tightened. My toes curled. I tingled all over. Pressure built up inside me, and it was all I could do to keep the volcano from exploding!

Tina had to leave for some reason. That precipitated Gene, Tina and Jim getting up to go, the way people do when no one wants to be the last to leave. Janie stayed in my lap. Gene trailed behind Tina till she was out the door. I could see his wheels working. Tina had to be somewhere; he didn't. Gene stopped and turned around. "You can come with us, you know," he said to her, not to me.

Janie bit her lower lip again, looked at me, and snuggled closer. "I'll stay," she said.

What happened next was purely non-verbal. We shifted from the chair to the floor, but soon we were on top of Carol's white dotted Swiss bedspread. Thoughts of Carol quickly disappeared. Janie was everything I'd ever fantasized about in a woman. She was mature beyond her years. She was eyesight to the blind. She was a powerful narcotic, and I was hooked. All I had ever wanted to learn about womankind, she taught me that afternoon. She was my ticket to adulthood. She brought out the primal scream in me and soothed it to a whimper. Love was an atomic explosion that vaporized my loneliness. No one could hold a candle to the free, playful, sensuous and expert Janie. Before the afternoon was over, she owned me, body and soul.

From that day forward, she was my own personal Medusa: All I had to do was look at her and I got hard. What if the attraction was purely hormonal? If so, bring it on! No more holding back as I had done with Em for four years. No more "saving ourselves for each other until we graduate and get married." Seize the day! Love the one you're with!

That night when Carol came home, I made a not-so-clever excuse about being tired and having a headache. Could we get it on in the morning? We did, but I just wasn't into it. At this point I'd had sex with Earlene, Janie, and Carol—all in a forty-eight hour period—but Janie had spoiled me for any other woman. I had been making some halfhearted attempts at finding my own place, but, after making love with Janie, all I could think about was how soon I could find a place and invite her to live with me. As well, I felt guilty living on Carol's good graces, taking from her but not giving anything back. Besides that, I was wondering if she had noticed the trace of a stain on her bedspread even after I'd run it through the laundry twice.

I told Carol about Janie. Reminding her that my stay with her wasn't about love didn't seem to help matters. She clammed up and I could tell it was time to leave. I made a graceful exit before getting booted out. A couple of days after making love with Janie, I was back on the street. I never saw Carol again, nor Earlene for that matter.

BACK IN THE VAN AGAIN

The events of the last month had all brought me to this point of urgency to find a house. The first time around, living in the van had gotten old fast; I was sure it was going to be even less fun this time. Between loneliness, boredom, inconvenience, and the threat of jail, the street was no longer an option. Also, I couldn't stop thinking about making a nest for Janie and me. That's why, as soon as I left Carol, I started going to the *Enterprise Record* every day.

The phone call to Mrs. Whitlow changed my life forever, but lying there in the van that blistering August afternoon, I didn't know how important the call would turn out to be. I only knew that I wanted to avoid another encounter with the cops, and getting to 2307 Mariposa on my bicycle was going to be a long, hot ride.

FINDING 2307

When I reached the point where Mariposa Avenue teed off East First Avenue, I stopped and looked down Mariposa. Peering through the telescope of my circled thumb and forefinger, I saw a tree lined street, several blocks long, running past moderate tract homes that looked like their lawns had all been mowed at the same time; then, a transition zone of lesser homes at the raggedy edge of town; and funneling out the other end, a countryside of golden brown savannah that ran out to the foothills of the Sierras.

This must be my new street, but it looks a little too nice.

About halfway down the length of Mariposa, a closer look revealed a sudden and dramatic contrast between the ranch style development and a mishmash of neglected properties on the other side of the city/county line. On the city end of the street, the trees were all of the same species, uniformly spaced, planted at the same time, and still immature. By contrast, on the county end of the street, an assortment of gnarly old trees formed an irregular pattern.

This looks more like it.

At the edge of the housing tract, the sidewalk ended, and a dirt shoulder began. Crossing over the line, I left my old life behind, and entered the Twilight Zone.

FINDING 2307 WAS EASIER SAID than done. Although the house stood immediately past the city boundary, I passed the house twice coming and twice returning. Then, locking my bike to a telephone pole, I walked past the house two more times, even though the front door was only steps away from the street. Once, I even looked right at it, and said, "That couldn't be it." For one thing, there were no numerals on the house or on the mailbox. In fact, there was no mailbox. Still, how could I miss a house that sat a few paces from the road's edge?

Only by process of elimination did I guess the address. *This must be the place.*

I stepped up on the front porch and knocked. The splintered, hollow door had the consistency of cardboard, and it wagged under my knuckles. A child could put a fist though it. No one answered, but I could hear children yelling and screaming, and loud thuds. Was someone hammering nails or beating their children? If I knocked hard enough to be heard over the din, the door would surely implode, so I went around back and stood at a distance from the back of the house, hoping the occupants would spot me and come out to see why I was there.

While I waited in a spot of shade under a huge black walnut tree, the squealing and pounding continued. Crossing my arms and slowly turning all the way round, I scanned the property. It was long and skinny, a weedy tract twenty lots deep and a hundred and fifty feet wide, maybe four acres in all. A uniformly built redwood fence lined the back yards of twenty-or-so houses, further defining the city limit. The fences along the other side of the lot separated the acreage from a ragtag of houses in the county. These fences formed a broken line of standing-up, falling-down, leaning-over barriers made of redwood, pecky cedar, dilapidated basket weave and plywood patches; old, older, and oldest; each one alike only in their dissimilarity. The contrast between the two fence lines gave an impression that the acreage where I stood was a buffer zone, a place of transition. An oasis of open space, it was neither city nor country, but decidedly more rustic than town.

Momentarily, I was transported back to a montage of childhood scenes at my family's ranchette in Van Nuys: climbing walnut trees; tending our menagerie of chickens (sometimes invited to dinner), ducks, geese, pigeons; milking the cow and the goats; riding our stiff-legged donkey and our stubborn burro; harvesting honey from the beehive; eating monstrous five-napkin cheeseburgers barbequed by our father on summer days; cranking the handle on the ice cream machine; playing touch football and hide and seek in the back yard; and setting off Fourth of July fireworks on the front lawn while grandparents watched; scenes that were simple and pure and trouble free; moments of perfection before my family came undone and we scattered to the four winds.

Coming back to the present, I took in the house.

Next to the house, I'll plant my garden.

The house looked as if someone had brought it there and set it down until they decided what to do with it, but they never got around to deciding. It had no foundation save some bricks holding the floor joists a few inches off the ground. Something was wrong with the picture: By all rights such a house should have sat way back from the road in a manorial manner, like so many farm houses in Butte County. Instead, the inverse was true—a house too close to the road, with a long tail of neglected earth.

The house is maybe seventy-five years old. Paint is peeling; probably hasn't been painted in fifty years. It could be jacked up and dropped on a new foundation, but the doors and windows would no longer fit. Anyway, I'll bet the windows were painted shut fifty years ago. Roof needs to be replaced; leaks, I bet. Hard-packed dirt driveway, muddy in winter. Landscaping, non-existent, or shall we call it "sylvan"? All that trash littering the yard looks like the aftermath of a tornado.

"Funky," I said out loud. "Downright *Tobacco Road.* Not worth $125, Mrs. Whitlow, but for no rent, a bit of paint and fixing, some elbow grease, maybe we can work a deal. The right people coming and going, this place could become my very own *Sweet Thursday*, a regular Chautauqua of ne'er do wells!"

Just then, the pounding and yelling stopped. When I started walking toward the back door, I saw a boy and girl, about nine and six, come running out. The boy was clearly running the show. "Here, hold the front of your dress out! There! Right!" She followed him around the yard as he excitedly picked up rocks and dirt clods, loading them into the makeshift basket of her dress. Then they rushed back into the house, and the yelling and squealing and pounding began again.

Were any adults around?

The back door was open. Stepping up on the back porch, I stuck my head inside and raised my voice. "Hello! Anybody home?" To my right, I could see that no one was in the kitchen, nor in the room next to it, nor in the bathroom beyond. Straight ahead, the noises came from the front room. I crossed the kitchen and stuck my head into the living room.

The bare wood sub-floor was covered with rocks and dirt clods. The boy and girl were throwing rocks and dirt against the living room wall.

I stepped into the living room and looked toward the bedroom to my right and yelled, "Hellooooo! Anybody home?"

The boy and girl ignored me. Only a few feet away from me, they were recycling the clods and rocks as they bounced off the wall onto the floor, but some of the clods shattered. That explained the trip to the yard for more ammo.

Looking through the bedroom door at the other end of the living room, I could see no one else was home, and there wasn't a stick of furniture in the house. Who would leave kids to throw rocks and dirt inside the house? Or, did these kids even live here? Had the occupants already moved out, leaving the house at the mercy of neighborhood mischief-makers?

Suddenly, I flashed back to days in Van Nuys when Jon and Tim and I made mud pies to throw at passing cars. Some we loaded with rocks, not thinking how dangerous that could be. No wonder we got caught—the street in front of the house was littered with mud and rocks. Kids will be kids, I thought, but throwing rocks and dirt inside the house? *Inside MY house?*

"Hey!" I yelled. "Quit throwing rocks!"

They paid no attention. I might as well have been talking to the moon.

"Where are your mom and dad?" I said, but they still ignored me.

Something fierce and primal awoke in my core and arose in my vocal cords. "HEY! STOP THROWING THE GODDAM ROCKS!"

The boy suddenly stopped and looked shocked, as if seeing me for the first time. The girl kept squealing and throwing.

"Why are you throwing rocks and dirt in the house?"

"Because there wasn't any mud," he said matter-of-factly. "We wanted to throw mud pies, but the water's turned off."

"And where are your parents?"

"We don't have a dad. Our mom's at work," said the little girl.

"Shut up! Don't tell him anything!" the boy scolded.

"Do you live here in this house, or somewhere in the neighborhood?"

"I don't have to tell you," he said, and started to pick up another rock.

Something in me was steaming. I was channeling a drill sergeant. I yelled, "Put the goddamn rock down *now*!"

He did.

"Now tell your sister to do the same. Then tell me when your mother is coming home, because I'm renting this place when you move and I need to find out from her when you're moving. You do live here, right?"

He stared at me, but then he got his sister to stop, and told me his mother would be home soon.

"Now clean up this mess, and quit throwing rocks in *my* house!" I said. It was kind of like when you name a stray cat: you take ownership, and there's no turning back. At that moment I knew I wanted the house, dirt clods and all.

"It's not your house," he argued.

"I know, it's Mrs. Whitlow's house, but it will be mine soon, and she sent me here to take care of it for her." Fearing I might wring the little guy's neck, I spun on a heel and went out back to chill out until their mother came home. Calming down, I found a piece of cardboard and took it back inside. "Here! Clean that up, *please*!" They both stared at me.

"Haven't you ever cleaned up after yourself?" I asked. "Look!"

I knelt down and started scooping up rocks and dirt onto the cardboard. "Now you do it! Come on, you can do it! I'm not cleaning up your whole mess for you." They both got on their hands and knees and started shoving debris onto the cardboard. Oddly enough, they seemed to enjoy the work.

We got it cleaned up, the big pieces anyway. I wasn't angry anymore. "Thank you very much. I'm sorry I yelled at you, but you weren't listening. Now please don't mess this place up anymore. I'll have enough to do to make this place livable. Here, shake hands." We shook and I thanked them again, and followed them outside just as a woman drove up behind the house.

Mrs. Smith—that's what she said her name was— seemed agitated and nervous. The sum of our conversation was that she was a single mother who couldn't afford a babysitter, so she left the kids to shift for themselves while she worked as a bank teller. At some point she had stopped paying for garbage collection. That explained the trash in the yard, and the combination root cellar/well housing she had packed to the brim with trash and covered with a piece of plywood. Where she was moving I don't recall, but she said she needed to find someplace cheaper. (I didn't bother to point out that she already lived in the cheapest place in town.) She wouldn't be moving for another week or two, and she couldn't guarantee that the kids wouldn't make more messes, but she'd try. To me, Mrs. Smith didn't seem mentally well.

I decided to sleep on it. A call to Mrs. Whitlow the next day sealed the deal. I would maintain and improve the place in whatever way possible, donating the labor. She would charge me $75 a month rent, but reimburse the cost of all materials. If I got roommates, she wouldn't charge extra because I would select guys who would work on the place. We never signed an agreement.

She took no deposit. I never wrote a check for the rent, preferring to hand-deliver cash to her in Forest Ranch, thirty miles away. Presumably, this arrangement saved her money on taxes. If the rent was late, even as much as three months, she never called to ask why. Living at 2307 Mariposa Avenue, in Mrs. Whitlow's honeymoon home, was strictly an old fashioned, handshake deal.

I could move in on August 15.

MOVING DAY

Moving in consisted of nothing more than parking my van in back and transferring my toothbrush, hairbrush, razor and towel to the bathroom. Jim did the same. While we were fixing the place up, the vans served as our respective bedrooms. A few more weeks sleeping in the van was no big deal.

The overstuffed chair I had kept from the Captain America house remained in my van, tethered to the floor by a short length of chain. We kept food in Styrofoam ice chests and sat on produce crates. Granola for breakfast, sandwiches for lunch and dinner. Once we both realized mayonnaise could spoil in melted ice, causing intestinal problems, we cut out the mayo till we got a refrigerator— two refrigerators, to be exact. Styrofoam coolers would have to be good enough for a while. As long as there was hot and cold running water and a flush toilet, we were set. I had survived with fewer amenities while backpacking the John Muir Trail from one end to the other and back when I was thirteen.

Here I could park off the street and not be hassled by cops, but the hope of Janie coming to live with me withered in the face of reality. The place was such a mess, no decent woman would put up with living there. With fall and winter coming on, the need to make the place habitable was urgent. When I moved in on August

15, I hardly knew Janie anyway. All I had was the memory of one hot sexual encounter, a shred of hope, and her phone number, which I had misplaced somewhere.

Quickly it became apparent that I couldn't fix up the place enough by myself in time for winter. Gainfully employed male roommates with handyman skills would be necessary. Jim had some of these skills. Then, without consulting me, he invited Mike B. to live in the garage out back. (not to be confused with the Mike who was my old college roomie whom I ran into in front of the newspaper office.) Jim wanted Mike to live at 2307 because the two planned to form a band. From that point onward, the whole scene became something other than what I'd imagined.

Mike and I were like oil and water, but I tolerated his presence for economic and pragmatic reasons, and because the music he played with Jim made us all happy. Mike had an eight-wheeler dump truck that we used to clean up the yard and haul away construction debris. Another factor was that Janie couldn't afford $37.50 a month rent, but these two guys could chip in $25.00 apiece, a net savings to me of $12.50 over splitting the rent two ways. In those days, $12.50 could buy a bag of pot, and a pastrami sandwich, which a guy was going to need once he got the munchies. So Jim stayed and Mike stayed and later Janie visited often.

Then came the crashers and hangers on, assorted unexpected visitors of all stripes coming and going at all hours—pot-smoking ex-cops, Jehovah's Witnesses, Mormon missionaries, martial artists, poets, musicians, jugglers, mimes, Native Americans, rednecks, actual "Okies" from Oklahoma, a country music guitar picker with a slicked back pompadour, hippies, Vietnam vets, farmers, a professional thief, and auditioning drummers.

Along with the kaleidoscope of characters passing through, we had a crew of regulars that included my sweetheart, Janie; Barney, a consummate martial artist; Steve, five years our junior whom we met initially as a purveyor of pot; Gene, who sometimes lived in a cave; various and sundry beautiful young women including Gene's girlfriend Tina and her two lovely young sisters; my brother Tim, released from prison on Bastille Day, 1969; stepsiblings; and my mother when she came up from L.A.

Friends of friends and acquaintances of acquaintances passed through our back door in continual procession during two falls, two winters, two springs, and two summers. 2307 Mariposa Avenue was an ever-mutating fractal of human geometry. The house, like its occupants, was an eccentric character that needed lots of love. It had fallen on hard times, but it wasn't hopeless. The house, like my psyche, was an unreconstructed mess. It was a fixer upper, and so was I.

Gertrude Stein had nothing on me. She had her salon in Paris with Picasso and the like; I had my gathering place on the edge of town.

3

I Didn't Always Live Here

I didn't always live in the house on Mariposa Avenue.

Sometimes it seems as if I had always lived there even before I arrived, and as if I've been living there ever since.

Before Mariposa there were two family homes, a stepfamily home, and various assorted college residences, including a dormitory for a year in Spain, then a few temporary residences post-graduation, and finally the big white bread truck.

Until I was twelve, I lived with my father and mother and two older brothers, Jon and Tim. To all appearances we were a normal, prosperous, nuclear family in post-WW II America. However, unknown to my innocent mind (beyond perhaps an intuitive knowing), dissolution and madness were growing in the seemingly safe womb of our family.

The first of the two places we lived, before my parents divorced and we all went in separate directions, was 1027 Euclid Avenue in Santa Monica, California. From my birth in 1946 until 1954, my future landlady, Mrs. Whitlow, was living with her husband and two children at 2307 Mariposa Avenue in Chico. Roughly two decades later, we met, and it seemed that she had been saving the house for me all along.

Early memories of safety, happiness, and normalcy in Santa Monica include Sunday drives, visits to our grandparents, a jungle gym in the back yard, my first tricycle, playing hide and seek with waves at the beach twenty blocks from our house, digging clams for Sunday chowder, and learning to read on my mother's lap. If there ever was a foundation that gave me a basis for a normalcy to return to, it was in Santa Monica.

On the not so happy side, I clearly remember the first violent fight between my two older brothers. It happened on a school day in the afternoon. I know this because they were supposed to escort me home from school, but they left without me. On my way home on foot, I was accosted by a gas station attendant offering me "candy." The man took me in the bathroom and showed me part of him that no youngster should ever have to see; and, he threatened that I would never see my family again if I didn't do what he wanted. Fortunately, he let me go before engaging in any sex acts. My brothers were supposed to watch out for me, but when I got home, they were having a knockdown fight and violence filled the air. Too embarrassed and afraid to tell my parents what had happened, I later asked my brothers to tell them.

Apparently they never said anything because a week or two went by and nothing happened. Finally I told my mother and she went to the gas station, but she was told the man didn't work there anymore. As far as I know, my father never heard about the episode. I mark the day of the molestation and the fight as the first day I felt unsafe in the world, a feeling that would persist for many years, especially as the violence between my brothers continued to escalate.

In 1954, a drive over the Santa Monica Mountains to Van Nuys in the San Fernando Valley led one along Sepulveda Boulevard and eventually to a cross street, Saticoy. Turning left on Saticoy and driving a country block past walnut orchards, vacant lots, and a scattering of homes, on the left stood a modest three bedroom ranch style home with a rail fence and a circular driveway: 15406 Saticoy. Driving farther down the block revealed a large chicken ranch. Even farther was Saticoy Street Elementary School, which my brothers and I attended, and at the end of the road was the incongruous Lockheed Aircraft.

Our house was situated on the front half of what is called a commercial acre, equivalent to about an acre and a half. Lining the perimeter of the property were thirteen English walnut trees, the source of many nutmeats and the site of much climbing for three active, towheaded boys. The front half of the property could be termed the civilized half, with a lawn, trees, and flowerbeds.

A chain link fence enclosed the back half, which my mother called "the back forty." At first this lot was barren except for some weeds, six of the walnut trees, and a funky shed. Over time it became a mini-ranch with a menagerie of chickens, ducks, geese, a cow, a burro, a donkey, and my mother's prized Alsatian goats, which supplied enough milk for our family. The milk and eggs and the occasional fowl invited to dinner, instilled the notion of self-sufficiency that coincidentally became widely popular in the "Back to the Earth Movement" of the late sixties and early seventies, during the Mariposa days.

Our second family home in Van Nuys was idyllic in many ways, despite the growing discord that would eventually scatter us all. Most vivid in my memory are the long family vacations. (Two weeks or a month seems very long to a child). Four summers in a row, we went to the southern High Sierras where we set up a base camp and went on daily excursions, fishing, hiking, and exploring. These experiences later led to my hiking the John Muir Trail and bonded a love of the outdoors to my soul, a love that carried through like a healing balm to the Mariposa times and beyond. A big part of the Mariposa experience was tied into the surrounding countryside, the hiking trails, and skinny dipping holes in nearby Chico Creek and Butte Creek.

It was no wonder that, when I found 2307 Mariposa with its long tail of fallow soil, I wanted to reprise the early self-sufficiency of my family's ranchette. Here on Mariposa I had a chance for a do-over. I wanted to recapture the best parts of my childhood, to get back to my good old used-to-be. I wanted to reclaim the happiness I knew before my family came apart at the seams and I became a sleepwalker in a long nightmare. I wanted to get back to the earth, back to my roots, to live simply and totally in the present. No wonder I sometimes referred to the acreage on Mariposa as "the back forty." Our vegetarian ways on Mariposa precluded killing any critters, though, so there were no feathers to pluck, only fruits and vegetables to pick, and endless pots of brown rice to share.

I've heard it said that you can never step in the same river twice. However, some things are constant and enduring, including change. At 2307 Mariposa I learned to go with the flow, to let go and keep moving on.

Looking back from a distance of four decades, I see that all my rivers and all my roads have led to and from Mariposa Avenue.

4

A Silk Purse

As Realtors like to say, the place had "potential." A contractor would call the place a knockdown. Anyone with a bank account and common sense would have razed the house to start over. It didn't take long for Jim, Mike, and me to realize the man-hours required to make the place habitable, divided among the three of us, would take us into the rainy season. We needed help.

We were discussing this fact one day in September when an image from *Seven Brides for Seven Brothers* popped into my head, and I said, "Let's have a barn-raising."

Jim knew what that was but Mike didn't, so I explained. "It's like this. We're living on the frontier, here on the edge of town. We invite others to scrounge materials and bring tools and muscle power, just like in the old days on the prairie. We pay them with food, like a big pot of spaghetti, and the job gets done. Then, if they ever need a place to stay, they can crash here. Maybe we'll break into song and dance while we work, and create our own musical!"

We had a lot of willing participants and, for a month or two, we were all ass and elbows. Two months of work condensed to one—and we did it on the cheap. Some major items donated: use of Mike's dump truck, two refrigerators, ten gallons of paint, a Formica kitchen countertop, a Wedgwood stove, a claw foot tub, scrap lumber for framing two new windows, and the windows themselves.

EIGHT-WHEELER DUMP TRUCK

As mentioned previously, I never cared much for Mike B., but the chief benefit of having him move into the detached garage was that he came with an "eight wheeler" dump truck. From the yard and the root cellar and inside the house, we took six loads to the dump. After that, the yard still looked messy. Jim made the observation, "It's not the big stuff that looks messy, it's the little stuff," and he was right on. For weeks we all went around picking up shreds of this and that until the yard really did look clean.

ORANGE AND GREEN REFRIGERATORS

We had a scrounge list. On any given day, especially a weekend day, everyone kept an eye out and asked around about items on our list. Soon we developed a pitch that worked like a charm: "We're young men just out of college…"—okay, I stretched it a bit. Mike was only a high school grad—"…getting a start in the world, not much money, fixing up a place for our landlord. What materials can you let us have for wholesale or better?" Every time I made that little speech, I felt like the kid with the paper route, trying to win a sales contest with the prize a trip to Disneyland, but it worked.

We needed a refrigerator, so one Saturday I came home with one I'd picked up for free, and so did Mike. Some discussion ensued as to what to do with the extra refrigerator. We decided to keep both, but it got confusing, remembering which refrigerator had what kinds of food items.

"Why not put stuff from the garden in one and all the other food in the other?" I suggested.

Everyone agreed, but it was still confusing. So one day I hauled both refrigerators out into the yard and spray painted one green for vegetables, and the other orange just for the hell of it, or, because orange matched the Formica on the donated countertop.

LATH AND BURLAP

By the time we peeled off several layers of wallpaper and even layers of newspaper from the 1930's, and removed tin can lids that had been applied to cover holes, and attempted to fill the holes with buckets of Spackle, which fell through the holes into the abyss, it became obvious that any further work would lead us to the skeleton of the house. It was like digging a hole all the way to China. Jim got the ingenious idea of buying burlap and covering the walls with it, fastening it down with stained lath and carpet tacks. Orange burlap and darkly stained lath formed a wainscoting in the bathroom—a little rustic, but cheerful. We painted the upper walls with high gloss butterscotch. Damned if it didn't look good!

TUB AND SURROUND

We had a bathtub to die for.

Someone scrounged an old-fashioned clawfoot tub. We painted the bottom exterior with high gloss black enamel. People pay big bucks nowadays for clawfoot tubs, especially for an oversized one like we had. It was so nice to sit and stretch out your legs or lie back without getting a crick in your neck. The tub was big enough that you could get your whole body under the hot soak at once. A petite woman could fit in there at the same time.

Jim found a stand of bamboo somewhere and fashioned a framework that he suspended over the tub with sisal twine. We hung an orange and white and yellow striped shower curtain that matched the wainscoting and wall colors, and cobbled a hose and spray nozzle onto the tap. Spray nozzles are another feature you see nowadays in the likes of *Architectural Digest*. For a few dollars, we had a setup that would cost thousands today.

If that tub could speak, what tales it would tell about shared showers and baths! People came over and said they had heard about our bathroom and tub, and could they take a hot soak? Many did. While they were in there soaking, we might bring them a mug of tea and a joint to smoke, and ask what music selection they would like to hear. It was almost a rite of initiation. After they got out of the tub, I might give them a massage if they wanted it. Then they could rest in the hammock, smoke a doobie if that was to their liking, and listen to music. Whatever they requested from our collection of one hundred fifty LP albums, we played for them.

It became a house tradition to invite guests to enjoy a shower or hot soak. Sometimes we would share, like children in the tub together. It was a way of reinforcing the sense of 2307 Mariposa Avenue as sanctuary or spa.

How much would you pay nowadays to take a hot soak, and then sit around in a robe while people wait on you hand and foot and give you a massage? The only difference was, none of us owned a robe.

Directly next to the tub was a small window where you could look out at the sunset while you were taking a bubble bath. Others could look in, but it didn't matter. Jim always said, "Ours is a bare-butt naked household!" Directly next to the window lived a persimmon tree. I remember soaking, smoking dope, and watching little sparrows flitting about in the tree. At harvest time, the yellow-orange globes of the persimmons seemed to go with the décor of the bathroom, bringing the outdoors inside. One day in particular I remember indelibly. The orange-gold light of the afternoon sun striking the bare branches of the tree made the persimmons look like a hundred small suns that reminded me of a Yeats poem. Blissfully, I recited:

And I will search,
Till time and time is done,
The golden apples of the moon,
The silver apples of the sun.

PAINT PARTY

When it came time to paint the exterior of the house, our scrounging pitch got us ten gallons of paint for five dollars. The paint store manager said he wasn't allowed to give it away; thus, the five-dollar charge, and he left it outside the store in back where we "just might happen to find it." There was no guarantee as to the color, he said. Some of it would be paint, some stain, but we could mix them together, and we did—and it all came out some sort of forest green. Actually, the mix was perfect, with the stain striking into the wood as a preservative and the pain providing a protective seal.

After we installed a couple of new windows in my bedroom, it took only a couple of days for Jim and Mike and Janie and me and sundry visitors to put two coats on the house, but touchups spread out longer.

One of those days, I was standing on a two-by-twelve scaffold when I felt a presence behind me. Turning, there at eye level in the branches of the persimmon tree I saw a gray and white kitten. "Piewacket," I said, and immediately thought the name trite, but it stuck. The kitten was pretty feral, but I raised her for a month until she got run over in front of the house. I felt sad and sorry, and I buried her under the persimmon tree.

Not long after that, an emaciated, scruffy feral gray cat appeared in the yard. I swore I wouldn't give her a name because that would mean I had bonded with her. First, I would try to turn her into a tame pet; then I would name her. I worked and worked with that cat until she stopped scratching and biting. After much coaxing and many scratches, eventually she let me brush her tangled fur, and pick her up by the head to swing her around my neck where she would ride loose like a scarf; but nobody else could touch her. She had a litter of kittens on the back porch, and they were quite feral too, but they didn't survive the tomcat that killed them off one by one. When all the kittens were dead, the mother got run over in front of the house. That's when I finally gave her a name, Maggie, because at the time Leon Redbone had a song out by that title:

"Oh, oh whoa, nobody cries when Maggie dies."

But I cried. That cat was a wild, abused, and kindred soul that just needed some love and care and time to heal. I buried her beside Piewacket and swore not to have any more pets as long as I lived in that house too close to the road.

WEDGWOOD STOVE

The antique Wedgwood stove was another one of those items designers nowadays pay thousands of dollars to acquire, but I got it free from the Quinn's, some old family friends who had moved to Chico. The only condition was that we had to get the stove out of their basement. It took four of us to wrestle it out of there and install it in the house. It must have weighed three hundred pounds at least.

What a great stove! Four gas burners occupied most of the stove top, but on the left side was a wood burning stove about a foot wide by two burners deep. Its thick cast iron top had two round plates resembling manhole covers. One could remove the covers with a special handle that came with the stove. We burned all our household paper in the stove, and sometimes that was enough. You hardly needed any wood; it was unbelievable how efficient that wood stove was. A few sticks and some paper trash would heat the house for hours. In the winter, we'd hang around the wood stove like old timers in a country store, sitting on produce crates, swapping stories. That stove was witness to a lot of talking and signifying. Many shared meals were prepared on that stove. The old Wedgwood was hearth and home.

KITCHEN COUNTER

At a cabinet shop, I gave the "young guys just out of college" plea and a nice man there custom-cut a burnt orange Formica top from a leftover piece. First he said it would be twenty-five bucks, but when I went to pick it up, he insisted I take it for free. We never figured out how to put trim on it, so the edge of the three-quarter-inch plywood remained bare, but, hey, it was functional.

KITCHEN CABINET TABLEAUX

To go with the countertop, I got some acrylic paints and painted amateur psychedelic tableaux over the ratty surface of the kitchen cabinets. One day on the street, I found a picture of Jesus holding his robe open to reveal an open heart crowned with thorns. In the picture, Jesus wore an expression of bliss. Something soulful about that picture got to me. I taped it on one side of the cabinet over the kitchen sink. Washing dishes, I looked at that picture of Jesus, and somehow I could relate to his pain and his bliss. I even learned a little chant to sing over and over while scrubbing dishes:

Door of my heart, open wide I keep for thee
Door of my heart, open wide I keep for thee
Wilt thou come, wilt thou come
Just this once, oh come to me?

That picture and that little song transported me to some otherworldly place where there was no more pain, only hope, and I wasn't even a Christian. Janie felt the same way about the picture, and being Mexican, naturally she was raised Catholic.

THE HAMMOCK ROOM

The hammock room was the heart and soul of the house. A smallish room, it was open to the kitchen with an eight-foot wide portal suggesting separation. Nowadays we call it an "open floor plan". Perhaps it was a dining area at one time, but we converted it to a relaxing lounge. First it received the burlap and lath treatment, but different than the orange and gold bathroom. Lavender burlap covered the walls entirely, held in place by the ever-trusty strips of lath.

I brought in the overstuffed chair I had salvaged from my previous residence and reupholstered in gold fabric. It was the most comfortable damned chair I've ever known, with wide flat arms big enough to hold a dinner plate on one side and a big mug of tea on the other. The chair was placed in one corner next to a window, which provided wonderful light for reading books and album covers. A high quality KLH stereo rested on an orange crate next to the chair. Next to the stereo were two orange crates full of LP records, an eclectic mix but mostly contemporary rock. I placed the speakers across the room, high up in the corners.

The crowning touch was the hammock. My friend Alyosha had brought the colorful, capacious, hand-woven hammock back from Mexico.

The problem with installing a hammock inside a house is how to make it bombproof so it doesn't fall down under weight. Our solution was to drill holes through the framing members of the house. The interior partition wall presented no problem in this regard. A trip to the hardware store scored the proper eyebolt, washers and nuts. The other end of the hammock wasn't that simple. To reach through the interior molding and the window frame as well as the exterior trim, the eyebolt had to be thirteen inches long, not available at any hardware store or building supply. Nor could I find a drill bit long enough. At work, Doyle Clemens fired up the acetylene torch and fashioned a custom bolt as well as an extension on an auger bit.

With that problem solved, we hung the hammock. It blocked passage to the bathroom, but that was no big deal. When the hammock was in use, people ducked on their way to and from the bathroom. As well, we could unhook one end and drape it with its mate from one of the eyebolts.

We had a special, athletic way of getting into the hammock that involved reaching under and grasping the edge farthest from you with your palms facing you. Then, gymnastic style, you would swing your legs over the top and lower your hips in.

The hammock carried etiquette similar to the bathtub. If someone in the hammock wanted anything, others would provide it. *Bring me a joint. Bring me some food or something to drink. Please put Pink Floyd on the music box. Come over here and talk to me. Make the hammock swing and sing me a lullaby. You want a turn in the hammock? Climb in here with me.* The hammock had a capacity of four persons. Getting in there and squirming about with three friends was quite fun, kind of like a game of Twister.

In the hammock by oneself was a bit of heaven. It was so

relaxing; you could get into such a meditative state that after awhile you'd notice a slight swaying of the hammock in synch with your breathing and heartbeat. Who needs the Maharishi when you've got a hammock?

Sometimes I'd come home and find a friend who had come over just to rest in the hammock. They would be so far "in the zone" that I wouldn't even realize they were there until they awoke and spoke to me while I worked in the kitchen.

Love in a hammock is not what it's cracked up to be. When you're pushing toward your partner and you want your partner to push toward you, the hammock is moving away, but it's worth a try at least once.

LIVING ROOM

The twelve-by-eighteen living room was pretty simple. One day I painted the walls light lavender, stood back, and exclaimed, "Lavender is the new off white!" I painted the exposed sub floor gray. We tacked old sheets over the windows for a year until we scored some donated curtains; brought in some rattan furniture donated by Mrs. Whitlow, some pillows, and a sectional corner sofa. Done.

Really, though, who needed furniture? The preferred angle of repose was to recline on the floor. We were like a houseful of lounging cats. (Even today, Jim says, "Do you realize the intimate conversations you can have when you're stretched out on the floor next to someone? It's just not the same as sitting in a chair!")

Later, a drum set, amps, guitars, a tambourine, and a nest of crisscrossing electrical cords on the floor occupied the space. The only thing I didn't like was when Mike got a little black and white TV after we'd been there about a year.

I wanted to take a hammer to that damned TV! I almost did, only I was afraid I'd start a fight. In my opinion, TV only detracted from social interaction, and I didn't like the noise, though I did like seeing a young Goldie Hawn on "Laugh-In".

NEW FRONT DOOR

Remember the front door that almost imploded when I knocked on it the first time? Jim solved that problem. He built some sawhorses in the back yard and used them to support his construction of a new door that he built from rough cedar planks. Heavy and very sturdy, it was more like a finely crafted barn door–"Frank Lloyd Wright Meets the Beverly Hillbillies." In lieu of a traditional door handle and hasp, he fashioned a barn-style sliding closure out of the same cedar. A piece of copper tubing inserted into the slider served as a handle. The door was a perfect fit, keeping out drafts., and sturdy as hell.

Just for fun, on the exterior of the door we placed a doorknob that had no function at all except to fool people. To strengthen the ruse, Jim placed the knob close to the side of the door that had the hinges, which were invisible from outside. Even if the hasp were open, someone pushing on that knob would have no luck opening the door.

In China this ruse has been practiced for centuries to ward off evil spirits. The door was as secure as the drawbridge on a castle. I quipped that all we lacked was a moat. Jim commented that the "vibes" around the house and its quality of invisibility were moat enough.

Only strangers came to the front door anyway.

NEW ROOF

The first winter, just as we were contemplating creating a sleeping space in the attic, the roof started leaking. Water sneaked into the roof peak and traveled down the rafters until drops fell off onto the ceiling over the kitchen. The pattern of the drops was predictable. We simply opened the trap door in the ceiling. The drops fell through the trap door into well-placed buckets, thus sparing the ceiling from damage. A temporary fix was to slather some tar up there, but it hardly made a difference.

Our joke went like this: *When there's a leak in your roof, why bother fixing it? It's raining outside! When it's not raining, why bother fixing it? It's not leaking!*

Come spring, Mike scrounged some asphalt shingles and roofing felt, and replaced about half the roof. For that Mrs. Whitlow gave us three months' free rent. We were like The Boxcar Children, taking shelter and "making do" in an abandoned car on a side track.

Here in this caboose of a house with floors bowed upward toward the middle, we made our stand.

5

The Run-Up to Bastille Day

It's in their eyes
It's in their very eyes
Looking glass to where their
Conscience lies
Even blinded eyes can see
release don't mean the same as free
It's in their eyes….

Brother Tim

One day a couple of years before finding Mariposa, I took a break from writing my thesis to go to the mailbox— you know, one of those old fashioned metal things on top of a post next to the street?

Among the usual junk, I saw an envelope addressed with a loopy scrawl that looked vaguely familiar. There was no return address, but the postmark said Van Nuys, California. I had lived there as a child, but who could be sending me a message from my past? Something about the envelope scared me and made my pulse rate climb. I set it aside and went back to work on my thesis.

Most theses are written to fulfill graduate requirements. However, my thesis was a requirement of the undergraduate Honors English Program. Without my thesis, my diploma would not show that I'd participated in this seminar-style program for four years, doing graduate level work as an undergrad. I was running behind schedule, having difficulty making "ibid's" and "op cit.'s" fit on the page in the days before the computer made footnotes a lot easier. In other words, I had other things on my mind than some scary letter from a stranger in Southern California.

The letter rested for several days, but periodically I puzzled over the familiar/not so familiar handwriting. Finally, I got around to opening the mystery envelope.

> *"I realize you might not want to communicate with me, but I thought you should know that I recently visited your brother in prison. He asked about you, and I thought you might want to get in touch with him. Doing so is not as easy as you might think. They have certain procedures. You have to be one of the people on a list of those from whom he's allowed to receive letters or visits. If you want to find out more about the procedures, feel free to contact me. Here's my address. Love, Phyllis"*

The first thing I thought was, who's Phyllis? Then I realized Phyllis was my mother! No wonder I sort of recognized the handwriting but couldn't recall who had written to me. I hadn't heard from her in nearly a decade. Compounding my confusion was the fact that she didn't sign the letter, "Your Mother." Her omission of a return address was, doubtless, a way of making sure I would not ditch the envelope without opening it first. I felt as if I'd received a letter from a far-away galaxy.

The last time I'd seen my mother was in the Los Angeles County mental hospital. When she and my father separated, she unraveled. There was some fear that she might do me harm. "You never know what a crazy person might do," said my father. "She might get a knife and stab you, and she wouldn't even know what she's doing." This assertion was, however, unfounded because she was catatonic, sitting all day in a chair with a thousand-mile stare, holding two or three lit cigarettes at a time, letting the ashes grow as long as caterpillars before falling onto her lap.

I was transferred to my father's care, and before long I heard about the men in white coats carting my mother off in a straitjacket. Not long after that, my maternal grandmother took me to see my mother, but she didn't seem to recognize either of us.

In later years my mother reported that, "The final straw was when your father put your brother Tim out on the street and neglected to tell me he had done so. I didn't know if Tim had run away or been hit by a car or kidnapped, and your father wasn't talking to me." Tim had some problems with juvenile delinquency, and our father's way of dealing with repeated offenses was to tell Tim to "Shape up or ship out," and eventually he shipped Tim out, telling him, "You're not my son anymore." Tim hit the street at age 13. Luckily, a friend's family took him in.

My father remarried and we moved to a wealthy community just over the hills east of Berkeley, California. My stepmother took over. She made it clear that I was not to have any contact with my mother or my brother Tim. My oldest brother, Jon, eager to escape the grip of our stepmother, joined the Marines, and I wasn't supposed to contact him, either. My mother and brothers and I were traveling in different orbits.

When I was a sophomore in high school, Brother Tim killed a man and got ten to life. The man he killed was our older brother, Jon. (Remember, I had a prescient dream on the night he died? In the dream I saw Tim as the shooter.) The crime was a culmination of a lifetime of conflict between the two and, in a way, it could be called self-defense because, as sick and violent as Jon was, eventually he would probably have killed Tim. It was a question of who got the upper hand, and Tim was tired of being beaten. The perennial victim became the perpetrator once and for always.

At first I didn't know what to do about the letter from my mother, so I mulled it over. In one of those "oh, duh" moments that comes across as an epiphany, it occurred to me that I was no longer beholden to my stepmother. She no longer held the purse strings for my college education. I was on my own, making my own way. I could choose to break the spell of nullification she had cast over me, and reconnect with my family.

There was another factor in my quest for connection. Almost a year before I received the letter from my mother, my college sweetheart had broken from me. She quickly married a local Chico guy whom she declared to be "more normal." With her departure went my connection to her family to whom I felt very close. I hated my stepmother. My father was distant and unavailable. I had no friends at school. Now, I was extending my college education into a fifth year for lack of anything better to do. Living alone in the country, I was miserable and depressed; and as if all this wasn't enough, the draft board was dogging my heels.

It was time to reclaim the missing pieces of my family, my mother and my brother, to cast off the mantle of Good Stepson. Without my mother and brother, and without my college sweetheart Em, I was a broken shell of a person. I knew that this Humpty Dumpty could never be put back together again, but I could at least try to right the wrongs imposed by my oppressive stepmother. I could try to regain a sense of connection basic to all human beings, a connection that had been broken by circumstances beyond my control. Clearly, a new geometry of relationships was in order.

Thinking back, my mother's move was masterful. To get in

touch with Tim, I had to contact her, but she placed no pressure on me whatsoever. Her years of psychotherapy hadn't been for naught. I wrote and requested her assistance. I submitted the required forms, and wrote to Tim. Who knows what I said, but here's his reply, blemishes and all.

> *Brother Bix,*
> *When in the course of 'Human' events it becomes necessary for one person to re-establish the ties which once connected him with another. And to assume, among the powers of the penitentiary, the seperate [sic] and equal station to which the law of family and its concepts do not necessarily entitle him. He holds this truth to be self-evident—that, all things being equal, even in the pursuit of happiness I am not naturally endowed with a natural or easy way of knowing what to say to you. Or, in the vernacular, I'm hung-up. Convention would seem to dictate that these words be friendly or at least cordial. However I have a certain amount of difficulty being cordial toward anyone with whom I'm not acquainted as a person. Also, I know you can dig this, as a brother I feel some amount of hostility toward you—conventions being what they are.*

He went on to say that he was in Toastmasters and a writers group. On the back of the page, he typed four of his poems. Here's one:

> *Different Deaths*
> *Everyday dying*
> *Different deaths*
> *I wander through living.*

Everytime I must say words
Which are opposite to my silent singing
I feel a chip taken
From my tombstone
And my song grows sadder.
10/22/68

(This was from a guy who dropped out of school in the seventh grade.)

Writing was our first line of connection. At our mother's suggestion, Tim joined a writer's group in prison, The Pen and Pencil Set. Tim asked me to contribute, and I did. I think he still has a copy of the publication, *Caught*.

Our mother had a neat idea. She and Tim and I began creating haiku poems, each of us contributing one line, and then forwarding it to the next writer. When a piece reached the third writer, he or she finished it and sent it on to the others for comments—kind of a Japanese chain letter. In this way, we established a connection by means of something fun, intellectual and artistic. Here's an example:

Darkness descending
Blank blackness covering me
Changing of the guard

On a sunny spring day, a guard let me through the perimeter gate and it clanged shut behind me. *Now I'm in.*

I walked up the steps and entered the visitor's lounge. I was shown to a seat and told to keep my hands to myself. My brother would be delayed; just wait here.

After several nerve-wracking minutes he came and sat down opposite me. I thought I was hallucinating. He was very thin, and his forehead looked enormous. His skin seemed especially red. His blond hair was combed back in a tall pompadour. His blue eyes looked luminous. We sat and stared and said nothing for a long time.

The first words out of my mouth sounded strange to me even as I said them: "Your skeleton is my skeleton."

What I meant to say was, "You are my flesh and blood down to the bone. We are the same. We are not different one from the other. We have no differences," but, "We have the same skeleton" is what came out. Perhaps it was a test, a sort of offbeat use of language such as our mother would invent. In this way, I could tell if the man sitting in front of me really was my mother's other son or a stand-in.

"Yes," Tim said, and we sat nodding for another few minutes. Several times I opened my mouth as if to say something, but no clear thoughts were in the queue, and I wound up just nodding and grinning.

When we did talk, it was all very superficial and surreal and unmemorable. The important thing was, we broke the ice. He told me he had a furlough coming up; a weekend when they would let him out to sniff around a bit, see what the world looks like, because he was up for parole. His sentence was ten to life, but he might get off in six for good behavior. Could he come to Chico and visit me?

"Indeed you can, brother."

Ironically, in those days, the number of California prisons matched the number of state colleges: fourteen. Some prisons worked a rehabilitation model. Vacaville was one of those. In fact, the sign next to the freeway still says, "Vacaville State Medical Facility." It has always seemed a euphemism. A prison by any other name would not be a prison.

Due to Tim's age when he committed his crime (at seventeen), he was sent to Vacaville where he could receive counseling. He completed his GED. He read voluminously, and listened keenly to music. One of his favorites: Bob Dylan. He got himself appointed as the visitors' intake manager, a position that netted him power and influence in the prison.

He came to Chico for forty-eight hours. Nothing much about that visit is memorable either. What do you say to someone you supposedly know, but don't really? Our lives were so different. Certainly we did not talk about Brother Jon. The important thing was, his visit was a beginning.

Tim was released from prison on July 14, 1969— Bastille Day. The symbolism pleased him. I liked the idea, too, of placing my stepmother's head in the guillotine alongside Marie Antoinette's. On that day, he and Mom and I were all liberated from a decade of estrangement. We were spiritual warriors storming the bastions of power that had kept us separated for nearly a decade. Come to think of it, Tim and I both graduated about the same time: he, from prison and I from college. Our mother had a graduation of sorts, too, only a few years earlier from Camarillo State Mental Hospital. We were all broken bodhisattvas on the road to recovery, and reconnecting with each other was essential to our progress.

By the time I found 2307 Mariposa, Tim and I had been getting to know each other, spending a lot of time together for almost a year. His quick energy, his worldly ways, his affection and generosity, and his sharp wit were a definite asset to the Mariposa scene. Our father, however, was unaware that we had reconnected. He and Tim were still estranged. It fell to me to broker a peace accord.

6

Two New Windows

When my bedroom windows fell out onto the ground, I knew it was time to see my father.

The windows were nailed shut and sealed with paint. Wanting to bring fresh air into the room, I pulled the nails out of the first set of sashes, and used a Stanley knife to slice through the paint, but they still didn't give way, so I pounded with a hammer and yanked down hard. All at once, the top sash gave way and fell to the ground with a crash of breaking glass. *What the hell*, I thought; I butted the bottom sash with the heel of my hand and that sash joined its partner on the ground. No sense holding back: I repeated this procedure with the second set of sashes, but they didn't break; they only cracked.

Leaning out to look at the wreckage, I thought, "Falling windows precipitate change." I knew what I had to do: Replace these windows and reframe my relationship with my father.

I leaped through the frame with a karate shout and smashed my work boots through the glass. Flexing and grimacing and grinding my heels into the glass, I saw myself as Bruce Lee delivering the final blow to his enemy.

THE CONVERSATION I HOPED TO have with my father had been a long time coming. So many things had gone wrong, so much loss and hurt. Our so-called relationship had become a stifled and broken down thing just as 2307 Mariposa had become a barely habitable structure; yet, the house was repairable, and I hoped our relationship would be, too.

Ten years of accumulated resentment had backed up in me like a clogged cesspool. It was time to clear the blockage. It wasn't going to be easy, but it had to be done. My father and I hadn't had a conversation of any substance in, well, I was going to say a long time, but maybe never, because first I was a little boy having little boy conversations with him; then I was a teenager having almost no conversations with him at all (unless you count the time when I was 14 and I stole a fifth of peach brandy from Safeway and he beat me with a switch till I couldn't sit down for a week); or, the time when I was sixteen, my father asked me what funeral arrangements I thought my brother might have preferred, military or civilian, and we chose military because it was cheaper and farther away where we would never visit the grave. Although my father and I had lived under the same roof during my high school years in the Lafayette stepfamily, we might as well have been living on separate planets.

DESPITE MY BRUCE LEE BRAVADO, it took several hours to get up my nerve to call my parents' house. As usual, the "evil step-monster" answered, claiming my father wasn't home and she didn't know when he would be. More likely, he was out in the yard and Millie was too lazy to get up, plus, she didn't want the two of us communicating anyway because in her world, love between my father and anyone but her must somehow subtract from his love for her, and that was not to be tolerated. (For all her bluff and bluster and seemingly confident, opinionated ways, I didn't figure out until many years later that she was secretly an insecure person in the way of bullies everywhere.) It seems she viewed herself as the dragon at the gate. I could enter the gate but an audience with the king was nearly impossible.

Therefore, I was to be kept at arm's length, merely tolerated by her. No way was I going to ask her to deliver a message stating that I wanted to have a sit-down with my father. Instead, I asked her to deliver the message that I would be coming down the next day. The need for two new windows was a good enough pretense. My father was remodeling their house and some remaindered windows might fit the bill. My taking some old windows off Millie's hands wouldn't cost her anything. Still, I doubted the message would be delivered, however innocuous my excuse for visiting the house in Lafayette.

THE NEXT DAY, I FIRED up the Gypsy Moth, which is what I called my Step Van, and headed south. Three hours to think: how does one talk to a stranger who is one's father? What if time and place and courage and opportunity to speak do not come together? Will I slink away in silent defeat yet one more time, with my consolation prize two crumby old reject windows; or, worse yet, will I explode like a plug volcano, venting a decade of stored rage, kick my father's ass, walk away and never see him again? Worse yet, I might murder my stepmother and end up in prison like my brother Tim. That would spoil everything I was trying to accomplish.

This trip wasn't just about me. I was also on a peace-building mission, to deliver a message from the "black sheep" of the family, Brother Tim. They hadn't spoken in twelve years.

Tim was even less popular with Millie than I was. If I was held in a far orbit, and merely tolerated, Tim was in a distant galaxy, and Millie would fight fiercely to make sure Tim didn't get any closer. Whatever I said, I would have to be clever and quick, and catch my father alone.

In the van on the way down, I also thought about the garden I was going to plant at 2307 Mariposa Avenue, and the image of a good and green garden reminded me of my grandmother's garden, and how she used to put up a lot of her own food for the winter: pickles, peaches, jam, relish and the like. Surely, my father would not disapprove, and would appreciate that I was doing something that his mother would do. *At least I can plant a seed*, I thought.

Nonetheless, by the time I parked in the cul de sac at the bottom of my father's long, steep driveway, I still had a case of the jitters. Some deep breaths calmed me down a little, and I recited some words from *The Little Engine That Could* which my mother read to me as a child: "I think I can, I know I can." Walking up the driveway, I huffed like a pufferbilly and recited the words. At the top I was disappointed to see that my father's car was not there.

For a moment I almost collapsed into my old habit of mental defeat One more time I would have to go in and fake nice and pass the time of day with Millie, waiting for my father who probably had no idea I would be there. Briefly I thought of turning tail and going back home. But, I gave myself a soothing talk until my mind got still and quiet, and a sea change occurred: *I am not a victim. I'm not a little boy anymore. I'm a young man, and I can make choices. I will speak with my father whether Millie likes it or not. Where there's a will, there's a way, and I will find a way.*

With that, I went into the house and found Millie watching golf. We practiced our phony civility, and then sat in stilted silence while Millie ignored me. *Thank God she's ignoring me.*

At length I asked, "Is my father expecting me?"

"No," she said, and went back to her golf.

Okay, I thought, *you play your game, I'll play mine.* I sat and felt light as a feather and strangely peaceful.

At the first sound of my father's car starting up the driveway, I got up and walked casually out of the den as if I were on the way to the bathroom. Once out of sight in the hallway, I broke into a silent sprint across the living room, slowing just long enough to keep the screen door from creaking or slamming, then doing a 25-yard dash, arriving at the garage just as my father pulled in.

When my father got out of the car, he was moving fast on his long legs and he appeared to be lost in thought. Though I stood directly in his path, he blew right past me.

I really am invisible to him.

For an insane second or two, I wondered what would happen if I just stood there. How long would it take him to realize I was there? Then it occurred to me that Millie would simply neglect to tell him I had arrived and I knew once he went inside the house and entered his orbit around Planet Millie, any meaningful interaction between us would be quashed this time around. If I didn't do this now, I might never.

Bolting after him, I shouted, "Pop! Pop!" He still didn't seem to notice me until I tugged his arm. He stopped, wheeled, and seemed to look right past me. Gradually, I came into focus in his one good eye.

In that moment, every thought I had rehearsed flew out the window. Tears pressed against the back of my eyelids like stinging needles. I couldn't cry, not now! He would think there was something wrong with me, think I'd gone insane like my mother, and leave me blubbering alone in front of the house.

The words came unbidden. "Papa, I've been waiting for you. Where have you been?"

"How long?"

It occurred to me I'd been waiting a decade. Fighting back tears, the words almost stuck in my throat. "Forever. A real long time, Papa."

"How long?"

"Don't you get what I'm saying? *Where have you been?"*

"I was over at the apartments, and I had a lot of errands…."

"No, Papa, don't you get what I'm saying? Where have you been *for the last goddam decade?* I missed you, Papa. Where did you go?"

"I had some errands. How long have you been here?"

I realized I was getting ahead of myself. "Just a little while."

"I'm going inside. You come inside."

"No, Pop, please! Don't go inside now, please!"

"I want to go in and see Millie."

"Don't you get it? I keep waiting for you to show up, but you're never there when I need you. We need to talk."

"What about?"

"About a lot of things."

"Like what?" Impatiently, he made a move that looked like he was about to go inside.

This was obviously too intense for him. I had to think of something quick to keep him on the hook. "Do you have some windows I can have?"

"I think so. They're in back of the house. Do you want to look at them now?"

"Sure," I faked it.

We started walking to the back of the house. Halfway around, in the breezeway between the house and the garage, I wheeled directly into his path.

"Wait, Pop, I have some other business that's more important than some old windows."

"What?" he said impatiently.

"I want us to have a good old fashioned father-to-son, heart-to-heart talk, but...." I pointed toward the other end of the house. "... that fucking bitch is always getting in the way."

"Do you want to look at those windows now?"

"No, goddammit! I want to have a talk with you, and I want it now, not tomorrow, not yesterday, NOW!"

"What about?"

"Too much to say all at once, but at least we can start today. For starters, I thought you might like to know what's going on with your son."

"What?"

I gave him a brief rundown of how I had found the house at 2307 Mariposa Avenue in Chico, and why I needed the windows. He seemed genuinely interested in the fixit aspect, and he was impressed that my share of the rent was just twenty-five dollars a month.

"Do you want to look at the windows now?"

"No, Papa. We have a lot of things to talk about."

"Like what?"

"For one thing, I want you to know I'm taking a year or two off from the career path. I'm real messed up mentally right now, and I need a year or two to sort things out."

"Why?"

I wasn't sure if he was asking me because he wanted to know, or because he wanted ammo to use against me.

"As you know, mental health has been an issue in our family. Look at my schizophrenic mother...."

"Are you schizophrenic?"

"No, but I'm all messed up from too much loss, too much sorrow."

"What's going on?"

I wanted to say, *Don't you have a clue?* But then it occurred to me this was the first open-ended question my father had asked me in a long time. Maybe he was finally tuning in.

"For one thing, Em left me."

"Was that the girlfriend you had in college?"

"Yes, and I'm not the only guy who ever lost a first love, but it's one loss too many in a string of losses, and I find myself completely without direction or hope."

"What losses are you talking about?"

"You lost your first wife to divorce and madness, and I lost her too. You lost a son. Do you remember him, the one named after you, your firstborn, the one who died?"

He got a faraway look. "Do you want to look at those windows now?"

"No, Pop. You had another son, remember, the one named Tim, who did a very bad thing?"

He said nothing. I plunged ahead.

"Mom and you split up and the shit hit the fan and we all flew to the four winds. We all lost each other, and you married that woman in the house there, and you left me alone with her to run the show. I was left here with that woman you call your wife, and her three kids, and you wouldn't believe some of the mean and cruel things she said and did, and you never stood up for me…."

"What things did she do?"

"You know what, Pop, I'm not going to be specific about that because you'll say I'm whining and sniveling, you'll tell me how good I had it, and what am I complaining about, then you'll point out why I'm wrong and that will be the end of the discussion, and you'll go in the house with that bitch you call wife, and we will have gotten nowhere but back to the same old shit."

"What did she do?"

I wanted to tell him that his current wife had forbidden me to have any contact with my mother or my brothers; that she had intercepted all my mail from my mother and my brothers, opening it and reading it before I did, or throwing it in the trash before I ever received it, and that I learned to comb through the trash to find my mail. I wanted to tell my father how, shortly after Jon died, Millie came into my room one day and reasserted that I shouldn't have any further contact with my mother and surviving brother, saying, "They're nuts and kooks, and they'll do you no good. Tim did Jon a favor by killing him because he was a nut and a kook too, and he was stupid and he's better off dead." I wanted to tell him how, in effect she had forbidden me to grieve, saying, "Don't you *ever, ever* talk to anyone about how he died because no one will believe you! And don't ever talk to your father about Jon."

But I held back. "Pop, if I told you all of the mean, bad things that wife of yours did, there's not enough time in the day—and I refer to her as *your wife* because she's nothing to me and never will be; she's not my mother and never was; and she's not my stepmother, either. She's not even a friend. I *have* a mother, the only mother I'll ever have, and her name is Phyllis Mailes…."

"Oh, did she remarry?"

"Briefly, for a year, but she kept the guy's name."

"Where is she?"

"She got out of Camarillo after three years…."

"That long?"

"Well, one year as an inpatient, then they released her but she committed herself for another year. Then she was an outpatient for a year. She works at the DMV in LA."

"That doesn't sound like her."

"You're right. A major in Philosophy and a minor in Library Science out of UCLA, working at the Department of Motor Vehicles? She's way too intelligent and sensitive for that line of work. Somehow she manages, but she hates it."

"I've often wondered what happened to her since she kicked me out."

"Anyway, as I was saying, if I told you the disrespectful things Millie said about my mother and your other two sons…."

"Like what?"

"I'm not going to get into that right now because if you heard the bad words she said, you would hate her as much as I do. And I'm not here to dwell on the past. The point is, you went away somewhere and left me here with her. I hated living with her, and I missed you. I want my father back. You turned over the reins…."

My father jabbed a finger at his chest and spoke belligerently, "My attitude was, I make the money, Millie raises the kids!"

"You see what I mean? You left me here with that dictator and you never stood up for me. You gave her free rein and she ran roughshod, and you let her. You kowtowed to her because she controlled you with her pussy, and she still does."

He jabbed a finger at his chest again. "My attitude was…."

"You said that already! Listen to your words. You made the money while she sat on her ass at home, drinking wine. You let her control the money, but it was *your* money."

"I don't recall there being a lot of money around here with you kids in college…."

"....While you went on foreign junkets and you had your clothes tailored in London and you stayed in five star hotels and you owned a Rolls Royce?"

"It was a used Rolls..."

"Look, I'm not here to argue. You had money, and plenty of it, and you let her control it. Why didn't you overrule her?"

"For example?"

"For example, she controlled my college allowance, and I never had enough to even take my girlfriend to the movies or buy her ice cream—and again, I'm not crying over spilt milk here. I got a college education, I got to do some interesting jobs and learn the value of a buck, I got to do the grand tour of Europe with Em, but to make it to Europe I had to work three jobs and borrow money. Then, to stay in Europe for the summer, I borrowed the last four hundred of my college allowance. Therefore, Millie said I would have to support myself in my last year at school, and I did, but due to the workload, I got mononucleosis and I missed my chance to go to the Nationals in swimming.

That just wasn't fair, it wasn't right, and you could have changed that."

"Millie and I never agreed about money for the kids."

"Then why don't you do something about it?"

"Like what?"

"Like tell her to deliver your phone messages when I call you. Tell her to get out of the way. Tell her I want my father back. I want us to be friends, like when we used to go fishing and hiking together. Remember the time when I was twelve and you took me to the racetrack at Santa Anita? I was too young to bet, but I gave you a dollar to bet on Judy Acres to show, and we won two dollars."

"Funny, I don't remember that at all."

"Let's do some things together, like go to breakfast. We used to go to breakfast together, and I still like pancakes."

"Okay, my boy." He might have meant well, but he said it dismissively. Somehow, that rubbed me wrong. I stepped close to him and got in his face.

"I'm not your boy."

"Yes, you are."

"I'm not your boy anymore, not in the sense of your Negro slave. Maybe you mean it in the British sense, which isn't so bad, but I'm a young man now, and I want us to be friends like two grown men."

I want to say I love him, but I just can't, not yet.

"Okay, *my boy.*"

It was just like my father to put in a jab to win his point. We had come a long way in this conversation, and I decided to move on and make the best of it. "You're right, papa. I am your son, and I always will be."

"Do you want to look at those windows now?"

"Sure, Pop." My anger suddenly dissolved.

Who knew what the end result of this conversation would be? Perhaps nothing would change. I couldn't control the outcome. I could only say what I had to say, and try to heal my own wounds.

But I'm not quite through yet. I came here on a mission today.

We went around the back of the house and there lay the two gate-style windows, one atop the other, still in their casings with the frames painted forest green. I bent over to inspect them.

They looked good. I had a sudden insight. "Whoa," I muttered.

"Will they work?"

After our conversation and now looking at the windows, I flashed back to the day before when I leapt through the window frame at Mariposa and smashed the glass under my boots. An encouraging thought came to me and I mumbled: "*Two new windows, and one frame of reference.*"

I turned to my father to share this insight, but all I could say was, "Whoa, heavy, dude! Symbolic windows! Symbolic windows...."

My father squeezed his eyes shut and shook his head from side to side like a dog.. I expected to see water fly off his ears. "Do you want the windows or not?" What could I say? "Yes, Pop. They'll do. Thanks."

POP SAID HE WAS GOING in now, and he started back around the house toward the front door, but I wasn't through yet. With his 36" inseam, he was moving fast, and I trotted along behind. "Wait, Pop, there's one more thing I need to say."

"I have to pee," he said.

"Pop, I came here on a mission today. You have another son, and he wants to get in touch with you."

"Oh?" he said, stopping to face me.

"Mom isn't the only family member of ours I've reconnected with. Your son, Tim, is out of prison."

"Oh? I thought he was in for life."

"Ten to life, second degree manslaughter; out on good behavior in six."

"What's he doing?"

"He was released to Davis near the prison last year. He works at the university on a bird research project— starlings." I refrained from saying that a big part of his job was shoveling bird shit.

"I thought an ex con couldn't get a job. And he doesn't have an education, does he?"

"He's read more books than you and I put together. He had a

lot of time to read. He got his GED. He joined a writers group in prison."

"What's that?"

"The Pen and Pencil Set."

"That's clever."

"Your son, Tim, wants to see you. He wants you to know that he's very sorry for what he did, and there's no way he can ever make it up to you, but he wants to see you, even if it's only once and you never speak again, to tell you to your face that he's very sorry. And Pop, I know he misses you, too."

We discussed this topic some more, and he agreed to see Tim.

"Where, Pop?"

"Bring him here," he said, heading toward the front door.

"Promise?"

"Yes."

"Then shake on it."

He turned. We shook hands. I hoped he would honor his word.

"I don't envy you the discussion you're going to have with your wife," I said.

As we stepped inside, mentally I ticked off three items on my agenda:

Agenda Item Number One: Have heart-to-heart talk with father. Check.

Agenda Item Number Two: Get two new windows for the house on Mariposa. Check.

Agenda Item Number Three: Arrange reunion between my father and brother. Check.

An optional item, maybe impossible, is to ask my stepmother to get out of the way.

We went into the house and joined Millie. We sat around making civil drivel with the golf announcer *sotto voce* in the background. Suddenly, Millie fastened the evil eye on me, and said, "What have you two been doing out there?"

I just stared at her while I contemplated whether it was any of her damned business.

"Talking," I said neutrally. "What about?"

Restraining my irritation, and ignoring her question, I inquired, "Millie, did you give Pop the message that I was coming down here to see him today?" She had already told me no, but this was for my father's benefit.

If she said yes, she would be caught in a lie. If she said no, she would be caught in wrongdoing. With Millie, the best defense was always a good offense. Jabbing a finger in my direction, she barked, "That's none of your damned business!"

"I came here to talk to my father, and that is my business...."

"Now, you listen here. You don't have anything to say to your father that you can't say in front of me. And don't ask your father for money. If you want money, ask me, Buster, and you know what the answer will be! There are no secrets around here, buddy boy!"

This time she went too far. I jumped out of my seat and flipped her two birds for the price of one. As I stood directly over her, she looked puny and weak.

I told her she could keep her goddamned money. I cussed a blue streak, making reference to her family origins in the canine species. I shouted that I was tired of her Dr. Jekyll and Mr. Hyde personality. I told her there were only two reasons I didn't kill her or beat the shit out of her right then. "One is jail, and you're not worth it," I said. "And the other is out of respect for my father who loves you, although I can't see any reason why anyone would love you." I told her in no uncertain terms that I wanted her to get out of the way of my relationship with my father. I caught her in a wringer your wife about the phone messages, and I told her I expected her to deliver my messages to my father in writing.

When I was through with my tirade, I sat down with a flourish, saying, "I rest my case, and I rest my ass." My adrenaline was still pumping hard, and I still wanted to strangle her, but for a change I wasn't ashamed. Matter of fact, I felt pretty damned good.

Agenda Item Number Four, subset A: Cuss out stepmother. Check.

Millie didn't say if she would honor my request.

Truly, the phone situation never did improve. If anything, it got worse as the years went by, but at least on that day my father got two important messages: One, I loved him; and, two, I wanted to have a relationship with him. As well, and equally important if not more, he heard that his son Tim wanted to reconcile with him.

I SPENT THE NIGHT IN my old room. The next morning I got the windows and something else entirely unexpected.

We loaded the windows into my Step Van. The frames were painted forest green, the same as my father's house, and pretty close to the color we were going to paint the house on Mariposa Avenue. (In fact, the color of this book.)

My stepsisters arrived and we went over to my father's rental apartments to see him. When we were about ready to leave, he called me outside one of the units.

"Here," he said, extending his down-turned hand. Something Pop said made me curious. "I've been meaning to give this to you," he said. "A late graduation present."

I figured he was giving me some gas money for the return trip. Five bucks would fill my twenty-gallon tank. I palmed the cash and stuck it in my pocket without looking at it. Looking to see how much he'd given me would be impolite.

I said, "Thank you, Pop," and we shook hands.

I want to hug you, Papa.

I'd already gassed up the rig, so I figured I was ahead of the game; maybe I would stop for some chow. Halfway home I got to thinking about the money, and my stomach was churning. A graduation present would be more than four or five dollars. Maybe I'd have enough to stop for a sandwich. Driving along, I slid my hand in the right pocket of my black Frisco jeans. I felt more than one bill folded over. I swore I could feel energy flowing out of the bills. Several times I put my hand in my pocket and took it out again, but I kept my eyes on the road.

Finally, I couldn't resist. I pulled out the folded bills. The first was a denomination I'd never seen before: a one hundred dollar bill. At first I thought it was Monopoly money, and my Dad was playing a joke on me. He was fond of gags. Then I thought I must be hallucinating. Since I was about to run off the road anyway, I pulled over and stopped. What denomination would the other bills be? One at a time, I slowly unfolded four crisp one hundred dollar bills! I rubbed my eyes to make sure I wasn't seeing double zeros on a ten-dollar bill.

After a while I shut off the engine. I must have stayed there half an hour, stunned, folding and unfolding and counting them; smelling them; kissing them. Then I wondered: was this money supposed to make up for the four hundred dollars I had borrowed from my senior year's college allowance? If so, my father was setting accounts straight, letting me know he didn't agree with Millie about everything.

Suddenly, I felt very sad. Was this how it was going to be, guilt money in place of open, honest communication? A spasm of pride made me want to return the money. I wished my father would talk to me more, let me know his innermost thoughts, but for now this would do. Four hundred dollars: sixteen months rent! This was his way of saying he loved me and he understood what I was going through. I'd have to settle for the money, at least for the time being.

Would things change between my father and me? The jury was still out on that question. I had captured two new windows, but the hope for a single frame of reference remained at large.

7

Doyle Installs the Windows and Introduces Bouncing Betty

Meanwhile, back at the ranch, Jim and I scratched our heads, trying to figure out how to install the windows. They were about two times larger than the originals. Jim said he could probably figure it out, but it would be better to get someone who had actually installed windows before. A few days later, Jim suggested, "Hey, how about Doyle?"

Doyle worked with us at the almond processing plant.

I thought of the four hundred dollars in the right pocket of my Frisco jeans. I hadn't told anyone about it, and I didn't want my penniless friends getting any ideas. If I flashed the cash, I was afraid I'd have a line of mendicants hitting me up. I was still savoring the sweetness of the gift as I pondered the many ways it could be spent; but, we needed to get the windows installed soon.

Love makes the world go round but money greases the wheels. I wondered if Doyle would take any cash. He wasn't the kind of man who would take money for a favor. In his value system, a favor was a favor, freely given. When he built the cabinets and a bed in the Gypsy Moth, he wouldn't take any money, so I owed him already. If he installed the windows, I could pay him twice. "Okay," I said, "I'll ask him when I see him at work."

DOYLE CLEMONS: SALT OF THE earth. Heart of gold. At 5' 8" and 225 pounds, he was stout and sturdy and not nearly as overweight as his dimensions might indicate. His good-ol'-boy potbelly made him look a little older than his twenty-eight years, but beyond that, he was just plain thick and solid, with a round, pleasant face and alert blue eyes. His folks had come out from the Dust Bowl in the thirties. They knew a few things about survival and fixing anything that needed fixing. I guessed I could trust Doyle to install my windows. A story he had once told me reinforced my trust:

Doyle was a tank mechanic in Vietnam. One day he and his crew were traveling in a jeep to fix a tank stalled on the battlefield. On the way they passed an abandoned jeep, and a bit later they got stuck in mud. The enemy started firing at troops in the area, and bullets whizzed past Doyle's ears. Doyle's jeep didn't have a gun mounted on it, but the jeep they had passed did. Problem was, the gun would swivel only a hundred and eighty degrees, and it was pointed in the wrong direction. Under fire, Doyle managed to unbolt the heavy gun. It took four men to rotate it and bolt it down again. While his crew fired away, Doyle "troubleshot" the jeep and got it started, allowing him and his crew to escape. Knowing Doyle, they probably fixed the tank, too.

A footnote is that Doyle didn't volunteer this story, nor did he tell it with bravado. I kept pestering him for a Vietnam story, and the details came out under my persistent questioning. A lot of guys didn't want to talk about their Vietnam experiences.

WHEN I SAW DOYLE AT work he readily agreed to help. He came over on Saturday. We gave him a tour of the property and a review of the things we had accomplished so far. He took interest in Mike's dump truck, and we told him about the six loads of trash we had removed from the property. We showed him the empty root cellar the previous resident had filled with trash. When we got to the garage, our conversation was suddenly interrupted. Mid-sentence, Doyle stopped talking. His eyes got big and round. "Oh, shit! Bouncing Betty!" he yelled, and quickly backed up thirty feet. "It's Bouncing Betty! Everybody back up!"

Clueless, we all stood our ground. Somebody said, "Betty who?"

"Betty" made me think of my friend Betsy, but that didn't make any sense. "Betty Boop?" I speculated aloud while Doyle kept yelling at us to get out of there.

Then we saw what he was talking about, something that looked like a hand grenade, and we backed away too.

Regaining his cool, he said, "It's all right for now. It's not going off, but stay away from it!" He explained that a Bouncing Betty was launched into the air by a soldier stepping on a triggering device. The shrapnel-filled grenade then broadcast its damage. "It's probably a dud, but you'd better get it checked out."

(The following week we had the sheriff come by and he declared it harmless.)

Clearing out of the garage, we figured the previous resident had bought Betty at an Army Surplus store for her kids to play with. Dirt clods in the living room, six dump truck loads of trash, and a Bouncing Betty for her kids. Strange woman, Mrs. Smith.

AFTER THE BOUNCING BETTY FRIGHT, Doyle got to work. He expanded the window opening to four feet high by six feet wide. "Let's hope the hole doesn't cave in," he said, and put in some temporary bracing. He had Jim and me fetch tools and scrounge some two by fours, while I inquired, "Scalpel? Suture?"

Doyle worked fast. It couldn't have taken more than two hours. Now I had a bedroom with cheerful light, a room with a view.

Fishing out two twenties from Dad's first broken hundred dollar bill, I offered Doyle forty bucks. Twenty dollars a window, not bad; but he wouldn't take it when I said it was for the windows *and* the previous favors.

"Fair enough," I said, "but you're not getting out of here this time without a reward for your efforts." Reluctantly, he took a twenty. "Doyle," I said, "since our wage at the nut house is $3.68 an hour, ten bucks an hour for skilled carpentry ain't bad, and well worth it. And you don't even have to pay taxes. Thank you!"

It's what my father would have said.

That night, I slept in the bedroom for the first time.

Two new windows installed for twenty bucks was a hell of a bargain. In the months to come, some of the guys must have thought so, too because I'm pretty sure Janie and I had some voyeurs watching us from time to time, but we were too busy to notice or care. I never did get around to installing curtains. The windows must have made a nice movie screen of sorts, and the admission was free.

8

Room with a View

Once we got the windows installed, Doyle left and Jim took off somewhere, probably to the gym. I sat on the edge of my five dollar garage sale bed and looked out my two new windows, enjoying the light flooding in, and the view of the weedy side yard and the dirt driveway, and the big old black walnut tree just outside. I thought, *This is going to be my thinking place as long as I live here, and I sat for a long time, pondering my situation.*

I wanted to thank my father for the windows and the four hundred dollars, but I was in a quandary as to how to go about that. If I called, I would get the same old runaround from Millie, and if I wrote, I couldn't mention the money specifically because Millie would intercept the mail ("There are no secrets around here, buddy boy!") and my father would be in trouble.

For one thing, I knew Millie was vengeful. She had kept me from having a driver's license until I was twenty-one because I wrecked her car when I was fourteen. I wouldn't put it past her to screen all my phone calls to my father from now on because I had recently cussed her out. She might never hand over the phone to my father or deliver a message again.

What if I write a letter and thank him for the windows but don't mention the money? That would seem unappreciative. Still, at one point I got up and searched the house for stationery and a writing instrument. There wasn't a scrap of paper other than a grocery bag, no envelopes, no stamps, and not even the stub of a pencil. There were no books either. I was, after all, taking a complete break from academia.

The sense of victory I took away with me from Lafayette now seemed hollow. I could only sit and think what I wished I could say to my father, and hope he was psychic. *I love you, Papa. Thank you for the money and the windows. I wish you would come up here and enjoy the view out the windows with me.*

Would the situation ever change between my father and me?

At least I planted a seed.

Meanwhile, the phone wasn't ringing and no letters arrived from Lafayette. I could only hope what I had said to my father might have an impact, because I thought it unlikely I would ever have the opportunity, time, place, and courage to speak to my father so clearly and passionately as I had during my last visit. The best I could do was chalk it up as a moral victory.

"I can only clean up my side of the street," I thought, quoting my wise older brother, the ex-con.

I sat for another hour in my thinking place on the edge of the bed, gazing out the two new windows and daydreaming about the times to come at 2307 Mariposa Avenue in Chico in California, in the United States of America, in the World, in the Universe and the Mind of God. I wondered how it all would look in retrospect when I retired with a gold watch and an engraved plaque.

I thought about Em, my college sweetheart who had abandoned me for another. *Only one time in life do we know first love. There is no love so intense as first love; no wound so deep and difficult to heal as first love lost. I'm still hung up on Em. Why don't I just move on? Why do I feel so empty and alone? I should just let go and move on, but it's impossible to let go of something so big all at once.* I entertained a gallant and delusional notion that she would someday come back to me, having seen the error of leaving me. Never mind that she was married and had a child. On one hand, I was determined to wait for her forever; on the other, I knew such a futile notion could lead me into deep depression. I tried telling myself she was gone forever, and it was time to move on, but I believed it only from the neck up. Acceptance was still many years away, despite numerous relationships with other women. Whenever I dwelt on the grief of her departure, I doubted I would ever meet someone of her caliber: all others were merely a consolation prize.

But wait a minute. What about Janie? We'd had a highly charged liaison one afternoon a month or two before and I hadn't seen her since. I was still thinking about her, but I had misplaced her phone number and I didn't know where she lived. By my parents' definition and my own rational thinking, she and I were a mismatch from the get-go, but what good would it do me to care about my parents' opinions at this point, and how much good had rational thinking done me? It was time to learn to trust my intuition. And what good was it doing me to pine over the lost Em? I just knew I wanted to be with Janie, and I was determined to find a way, if only I could scare up her phone number or find out where she lived.

I suddenly remembered something. Excitedly, I ran out to the van and rummaged around in the glove box. There was Janie's phone number!

Although very excited, I went back and sat on the bed to calm down, and I wondered: *Do I really want to get involved? And what about this Free Love I've been hearing so much about?* I was definitely willing to continue contributing to that social experiment. Would it be compatible with a relationship with Janie?

I had scant idea where life was taking me. Meanwhile, I knew this was where I belonged, here on the edge of the bed, in this little shack on the outskirts of town. I was just happy to have a room with a view, and a place to sit and think.

The next day, I called Janie.

9
Meeting Barney

One day that first fall on Mariposa, Jim came home all excited. "Did you meet that new guy in janitorial—young blond guy, martial artist?" I hadn't.

Jim couldn't stop talking about Barney. "There I am at work in the shelling room, and I see this young guy come through pushing a broom. He was limping pretty bad, but you wouldn't believe how fast he was sweeping the shelling room. All that almond dust under those machines, and all those nooks and crannies—I've never seen anyone get the job done so fast, yet he made it look easy, like he wasn't in a hurry at all, and the whole time he's doing his job with a limp, so I asked him what was wrong.

"He says, 'Oh I injured myself, but I'll get over it.'"

"I kept asking him for more details about what happened, but he wouldn't tell me, and finally he says, 'See, I'll get over it, and I can still kick.'

"Right then, you wouldn't believe it. I'm not kidding, he unleashed a karate kick that reached at least, and I mean *at least* twelve feet in the air! I said, Jesus Christ, how in the hell did you do that?

"And he said, 'I've had some training.'

"Well, damn, right away I said I wanted to know how to do that too, and would he show me sometime? So I invited him over."

That's how the karate demonstrations, lessons and sparring

sessions began in the back yard, and Barney became part of the core group that was Mariposa Avenue: Jim, Mike, Barney, Brother Tim, Calhoun, Gene and Tina, Janie, and Steve. Notwithstanding the fact that everyone else was incidental or just passing through, they were all unique in ways that made life on Mariposa endlessly entertaining.

Barney was a counterpart to Jim and me. While Jim and I were college educated, Barney (like Janie) dropped out of high school in the tenth grade, but he was clever and funny, street smart and tough as hell. With his unique qualities, he became a regular on the Mariposa scene.

Barney was born in 1951 in Chapman Town, Chico's poor white ghetto. That neighborhood, like the Mariposa property, lived on the margin of Chico. (In this sense, Barney's arrival at 2307 constituted a kind of homecoming for him.) Chapman Town was set apart by Little Chico Creek and further defined by open fields to the east, Twentieth Street to the south, and Mulberry Street on the west. Like our neighborhood, Chapman Town was a world apart.

Chapman Town constituted a mere ten square blocks, but was no less obvious for its tattered earmarks: travel trailers cobbled together with makeshift additions; broken down cars in the yard. Residents of the Better Part of Town might spend their Saturdays mowing the lawn or touching up the paint job on their houses. Chapman Town folks socialized while helping each other fix their cars, horse-trading, and what Barney called "bullshitting," or just hanging out and swapping stories. Nobody was in a hurry.

An ethic of self-sufficiency prevailed. Nobody in the neighborhood would ever consent to being on welfare. The folks in Chapman Town had real core values, pioneer values, Bible Belt values. A certain raw honesty ran as a common thread amongst them, the kind of abrupt honesty you find in people who live close to the bone and have nothing left to lose but their integrity. This was where Barney came from. Coincidentally, Barney and Jim grew up in the same neighborhood, but Jim was five years older.

Of Chapman Town, Jim says, "The men who came there after WWII had some things in common. They had all survived the war on the front lines. They'd been in the army and they were fed up with rules. They didn't want the city government telling them how they could live or what kind of dwellings they could inhabit, so they set up shop on the other side of the creek that marked the city boundary. Another thing these men had in common: They were all big, and I don't mean big because I was little and they all looked big to a little kid, but I mean *big;* all over six feet, big chests, big bones, and they ate big."

It wasn't until Barney had been around 2307 a while that he and Jim compared notes and realized they had both been born and raised in the same neighborhood. With Barney being younger, the two boys didn't have much reason to associate with each other despite the defined area that was Chapman Town. As well, Jim moved to another part of Chico for a time before moving on to a remote corner of Northern California and subsequently to Reno and Redding before returning to Chico for college. What began to create a linkage of memory between them was martial arts. They had both had the same sensei, Bud Estes.

Bud and a friend named Lamar Fisher had studied jujitsu and tae kwon do, respectively, when they were stationed in the military in Hawaii. After WWII, they decided to return stateside and bring their particular forms of martial art to the U.S., and they ended up in Chico. By the time Barney was seventeen, he held a black belt in both jujitsu and tae kwon do, having studied under Bud and Lamar.

The more Jim and Barney compared notes, the more they remembered snippets of seeing each other. Jim remembered Barney as "a wiry blond kid, a virtual blaze of can't-sit-still energy, as curious as he was energetic."

Another thing he and Jim had in common was that they each grew up without a father. Barney's father split when he was maybe two years old. Jim's father, a fighter pilot instructor in WWII, went down in a training exercise just after the war due to mechanical failure, the day Jim was born.

(Come to think of it, we all had father issues—a rite of passage. Calhoun's parents split up and put him in foster care. My father was distant and unavailable. Steve's father was a kind and humorous man but a stern disciplinarian. Gene was often pissed off at his father. The only one with a healthy relationship with his father was Mike.)

Barney's mother, Maxine, raised him mostly on her own because his eventual stepfather Rufus was a sort of yo-dee-oh-doe thumb twiddler, a good breadwinner but a bit low on the intellectual scale, and he didn't participate much in parenting. He was more like an older pal to Barney. Maxine was definitely salt of the earth. She was built like a bowling ball, and you got the sense that if offended, she could knock you over like a bowling pin. "Don't mess with Mama," I heard her say on more than one occasion.

Her face was round and marbled and sometimes shiny from a shot or three of whiskey. One time I went to see her because I was concerned about some problems Barney was having. She said, "Oh, really? You think he has problems? I thought he was just wet behind the ears and didn't know how to wipe his ass!" Before long she had me in stitches and I forgot about Barney's temporary heroin problem, and Maxine fixed me some biscuits and gravy. Maxine was by equal measures kind, crude, funny, tough and willful, and you couldn't put anything over on her; like mother, like son. One of Barney's favorite expressions, which he learned from his mother: "Don't try to con the con man."

Aside from his mother, Barney described his origins as "Heinz 57—a mongrel, and mongrels are the best." His grandfather was full-blooded Cherokee, six-foot-six and thick through the chest. If there's such a thing as ancestral memory, Barney's intolerance for injustice and his willingness to defend himself and others must have come from his Cherokee ancestors who walked the Trail of Tears. His hot temper must have come from the Scotch-Irish. Another measure of his "Heinz 57" must have derived from Nordic roots, as evidenced by his blond hair and light complexion.

Pound for pound, Barney was the most powerful human being I'd ever met. A carpenter's grip is nothing compared to Barney's. He was also the fastest human I ever met. I have timed him in the 100-yard dash in the low ten seconds—Olympic caliber. When he ran, it wasn't one foot in front of the other. Rather, he leaped and bounded like a deer. He was a fast worker too. I once saw him paint a two-bedroom apartment in two hours, without using a tarp, and he did a good job without spilling a drop. The whole time, he kept up a running patter and didn't look like he was hurrying in the least.

When Barney arrived at Mariposa, he was one of the least likely persons with whom I'd ever form a friendship. He wasn't someone I would have met if not for Mariposa and Continental Nut and Jim (but it seemed somehow fated that he and Jim would come together in a reprise of their mutual origins). I had no idea that we would be friends for over twenty years, let alone how our friendship would end.

Some sort of glue held Barney and me together. Where I shriveled in the face of conflict, he welcomed it. Where I played possum or ran the other way in the face of danger or physical confrontation, Barney stood and faced the enemy. Barney didn't look for trouble but if it found him, with his intuitive sense and his martial arts, he was fearless and ready for battle. Because he projected fearlessness, and he could read people like a book, the fight was over before it started.

Where I hesitated to speak up lest I descend into psychobabble and puerile attempts at nicety, Barney cut through the bullshit and told someone to go fly and get out of his face. In a pack of wolves he'd have been the Alpha. He was quick to anger but quick to forgive. I found this refreshing and reassuring, because like his mother, underneath the gruff exterior was a heart of gold, someone you could trust. Often I heard Jim say, "I trust Barney with my life." Barney was the guy you'd want watching your back in a dark alley.

In Barney I found an antidote to my crouching fear of confrontation. Thus he became my alter ego, and I followed around in his wake for many years. Our paths diverged when he became a dyed-in-the-wool survivalist. (Parting our ways is a story in itself.) For all his uncouth manner and the nuttiness that overtook him in later years, there was comfort in his raw honesty for as long as I knew him.

One day someone uninvited came knocking on the door, and I learned a lot more about Barney, something that created a tighter bond between us.

A STRANGER UNINVITED COMES AND FILLS THE DOORWAY

One day not long after Barney first appeared in our lives, someone knocked on the front door so hard, I thought it was going to explode off its hinges. It scared me. I didn't like the "vibes", so I didn't answer. After a minute, I peered out the front window to make sure the caller was gone. Tentatively, I slid the hasp and opened the front door a crack. Just as I was doing this, I heard another explosion at the back door, and I just about jumped out of my skin. Damn! Now I was not only scared but pissed off. Keeping my steps silent, I stole to the little window over the sink by the back door, and peeked out. It appeared no one was there. Just in case, I flung the door open.

I was loaded for bear, but quickly withered in the face of the imposing stranger filling the doorway like a wall of bricks. He looked like Mr. Kleen in a tight white tee shirt with a pack of Marlboros rolled up in one sleeve. He was blond and shaped like an acute "V". He appeared totally unmoved by my aggression. Standing a step below the threshold, his stare seemed to pass right through my chest. It was I, not he, who backed up a step. I felt an immediate sense of defeat and intimidation.

There was something decidedly martial about him. He was standing in military at-ease posture with his hands clasped in front of his belt. "Where's Barney?" he barked like a drill sergeant.

I thought the friendly approach might throw him off guard since nothing else was working. "Hey, what's going on?" I said. "Come on in, set a spell."

"I'm not coming in."

"Well," I stalled, "Jim's not here, and neither is Mike...."

"I don't give a damn! Where's Barney?"

Now I was starting to worry that Barney might have gotten mixed up in some bad business and this goon was coming to break his knees.

"Well, I don't know any Barney, whoever that is. We're all out of pot," I telegraphed in case he was a narc, "and nobody here has any money…."

"Where's Barney?" he pursued even more forcefully. At this moment a whole flood of feelings and impressions started overloading my senses. For one thing, I was instantly pissed off at Barney for attracting this kind of hostile energy to The Ranch (as we sometimes called 2307). There always was something lowlife about Barney, some kind of skeleton in his closet I couldn't figure out, and now he'd attracted violence to my doorstep.

Another impression that came through on a gut level was that this man at the doorstep was my brother Jon incarnate, come back to haunt me with his cruel ways. My visitor's presence brought the same creepy feeling that I used to feel when the sadistic Jon picked on Tim, and the fight began, and they chased each other around with knives or baseball bats. All in an instant while the stranger filled the doorway, I had a flashback: Jon throwing a steak knife, the knife finding its target, and twanging back and forth in Tim's thigh. In another flashback, I felt the sting of b.b.'s when Tim shot me with the b.b. gun to take out his frustrations toward Jon.

"Like I said, there's no Barney here; haven't seen him, haven't heard of him, don't know who you're talking about, and if he's ever been here I don't know if he's coming back or when that might be. Besides, you haven't said who you are, and you haven't stated your business, but you're welcome to come in and look around…."

"I don't give a fuck!" he said. His words were not yelled but they went through me like a piece of straw penetrating a tree in a hurricane. "Just tell him I was looking for him." With these words, the stranger did an about face and was gone.

Calling after him, "Who shall I say was looking for him?"

Without turning around or slowing his pace, he said, "He'll know."

A few days later, Barney showed up. When I began describing the scary stranger, he interrupted. "Blond guy, white tee shirt, cigs rolled up in his sleeve?"

"Yep. What's he got against you?"

"Oh, that's my brother Louie. He always acts likethat."

I told Barney how much Louie reminded me of my brother Jon; how my guts seized up in Louie's presence same as they used to do in Jon's; how I felt helpless whenever the fights started between my brothers. I confided in him what had happened between Jon and Tim, and why Tim had to go to prison.

That was the day Barney and I became friends, as we shared the miseries of our past. Barney told me how his older brother would wake him up at five a.m. by slapping him on the soles of the feet with a willow switch and ordering him to "roll out and give me a hundred pushups!" If Barney refused, Louie would start beating on him. This information corroborated the helpless feelings and flashbacks I'd had when Louie came looking for his brother. We both had older brothers who were sadistic. My brother Tim and Barney had faced continual abuse. Barney's response was to take martial arts so that he might stand a chance against his brother. Tim's response was to fight back as best he could, and one day he put an end to the fights for good.

"Do you ever feel like killing Louie?" I asked. "Sometimes I've wanted to, but he's my brother. If the two of us ever really get into it, only one of us is going to walk away."

Another thing Barney told me was that his brother had just returned from Vietnam where he was one of only a few in his unit to survive after he'd been pinned down for days on a hilltop, the infamous Hamburger Hill. "Louie finally said, 'To hell with it, I'm going to fight my way out of here or die trying,' and he fought his way out" with a combination of weapons and hand to hand combat. It was not long after that battle that Louie came to 2307 and filled my doorway with his deadly presence.

BARNEY INVENTS THE LETTUCE SANDWICH

"Whaddya you got to eat around here?" Barney bounded through the back door one spring day with nary a "howdy" and headed straight for the orange refrigerator, which was empty except for half a stick of butter and a block of Jack cheese.

He slammed the refrigerator door.

"We're out of everything but Romaine lettuce and cheese," I managed to fit in before he flung open the green refrigerator, "unless you can figure out how to make a cheese sandwich without bread," I said sarcastically.

Barney leaned over with his head buried inside the green fridge.

"I told you, man, there's nothing in there that you'd want. Why don't you drink some Trappey's hot sauce like you usually do?"

Barney had a habit of leaping through the back door and making a beeline for the Trappey's on a shelf over the stove. He'd screw off the top, tilt his head back and shake a jolt of Trappey's directly into his mouth. Then he'd replace the lid and put the bottle back on the shelf before repeating the whole procedure. (It never made any sense to me, why he always put the bottle back only to open it up again, but he explained to me once that he didn't want to be greedy with the sauce.)

"Goddam rabbit food," he said, taking out a leaf of romaine and crossing the kitchen to the sink where he washed the leaf quickly, and returned to the table by the window.

"What are you going to do with that? I thought you didn't like rabbit food," I said.

Getting the cheese out of the orange fridge, he replied, "By god, I'm going to have myself a sandwich!"

"You call that a sandwich? I told you we don't have any bread. Why don't you just wave a magic wand? And when you're through doing that, why don't you go to the store and pick up a loaf?"

"I'm too hungry to go to the store, and I just told you, dammit, I'm going to have a sandwich. Now shut your trap and hand me that hot sauce."

By the time I reached the Trappey's and passed it to him, he already had the cheese laid out on his new invention. "Here," I said, "be my guest, and I hope you burn your guts out."

"I will, and I'm going to enjoy it, and have myself a sandwich, and when I'm through I'm going to fix you one too, and you're going to eat it and you're going to like it and you're going to thank me for it."

Barney shook some hot sauce onto his creation. He folded the leaf over the contents of his "sandwich" burrito style, and ate half of it in one gulp. Not quite satisfied, he shook some Trappey's directly down his gullet and chased it with the rest of his Barney D. Lettuce Sandwich. Before I could say Cheez Whiz, he had fixed another one, and polished it off, and was working on yet another one for me.

"No hot sauce, please."

"It's no good without hot sauce."

"Put hot sauce on it, I won't eat it."

He handed me the "sandwich" with instructions to hold it so the lettuce, folded end to end and side to side, wouldn't come undone. I ate it, and declared it good but somewhat bland.

"That's because no hot sauce."

"Get off the hot sauce!"

"Then, by god, you'll have it with something else.

His head was inside the orange refrigerator again, and out he came with a small jar of sauerkraut.

"Well, I'll be damned. Where did you get that?"

"It was stuck in the back where you couldn't see it."

You guessed it. Next he made us each a lettuce sandwich with sauerkraut and cheese. He found a little mustard and applied it. I pronounced it quite good; delicious, in fact.

What followed was somewhere between a royal feast and a feeding frenzy. We polished off the whole supply of lettuce, a block of cheese, a jar of sauerkraut, and a bottle of Trappey's. (I refrained from the hot sauce, though.) By now I was actually convinced I was eating some kind of sandwich, despite the lack of bread. One day it occurred to me Barney's initials were BLD, so that's what we called the Lettuce Sandwich—a BLD.

The next day I picked some more lettuce, scraped together some change to buy another jar of sauerkraut and a block of cheese, and waited for Barney to show up. When he arrived, Jim was there, and I sat back and watched Jim go through the whole initiation into the Barney D. Lettuce Sandwich. The dialogue was pretty much the same as the day before, but Jim didn't argue as much, and before long he said, "Damn, that's good. Gimme another one."

After that day, we kept fixing lettuce sandwiches, trying out new combinations such as a lettuce sandwich with kippered snacks or anchovies. "How do you want your lettuce sandwich this time?" Barney would inquire.

"Make mine medium rare with sauerkraut, and hold the hot sauce. No bread."

We fixed them with great ceremony and reverence.

Soon it became our custom to offer a lettuce sandwich to all our guests.

"Lettuce sandwich? What's that?" At this point we'd regale them with the entire cumulative history of the BLD. The story got longer and longer every time someone new tried a lettuce sandwich because their responses were added to the tale. It almost got to be a shaggy dog story.

I even stretched it out on purpose sometimes, just to see how long it would take before the listener said, "That sounds awfully good. You're making my mouth water. Does this story have an ending? I'm getting hungry." I was declared Master of the Shaggy Dog Department. Jim was elected Expert of Sensuous Description of all the juicy details of preparing, smelling and eating Barney's invention. While Jim narrated in great sensory detail, Barney made the sandwiches. It was like having a famous chef in your own kitchen, having Barney there to prepare your sandwich.

Jim insisted the listener hear the whole description before actually taking a bite. "Chew each bite forty times, and notice the many subtle changes in flavor."

"Damn," the visitor would declare. "Let me try one."

And hold the bread.

10

Meeting Calhoun

My first recollection of Calhoun was when I saw him sunbathing on the hood of a creamy white Lincoln parked at the curb next door to 2307. Arriving home on my bicycle, I made note of his presence, nodding as I swung past him into the driveway. Parking the bike on the back porch, I went into the house to put away groceries, half expecting the young longhair to show up on the back porch just as so many others had done since Jim and I moved in a year before. After all, I had seen him around town for a few days, standing out like a sore thumb in the fancy car. When I saw him driving around I had a hunch he might show up at the house.

By the time I went back out to check on the guy on the hood, there sat Jim alongside him. Jim always acted like he knew people, even those he'd just met, so it came as no surprise to find him there, sunbathing with Calhoun and shooting the breeze.

To my perception, Calhoun was just some guy who happened along but Jim recently set me straight on that, and the story was much more interesting than my limited recall:

> *I first met Calhoun after a vision quest at Pyramid Lake in Nevada in August of '69. I spent a few nights under a full moon, and as it turned out, that was the same full moon that was shining on everyone at Woodstock. I hitchhiked back. While I was waiting*

> *for a ride at Hallelujah Junction, near Susanville, there wasn't a car in sight for at least an hour. Then I saw in the distance a little black dot growing bigger as it came closer. Soon I could make out a black and silver Chevy Impala truck, and I squeezed in alongside this tall skinny longhair kid. His uncle was driving. Nothing much was said for miles, but when we stopped in Quincy for coffee, we talked a lot. When I asked about Calhoun's occupation, he was a bit vague. He mentioned he'd been in the army in 'Nam, but when I asked questions he just said, 'I got out of there because my days were numbered.' I found that intriguing, but I didn't press the point. Turns out Calhoun was AWOL from the military, hiding out at his uncle's place in Greenville. We got to talking about music. Calhoun said he wanted to learn blues guitar, so naturally I told him to come on down; I'd teach him. It took him quite a while to get around to it—almost two years—but he finally showed up.*

There you have it: The serendipitous convergence of Woodstock, Jim's vision quest, and a young private gone AWOL while thousands of our peers were being blown away in 'Nam. That's how Calhoun came to sunbathe on the hood of the Lincoln, which turned out to be his uncle's, and Jim really did know Calhoun already. The music lessons began that day, and continued perhaps a year. Calhoun really did have a talent for the blues. The music connection was how Calhoun became a member of the Mariposa scene.

DROOPY-EYED, BROWN-HAIRED CALHOUN was long, loose

and lanky. He walked like a slinky, with his feet leading and the length of his body slowly catching up. Because of this, I came to call him "Sidewinder," which was as much a reference to his character as to his unique mode of moving about. Without compunction, he'd steal your woman, eat your food, smoke your dope, and laugh in your face. Satire was a way of life for him.

When I found out he'd been a private in the army I started calling him "Privates."

"Stand at attention, *Privates*!" I commanded, but Calhoun always hung loose. If he got the stupid pun, he didn't let on.

Calhoun was a "wannabe" black man in a white man's body. "What's up, fool?" was his favorite greeting; only, he said it more like, "Whassup, foo'?" I always thought his emulation of black ghetto speech, mannerisms, music, and sense of humor was his attempt at being hip and soulful. It was all part of his clown act.

Jim got a big kick out of Calhoun the Clown, but in his act I sensed a cover-up for an angry young man who could turn volatile. One thing for sure, and Jim even said it: "You can't trust Calhoun any farther than you can throw him." But he was hilarious at times, iconoclastic, holding nothing sacred, making fun of anything and everyone.

Calhoun could improvise blues lyrics out of any everyday situation, usually with the obligatory sexual innuendo. He lived his life as one continuous soulful blues riff and jam session.

For reasons I still don't wholly understand, women found Calhoun attractive. With his unique mannerisms and his devil-may-care attitude, I guess women thought him charismatic, a refreshing change from fawning men with cliché pick-up lines. As soon as he'd meet a woman, the playful insults would start; he'd get them laughing, and that turned them on. Next thing you knew, Calhoun disappeared for a week or two, and it wasn't too hard to figure out how he was spending his time. Maybe he had a magnetism seen only by women but not by guys. But Calhoun couldn't keep a woman around, or maybe he didn't care to. It seemed with Calhoun that the conquest was more important than a relationship. If a woman stayed around too long, that might cut into his next prospect.

Unlike Jim or Steve or Barney—real friends who respected my boundaries and stayed clear of Janie despite her flirtatious ways and their obvious attraction to her—I sensed that Calhoun would have no hesitation about a fling with Janie if the opportunity arose. Over time, I could see Janie getting interested in him, and that worried me.

Calhoun was a snake in the grass.

11

Tyrannosaurus Rex and Other Ways To Beat the Draft

Each of us on Mariposa Avenue dealt with the threat of forced conscription in our own unique ways. Some, like my stepbrother, joined the army and came back mentally unhinged. Some got lucky and never got called. Calhoun joined, went to Vietnam, and went AWOL. Some managed to get declared unfit for service. Here's an account of how several of us exercised our right to avoid military service in a war we didn't believe in.

JIM

Jim was classified unfit for service because of his close acquaintance with Tyrannosaurus Rex.

"When I got to the induction center in 1968, they handed us a medical history form. Well, I looked around and saw a lot of guys checking off every malady you can think of—heart murmur, measles, you name it, but I know a few things about filling out forms. I was much more selective, and I knew that it had to be the truth. So when I saw 'Nightmares,' I checked that.

"At some point I was pulled aside and placed on the Group W Bench with a bunch of other misfits—you know, the mother rapists and father stabbers—waiting for an interview. My turn came, and I was called into the shrink's office on the other side of a partition. He must have been a licensed psychiatrist because he even had a couch in there.

"He was very sincere and he seemed truly interested in my dreams, the way a real psychiatrist would. 'So,' he said, leaning forward, his eyeballs looking very large behind his thick glasses, 'tell me about your dreams!'

"Well, I saw that couch and thought I'd get in the mood, and I said, 'how about if I just lie down here?' So I stretched out and started telling the good doctor how all my life I'd had these dreams where I went go to sleep, and within the dream I dreamed that I woke up and went back to sleep. I told him how this pattern kept repeating through several levels until I was several levels down in the dream. For effect, I yawned there on the couch and acted very sleepy as I mumbled my way through my recitation. I *was* a bit sleepy, so it wasn't hard to act the part.

"There I was all sleepy and yawning and telling him that once I got into the deepest level of the dream, in order to fully wake up I had to come back up through all the levels before I was actually awake. Sometimes my mother found me sleepwalking, or if the dream was a bad one, I was out of bed sleep-fighting imaginary monsters and she couldn't wake me up because I still had to come back up through all the levels of the dream. Then I told the psychiatrist how, in the deepest level, I sometimes dreamed that I sat up in bed and looked out my window and there, looking me in the face was....

"At this point, I jumped off the shrink's couch and shouted, '...TYRANNOSAURUS REX!!!!!!!' and I started shadowboxing T. Rex while I screamed and yelled right there in the shrink's office. I think I knocked some stuff off his desk. You should have seen his reaction. He was so freaked out, he wrote me off then and there. That was the beginning and the end of my military career."

THIS MAN'S ARMY

Another friend, Alyosha, paid a visit to the psychiatrist's office just as Jim did. The way Alyosha told it, when the psychiatrist asked him why he claimed to be unfit for military service, 'I stroked my mustache like this, first one side, then the other, and said, 'Because, you don't want me in this man's army.' Upon further questioning, Alyosha implied that he was interested in his own gender, and he said, 'All those fit young male bodies....you never know what might happen in the barracks after lights out.' Alyosha was immediately classified unfit for service. Alyosha, by the way, was one of the most masculine, heterosexual males I ever knew, a former halfback on the UCLA football squad.

GENE (THE CAVEMAN)

Gene stumbled on a very simple means of being classified 4-F.

"At the induction center, just before the blood pressure station, I sat on the floor right there in the midst of all that commotion on the gray linoleum, and I meditated. Hundreds of guys were coming and going, and I just sat there cross-legged on the floor and closed my eyes, pretending I was back in my cave in Deer Creek Canyon. After a while, I opened my eyes and got in line, trying not to move around too much or get excited. When my turn came, my blood pressure was so low, they thought I was dead, and they declared me 4-F."

HOW CALHOUN WENT AWOL

I mentioned that Calhoun had gone AWOL from Vietnam.

Jim recently told me more about Calhoun's exit from 'Nam. Here is that story:

Calhoun sat on the tarmac in the shade of the general's jeep and contemplated his situation. Even in the shade, the heat and humidity of Vietnam had him feeling like a limp biscuit.

On this particular day, Staff Sergeant Joe Bob Wright gave Calhoun a direct order: rotate the tires on the general's jeep. This task was, of course, completely superfluous. It was just a way for Joe Bob to pull rank and harass Calhoun, whom he hated with a passion.

Certainly, Calhoun had given the S/Sgt. reason enough to hate him, all the way back to training camp at Fort Bragg where the indolent Calhoun earned his stripes as the world's greatest slacker. Staff Sergeant Wright was a southern cracker, career military, son of a military family going back generations, and Calhoun was an eighteen-year-old don't-give-a-damn kid who irritated Joe Bob no end.

One example of Cahoun's passive/aggressive antagonism occurred one day when Job Bob ordered him to "sweep this barracks now!" Ever so slowly, Calhoun reached for the broom and began sweeping at a glacial speed. Calhoun's speech matched the pace of his work. "Yooou meeean yooou want meee tooo sweeeep liiiike thiiis, mister staaaaff seeeer-geant, sir?"

By the time boot camp was over, Joe Bob was looking forward to being shipped out, just to get away from Calhoun. But as fate would have it, Calhoun and Joe Bob were assigned to the same base in 'Nam. Not only that, Calhoun was one of Joe Bob's charges. One day, Joe Bob was looking for Calhoun who happened to be blowing reefer in the tent where the black guys hung out. Joe Bob, being a good southern cracker, would not be caught in the same tent with all those black dudes, let alone smoke pot.

Sergeant Joe Bob shouted, "Calhoun, I know you're in there! Come out NOW!"

Calhoun, in his best imitation of black dialect, said, "Calhoun? Dey ain' no Calhoun in heaah." Joe Bob stormed off and Calhoun remained in the tent. (This is an example of how Calhoun took on black mannerisms as a kind of protective coloration.)

The situation escalated until Joe Bob openly threatened Calhoun's life. Calhoun was Inspector Clouseau to Joe Bob's Inspector Dreyfus of *Pink Panther* fame. I can just imagine Joe Bob being steadily driven crazy by Calhoun, and being hauled off in a straitjacket to write, "Kill Calhoun!" with his toes on the wall of a padded cell. (That must have been what Calhoun meant when he first met Jim and explained that he got out of Vietnam because "My days were numbered.")

TRUE TO FORM, THE DAY Joe Bob gave Calhoun the order to rotate the general's tires, Calhoun said laconically, "Yessssiiiir, Mr. Sergeant man, comin' right up." Then he sauntered off to his tent to roll some joints, took off his shirt, grabbed his suntan lotion and his boom box, and made his way to the jeep. He proceeded to rub suntan lotion all over his torso, ever so slowly. It was hot, after all. One had to move slowly in this kind of heat, and one had to have lotion. Then Calhoun jacked up the car one wheel at a time, taking frequent breaks and toking a joint, until the whole jeep was up on blocks. While he sat smoking a doobie and listening to Jimi Hendrix, Calhoun thought about Joe Bob's threats, and how damned hot it was out there on the tarmac.

Suddenly, Calhoun had an idea. "Fuck this," he said. Leaving the general's jeep up on blocks, he stood up, clicked off his boom box, and walked to the base commander's office where he sometimes did clerical work. No one was around. He went to a particular file cabinet and fished out a form. Filling it out expertly, he wrote himself a two-week furlough. In the appropriate slots, he indicated that his grandmother was deathly ill, and he was the only surviving male family member. He knew those facts would trigger an immediate mandatory return to the states. He especially enjoyed that last bit of creativity. (Calhoun's grandmother was alive and well, and he wasn't the last male in his family.)

Then he expertly forged the base commander's signature. At the CO's request he had signed the CO's signature on other occasions to requisition goods. Calhoun learned that he could acquire pretty much anything he wanted to use or sell or trade for dope. Once he even gave himself and some buddies a furlough in Saigon, and requisitioned the general's jeep to get there! His plan to sell it failed, so he ran it into a ditch and left it there. Knowing Calhoun, he probably came up with a plausible explanation for the missing jeep. Now, with the general's latest jeep up on blocks, Calhoun fed the newly forged form into proper channels. Within the week, the relieved Joe Bob ordered him to board a flight for the states.

Calhoun never returned to military service. Eventually the army caught up with him and he was threatened with dishonorable discharge, but the forged signature was so well done, he was given the benefit of the doubt, and he was upgraded to a plain discharge—which Calhoun righteously protested. In the end, he got an honorable discharge with full benefits. The last time I saw him, in 1974, he was using his GI Bill to attend classes at Butte College.

And that's how Calhoun avoided military service. "If you can't beat 'em, join 'em, and then outfox 'em at their own game." That was Calhoun's credo. Come to think of it, he must have been looking over his shoulder the whole time he hung around Mariposa.

YOURS TRULY
VS.
THE U.S. GOVERNMENT

"The war can't go on forever. If you just keep stalling, it could be over before they call you."
John Whitcomb

The draft in those days was a death sentence that I was not going to accept. As far as I was concerned, there was a good reason the draft was called 'Selective Service', because I was going to be very selective about the service I was willing to perform--selective as in zero.

In my last year in college, I lost my student deferment, and applied for Conscientious Objector Status. The saga lasted nearly four years and involved lots of paperwork, which was my way of beating the government at its own game. My basic strategy was to use the bureaucracy against itself.

I began by writing a letter requesting an application for C.O. Status. By law, as long as that request was in the works I could not be drafted. The government being what it is, every step of the way took thirty, sixty, or ninety days. I sent the letter off and waited sixty days. When I got the application back, I had thirty days to file it. I waited till the twenty-ninth day and sent the application certified, special delivery, return signature required. Every time I added something to my file, or took another step in the application or appeals process, another thirty, sixty, or ninety days went by. I always sent the return on the last possible day, and I went on with my life. I kept copies of everything, even the return signature cards.

The process went on like that for three years. Then my request was denied. That was a mere formality that opened the way to appeals, but I grew tired of the game. I was prepared to go to jail or Canada. Legal steps were still available to me, but in our little game of chess the draft board had put me in check. To stay in the appeals game I needed a lawyer, which I could not afford.

When the notice to appear for a physical arrived in the late fall of '70, I simply failed to appear. That was good for another sixty days until I received a letter saying I'd been bad, and I should appear thirty days after receiving the letter.

I hitched to Sacramento and got on a bus that took me and a bus full of potential inductees to the Induction Center in Oakland. What a scene! When we arrived, we were greeted by sign-bearing protesters and a troupe of clowns.

I went in, took some parts of the test, skipped others, and left. Thirty days later...you get the idea. Eventually, I completed all tests in late spring of '71. In June of that year I received a 1-A classification, but my stalling strategy paid off. Thirty days after I got my 1-A, the lottery system was put in place! Mostly nineteen-year-old draftees with numbers one through nineteen were inducted. By then I was twenty-five years old, and my lucky number came up 276. The odds of my being drafted were one in several million. Once I received this news, the shining times at Mariposa began. I was finally able to relax and enjoy my remaining time at Mariposa.

On some level, I wasn't satisfied with that outcome. I wanted to be officially sanctioned as a pacifist, but actually, had I been granted Conscientious Objector Status, I'd have been required to perform some form of alternate service, something I did not intend doing under any circumstances. In many cases, alternate service meant CO's became medics, getting shot at in 'Nam without carrying a gun for self-protection. In other cases, CO's worked in Veterans' hospitals. I regarded alternate service as condoning the war, which

I refused to support in any way. In retrospect, the stalemate actually became a complete victory.

I never disputed the right of the individual to join the military according to the dictates of his own conscience. We each exercised our right to choose, and I'm thankful for that. In the long run, I believe I served my country better by refusing to participate in a futile and fruitless war costing 55,000 lives. I survived, and for twenty-five years I gave back to society by teaching youngsters in public schools. If that's not good enough alternate service, I don't know what is.

12

The Legend of Crazy Earl

One day I came home and found two off duty police officers sitting on Jim's weight bench in the back yard.

In fact, I was soon to find out they were so off duty, they weren't even on the force anymore. Before I became aware of that, though, their appearance made me paranoid. As I rolled up on my bicycle, I speculated, are they narcs? On furlough from the Marines? What brings them here? The last time anyone so martial looking had appeared at the house, Barney's brother Louie had filled the doorway and scared the shit out of me.

They looked like twins with their matching tight white tee shirts, blue jeans and athletic physiques. Their short neat hair and well-trimmed mustaches made them look as if they'd just visited the same barber. As I parked the bike and approached them on foot, I felt something was wrong with the picture. Aha! They were passing a joint back and forth! I thought maybe they were working undercover. If so, I thought it was pretty unfair. *They can get stoned on the job and I can only watch because I don't want them to arrest me.*

Jim came out of the house and introduced us. "These guys came over looking to score some pot," he said.

"And you believe them?" I said to Jim. Turning to our visitors, I said, "We ain't sellin' and we ain't buyin', and we ain't smokin'—not with you two here. Stick around, though, and shoot the breeze if you feel like it."

What emerged from the conversation? In short, they had been cops but they had quit their jobs. They liked smoking pot; sometimes they even smoked on duty, but it made them paranoid. After a while they felt like hypocrites and quit the force.

One incident in particular precipitated their resignation from the police department.

"We were called out by the sheriff to join county sheriffs, highway patrol, and other cops to clear a pot plantation by the river near Princeton. The plants were so big and tall, we had to use chainsaws to cut them down. We filled a dump truck with the stuff, but guys were stuffing it in their pockets and saying things like, "You can sell this for money, right?" We shoved some in our pockets too—but we felt like hypocrites and we were disgusted with the other cops, so we quit the force. We'd rather get stoned than be dishonest cops."

This was either a convincing undercover story or the truth. The longer they stayed, the more I became convinced they were sincere, but just in case, there was no way I was going to torch up in their presence, or tell them who our supplier was.

A day or so after we received a visit from the pot-smoking ex-cops, our friend and sometime marijuana salesman Steve came over, and we told him about our visitors.

"Oh, yeah," said Steve. "The pot plantation they cut down was Crazy Earl's."

Crazy Earl was the "Johnny Marijuana Seed" of the North Valley. He had a reputation as a consummate pot grower who never got arrested, despite narrow misses. He was clever and kept his cool. He had the gift of gab, and being born and raised in the tiny farming town of Princeton, he knew everyone, or everyone's brother or sister or cousin within a fifty-mile radius, including the local sheriff.

His reputation went beyond his wily ways. His product was phenomenal. Earl's pot was definitely not your run of the mill Mexican ragweed. Smoke a little of Crazy Earl's Colusa Homegrown and you hallucinated rainbow mandalas as if you'd dropped a tab of LSD.

Word circulated about Earl's farming methods. It could be that the story got better with circulation, but it was said he caught fish from the river and placed one under each plant. He also knew where to plant his seeds in the riparian forest that lined the banks of the Sacramento River such that the plants were camouflaged yet received optimum sun and the best nutrients. He never concentrated the plants in one area, instead spreading them throughout the forest. He brought in no irrigation pipes, camping gear or other paraphernalia that might give away his plantation. With his local knowledge and having hung out by the river his whole life, his crop was well placed and well hidden. The only way his crop was going to be discovered was if some local voiced suspicion to the sheriff, but the same grapevine that led to the cops led back to Crazy Earl, so he was always a step ahead of them. That's why he abandoned the crop that got harvested by my pot-smoking cop friends and their associates.

Crazy Earl was not deterred by this loss, nor did his satisfied customers experience a pot famine because of it. He had other plants widely spread along a twenty mile stretch of the river.

Steve was one of Crazy Earl's cohorts; he recently filled in some details for me. "When the cops found Earl's plantation near Princeton, he changed tactics. That's why they never caught him. He was always changing up on them. He moved his plantings alongside irrigation ditches next to farmers' fields. In fact, I remember being a lookout, staying with the cars on a bridge at two a.m. while he and another friend passed the giant Hefty bags full of pot up to me. Later, when Earl got a little nervous about that kind of location, he moved the plants between rows of corn. That worked really well. That's how he got the idea to go to Kansas. We went back there and planted seeds in the cornrows and just left them there. They were irrigated for free. Later, we went back and harvested. Transporting trunk loads of pot across state lines was a little risky, though. That's when I got out of the business."

One of his return trips from Kansas added to the legend of Earl's invincibility. After driving all the way from Kansas with a trunk full of pot, he was pulled over just south of Chico. The cop let him go. What questions were asked of Earl or what he said, we never heard.

Another thing that enhanced the legend was the fact that we never met Earl during the Mariposa days. It was only under the influence of his potent product that we became aware of his prowess, and when someone would ask, "Man, where did you get this shit?" the Legend of Crazy Earl was sown.

A couple of years after I moved out of 2307, Jim and I finally had the opportunity to meet Crazy Earl. We were invited to play a gig at the Portuguese Hall in Princeton (population 214). The occasion was a class reunion, but in order to muster enough attendees to justify renting the hall and paying our band, everyone who'd ever graduated from Princeton High School was invited. What resulted was a cross-section of Princeton society circa 1950 to 1974, everyone from farmers to IBM execs to copy machine salesmen to our favorite token hippy, the legendary Crazy Earl.

When I heard Earl would be attending, I could hardly wait to thank him for his Colusa Homegrown and the pleasure it brought, but I was even more amused by the scene I witnessed when he arrived.

Earl walked in with two lovely young women, one on each arm. He wore a peasant shirt, jeans and huaraches. The women with him were dressed in handmade clothing that I recognized as being from Guatemala. He was greeted enthusiastically by a very straight-looking portly local wearing an ill-fitting three piece suit and shiny shoes.

"Earl! Earl!" exclaimed the man, pumping Earl's hand. "It's good to see you! What are you doing these days?"

Earl, smooth as ever, said, "I'm in the import business."

I could well imagine what kind of goods Earl was importing from Guatemala.

The clueless man said, "Oh, great! What are you importing, Earl?"

Earl looked left at one companion, and right at the other. Without missing a beat, he said, "Women's clothing, and these are my models."

13

The Woman With No Name

"It's too late, she's gone too far,
she's lost the sun,
she's come undone."
"She's Come Undone"
by The Guess Who

She seemed to come from nowhere. One fall day she wandered up to the front door and knocked. Nobody ever came to the front door unless it was Mormons or Jehovah's Witnesses or someone who'd never been to the house before. Nobody knocked, either. Just go around back and come on in, help yourself.

I swung the door open and saw a young woman with short blond hair, blue eyes, and a peaches and cream complexion. She wore an emerald green dress that fit her figure well.

"Is Larry here?" she asked.

I didn't know anyone named Larry, but suddenly I wanted to be Larry.

"I'm Larry," I said. It was worth a try. "Where's Larry?" she repeated.

"Am I the Larry you're looking for?"

The next several moments were like a frame in a cartoon where both characters are silent and one has a blank bubble over her head with a question mark in it. In the next frame, the dialogue resumes.

"My Larry…." She trailed off, confused.

"Come around back, and I'll help you find Larry," I said. Shutting the door, I went straight to the back door, opened it, and waited a full minute.

Maybe she left.

I went back to the front door and opened it again. Frozen in time, she stood perfectly still. That's when I noticed she had the look I knew so well. A lavender aura ringed her irises and she appeared to be staring into a far galaxy.

I asked her name. After a long pause, she said, "I don't know."

Suddenly I felt protective of her. She was like a beautiful little kitten that wanders up in your yard without an i.d. tag. You love her, and want to keep her, but you feel obligated to reunite her with her owners.

"Come around back, and we'll see about finding Larry," I said. I started to circle the house, but she didn't follow. I went back and gently took her by the arm. "Let me give you on a tour of the property." She followed me around the house while I narrated tales of two new windows, six loads of garbage in a dump truck, and finding Piewacket in the persimmon tree during the paint party. I knew she wasn't really taking in anything I said, but it was more about my tone of voice: I just wanted her to feel comfortable. We stepped up on the back porch, and I went inside. She hesitated.

When I wheeled around to face her, it was as if I saw her for the first time. We connected in a way that went beyond words. I looked into her eyes and saw her soul. She was lost and needed help. She must have seen into my soul, too, because I felt a tingle spreading from my eyes out to my extremities—a contact high.

I held out my hand. She took it, and stepped inside. I stroked her third eye with my thumb. We hugged, and she smelled like a warm day in a meadow. We went to bed, and we stayed there for a week or more. Whenever I wasn't at work, we were in bed together, sharing a love feast; and, whenever I woke up, I kept expecting to find her gone, but she'd be there beside me. We lived totally in the moment. I told her I would tell her my real name when she remembered hers. At times I wondered if I was Larry or Bix, but who cared?

THE WOMAN'S VULNERABILITY REMINDED ME of the time I had amnesia in Germany. When the academic year was over at Em's and my respective universities in Sweden and Spain, I was supposed to rendezvous with her in Munich; but, after an insane thirty-six hour hitchhiking trip from southern Spain without food or water or sleep, I checked into a hotel and slept eighteen hours. When I woke up I was completely disoriented. I didn't know what day or what time it was, or what country or city I was in. I went out looking for breakfast, but it was noon and it must have been Sunday because the town was shuttered, the streets bare. I felt like the last man on earth after a nuclear holocaust. Then I came to the frightening realization that I couldn't remember my name.

At this point I'd had nothing to eat for fifty hours or more. Dazed and confused, I stumbled through the empty streets and wandered by the Zuider See all day, trying to puzzle out who I was, where I was, where I'd come from, and where I was going. That evening I finally ate something at the hotel—Stroganoff, I recall—and got the idea to look at my passport. That in itself made no sense to me but at least it dawned on me where I'd come from. In my suitcase I found a letter from Em with instructions for our rendezvous, and I realized where I was going. Arriving two days late in Munich, I almost missed connecting with Em. She had checked out of the hotel, but luckily I caught up with her. Only upon hugging my sweetheart, and nuzzling her neck and smelling her, and hearing her say my name, did I regain my sense of who I was.

I KNEW HOW SHE FELT, the woman with no name. Although I loved having her with me, I wanted to help her recover and find Larry. (I remember thinking, *I want this home to be a sanctuary.*) Trying to jog her memory, for several days we played a game that was kind of like "Twenty Questions". I asked her to tell me any image, sound, or smell that came to mind, hoping to trigger her memory of who she was. This resulted in surreal verbal exchanges that made sense to us but must have sounded like a scene from *Waiting for Godot*. Gradually she became more lucid. From her occasional lucidity, I was able to piece together that she and Larry were from Chico. They had been living on a houseboat in Sausalito for two weeks, taking LSD every day. Larry took a notion to return to Chico on his own, leaving her behind. Somehow she had managed to find her way back to Chico. As to exactly how and why she found her way to our doorstep, I never did find out.

One day, while we were lying there in silence, she said, "Helen."

"Helen," I said. "Nice to meet you, Helen." We shook hands. Then, as promised, I told her my name. We celebrated with a hug and I felt very happy. In fact, I got so damned excited we made love again right away.

Our next project was to reconstruct her identity. When I asked if she had any sense memory of her mother, she recalled nursing as a child, and she remembered her mother's face. From there we pieced together enough images of her childhood home to realize that her mother no longer lived there; she had moved somewhere across town. More questions and more clues led me to hazard a guess as to where the new house was. We got up the next day and drove out West Fifth Street past the edge of town.

This was one time when my intuition paid off. At the first likely place, I stopped at the entrance to a gravel drive that led through an orchard to a gray stucco house. "Is this it?" Helen wasn't sure but we drove up and knocked, and her mother answered the door.

Her mother didn't exactly greet us like we were selling vacuum cleaners, but she didn't seem overjoyed either. She looked us over for several seconds. "Oh," was all she said, and she stepped aside, letting the door swing open. "I'm in the kitchen," she said, and we followed her through the living room.

"I'm cooking something for your sister," she said to Helen. "She's coming home this afternoon."

Although I had some trepidation as to what her mother would think of a longhair showing up with her daughter in a hippie bread truck, her mother and I clicked with each other. Without alluding specifically to Helen's LSD binge and her temporary amnesia, I said her daughter seemed disoriented, and might need help from some resources beyond my reach. "Can't you give her a place to stay while she gets her head straight; till she can get a job, and a place of her own?" I asked.

"I'd like to help Helen, but she doesn't want help. Her sister is coming home, and she doesn't want to share her room with Helen. They don't get along."

It seemed obvious to me Helen's mother was passing the buck. This was clearly a case of Good Daughter/Bad Daughter. Good Daughter was working on her teaching credential; Bad Daughter was a drugged-out hippie.

HAVING STRUCK OUT WITH HELEN'S mother, we returned

to 2307, but taking her back to the house presented a problem.

My motives for trying to reunite Helen with her mother were not completely selfless. My scheming little brain had hatched a plan to juggle girlfriends. When Janie wasn't available, Helen might be. If neither one knew about the other, what harm could result? But the plan would work only if Helen wasn't living at 2307. Also at odds with my scheme, Helen still wanted to get back together with Larry. There wasn't much hope for a real relationship with her, and I was beginning to feel sad and empty whenever we had sex—mind you, not so sad or empty that I abstained.

Bottom line, I wanted to cultivate my budding relationship with Janie. I realized that hedging my bets with Helen wasn't going to work, but I didn't have the heart to put her out on the street.

Driving along with Helen, I chided myself. *You idiot! Look at you, plotting this and that. You have no control over these two women. And just look at this beautiful one beside you. Live in the now. Appreciate her, you ungrateful fool!*

Still, my self-criticism didn't solve my immediate problem. If Janie found us together, I wasn't sure if the Free Love Airplane would fly or crash land. I had to come up with another plan. That's when I came up with a new double standard for the Free Love Era. Someone I really cared about, and wanted to be with, like Janie, would be off limits to my friends. Someone like Helen could be a communal love bunny, if she was willing

A day or two after taking Helen to her Mom's, I shared my idea with Jim. While I was at work, he could make nice with Helen, and who knew what might happen? It was, after all, up to her. She and Jim did have the makings of a relationship; they already talked a lot when he was home and I was at work. I was just letting nature take its course, with a slight nudge. Now, if Janie happened to come over, my foil would be that Helen was with Jim.

Apparently Jim took the notion to heart, and expanded on it with an unexpected twist. When I arrived home the next morning, I followed the sound of happy voices to my bedroom.

I found three naked people on my bed: Helen, Jim, and, to my surprise, our other roommate, Mike.

For one or two shakes, I was a little pissed off. I still didn't like Mike, and now here he was on my bed. I was willing to share with Jim, but not with Mike. I shrugged off my resentment, reminding myself that Helen wasn't my property; Helen could make her own choices; that's the way of the world, and the way of women.

I just wanted to lie down and sleep, but mine was the only bedroom in the house, and the only bed. (Mike lived in his own space in the converted garage out back.

Jim slept on the living room floor, or he used my bed when I was at work.)

I stood in the shower thinking, *without enough beds to go around, maybe Free Love isn't such a good idea after all.*

The two guys cleared out and I lay down next to Helen one more time. I asked her if she'd had a good time, and she said yes. "Well, good," I said, and stroked the contours of her body, which I'd memorized; I kissed her tenderly, and sleep slipped over me.

THAT AFTERNOON WHEN I WOKE up, Helen was not in bed. This was the first time I remember her getting up and moving about during the day. I got up and dressed and found her in the back yard, talking with Jim. It was a sunny fall day, and she was dressed in a nice dark blue cotton dress she had picked up on our visit to her Mom. In the early afternoon sunlight under a baby blue sky, Helen looked radiant, and her radiance formed a circle of love.

Jim and I stood together in Helen's circle of love, which became a golden glowing dome. We all stood there a long time and hugged and laughed joyously and said nothing. I remember nuzzling her golden hair; she smelled fresh and clean, like peppermint soap.

I knew she would be gone soon. When I came home from work the next morning, she was nowhere in sight. I took a shower. Jim, sleeping on my bed, woke up and apologized for oversleeping. "That's okay," I said. "Move over." We lay there, two naked, happy bucks, talking about Helen and this and that until I fell asleep like a baby and Jim got up and went about his day.

I didn't know where Helen went on that last day. I thought maybe she went to her mother's house, or caught up with Larry.

Weeks later, still on the graveyard shift, I climbed up in the warehouse rafters above the sorting room to amuse myself. I lit up a doobie and watched guys walking by below. Fishing out some almonds stashed in the pocket of my chambray shirt, I practiced pelting my buddies on their hardhats as they walked by. (It was always funny to watch the reaction. Ping! The nut would bounce off a helmet, and land on the floor. They would stop in their tracks and look around. Then they'd start walking again. Some guys wouldn't even notice at all, even if I missed and the almond bounced off the floor right in front of them.)

After I ran out of nuts, I started watching the ladies working at the sorting table. They sat on tall stools as the nuts went past on a white conveyor belt. The ladies picked out the nuts that were wormy, too small or broken, and the occasional pebble. The room around them was dark by contrast to the bubble of fluorescent light that hovered over their work station. There, among the frumpy women who usually worked the belt, I saw a new employee, a good looking young woman with a head of glowing, short blond hair. She seemed to have a golden aura about her. She worked listlessly, missing a lot of pieces that should have been culled. The new employee was Helen.

From time to time in the next week or two I walked through the sorting room, but Helen never looked up from her mesmerizing task and we never spoke again. She didn't last long on the job, though. I still have no idea where she went, or where she ended up after that.

14

Thanksgiving in a Cave

The sun was shining; the house, empty. It was Thanksgiving Day, 1970. I got up in the morning and realized the grand hippie-spontaneous-gathering-and-potluck-feast I had imagined wasn't happening. I was still too new with Janie to be invited to her family festivities. Jim had said he might stick around, or he might go to Shingletown to his godfather's. He was nowhere in sight, so I figured he got up early and left. My mother and brother had their own plans, and I had been playing a game of emotional chicken with the folks in Lafayette. Ambivalent as I was about the setup in Lafayette (nowadays we say "family dynamics") I had determined to wait and see if I got an invitation: Go ahead, don't invite me, see if I care; I have my own life now.

So there I was in my little shack on Mariposa Avenue, wondering what to do. Roam around the house, check to see that the orange and green refrigerators and the cupboards are indeed bare. Do yoga and meditate until I can hear the walls breathe—there goes an hour, and only twenty-three more to go until this time tomorrow when everything will be back to normal.

I might as well enjoy some sunshine. I sat on the edge of the back porch and tried to convince myself it didn't matter that I was spending the holiday alone. *I am choosing to break from everything familiar, to empty the earthen vessel of the past, to make room for new experiences, and today is one of those experiences.*

Sitting there in the crystalline sunlight wiggling my bare toes in the dirt, I had an epiphany: "I am at choice. I chose this day, this moment. If I hop in the van and drive to Lafayette, I might get a scolding for showing up unannounced, and who wants that? Go with your gut. Better an empty palate than a full plate. I don't want to be there anyway, as long as my stepmother is part of the equation."

Suddenly I felt joyous. Any day without my stepmother was a happy one. I wasn't a victim; I was making a choice, and I was happy about it. I began to count my blessings, determined to think of nothing else. Suddenly I thought of the koa beads my stepsister had brought me from Hawaii. I ran into the bedroom, got them, and returned to the back porch. Using the beads as a rosary, I sat and counted my blessings. Sometimes before I could think up a new blessing, I would have to repeat old ones, just to stay focused on the positive, and this reinforced my belief in my good fortune. After a quarter hour or so, Jim rolled up on his Schwinn, and I counted him as a blessing, too.

"I thought you went to Shingletown."

"Decided to stay. Went to the gym instead. Nice workout, feeling great. What are you up to?"

"Counting my blessings on Thanksgiving Day. What are we going to do today? Feast or fast?"

Jim sat on the edge of the porch next to me. For an hour we counted our blessings together, swapping stories of happy times and Thanksgivings past. We determined to make the best of this day. We decided to live the entire day as a rite of gratitude.

If anyone had a reason to feel forlorn on this holiday, it was Jim, whose father died the day he was born and whose mother had only recently died of alcoholism. But instead, he too remembered the good. Eventually, we decided to go for a hike and look for Eugene. He was living in a cave beside Chico Creek, about a mile past the end of the Upper Bidwell Park dirt road.

I first met Eugene, aka Gene or Geno, in Modern Dance class at Chico State. All those nubile young women in tights...and Gene and I were the only two men in the class.

Geno was the definition of tall, dark and handsome. At five feet eleven inches, he seemed taller due to his excellent dancer's posture and sleek physique. At 165 pounds, all smooth muscle and sinew, he looked like a longhaired Clark Gable, a charismatic girl-magnet. I can still see Geno on graduation night, diploma in one hand, a young woman's hand in the other. I watched them run off into the dark, mortarboards flying off their heads, their black gowns flowing behind them as they disappeared across the playing field. He never did tell me what happened between them, out there in the dark, but I can imagine. Graduation was a time to celebrate.

Jim and I wheeled our matching Schwinn five-speed bicycles out to the end of the paved road and locked them to a post. From there we ran the Yahi trail that parallels the creek another four miles to the end of the dirt road, and hiked the next mile to the area where we thought we might find Gene's cave. With a few hints from Jim's recollection of Gene's instructions, and following our noses, we found what we thought might be Gene's abode. What confirmed it for me was Gene's prior description of a particular rock where he'd had a tryst with a beautiful young woman.

He wasn't there when we arrived, but Jim and I hung out and sheltered in the cave for an hour or two, and Geno appeared. He was barefoot and wore a pair of denim coveralls.

Nothing much was said. In those days Gene, Jim and I worked

on mastering the art of non-verbal communication. A slight tic of Gene's head said he wasn't expecting us, but he went about his business and we all fell into blissful silence, listening to Mother Nature.

The cave consisted of a house-sized boulder of basalt sitting atop more basalt. The interior shape of the cave can best be described as having the shape of a sock. The "ankle" formed a natural chimney. The coals at the base of the chimney were cold to the touch when Jim and I arrived. We thought maybe Gene had gone home to the family farm in Grimes for the holiday. The "heel" formed a small living room with a natural ledge for setting the fire and sitting by it. The "toe" had a hole in it through which light and breezes flowed. Gene sat in the living room, Jim on a ledge by the cave entrance, and I stretched out in the lumpy toe or "bedroom" with only a couple of feet of clearance above my face.

"What's this?" asked Gene, disdainfully picking up the one-pound can of USDA surplus turkey meat we had brought.

"We thought since it's Thanksgiving, we'd bring some turkey," I replied.

Clearly, in his residence, Gene was not interested in having anything unnatural or any food that used to breathe and walk on legs. He set it aside and that was the end of it.

"Oh, hey, you guys brought some almonds. Thank you!" He popped some in his mouth and passed the leather pouch that I had inherited from my great aunt. Embossed in gold leaf on the outside, it said:

BANK OF GILLETTE GILLETTE, WYOMING

I remember looking at that and thinking that our friendship and a sack of tasty almonds made us richer than all the gold in the Mother Lode.

We all sat and munched our Thanksgiving dinner, and Jim started asking Gene some questions about the cave.

Gene gave us a quick rundown. "First I was in a smaller cave farther downstream, but too many people kept coming by and I didn't want to see anybody. If Tina or some other young lady came to visit, we had no privacy. "Then last Spring the cave flooded in the middle of the night. It was raining hard and I knew it might flood in the night but I just lay there listening. It was beautiful! I felt safe. When water started flowing into the cave, I could feel it on my back, but I still didn't leave right away. I stayed there feeling like part of the river. When I got completely wet, I got out of there and went to higher ground. I walked around in the woods for a while, and I swear I could see every drop coming down—like crystals! It was raining diamonds and crystals! I hung out under an overhang the rest of the night. In the morning, I moved a mile upstream and I could see this cave was above the high water line. So I moved in. It's okay, but I want a bigger place, something I can stand up in, farther from civilization."

Jim asked him how he spent his time.

"Mostly I hang out. I pray to Mother Nature. Sometimes I go into town to get supplies, and sometimes Tina comes to see me."

Tina was a lovely seventeen-year-old, one of three Italian sisters born and raised in Chico.

As Geno recounted his doings, I could discern some scratches in the basalt above my face. It looked as if someone had been trying to write a message. I asked him what it said.

"Oh, that. Maybe I shouldn't have put that there. I'm defacing the rock, but nobody will ever see it. It's not as if I'm painting graffiti or anything."

I sensed I had stumbled on something secret and personal to

Gene, but I pressed ahead. Once he told me what it said, I could better discern the words: *Teach me.*

"Teach me. That's what it says. It took me a long time to scratch that there, but I was lying there with nothing to do, thinking. I just want Nature to teach me how to live, how to be, what to do, how to do it, so I wrote that. 'Teach me,' it says." Then, sotto voce, "Teach me."

Teach me, I thought. *I get it!* I lay there mouthing the words: Teach me, teach me. Out of the corner of my eye, I could see Jim nodding yes.

When Jim and I got back to the house around dusk, it still looked empty and more cave-like than ever, but unlike the hopeless morning, the house seemed pulsing with possibility. I thought of inscribing "Teach me" on the lavender living room wall, the same wall where the previous resident's children had thrown dirt clods only three months before, but the meaning was clear without graffiti: *I have come here to learn, to be transformed. I want to overcome my grief; to banish all falsehood and deceit from my life. I have dragons to slay, and truths to seek. Gene has his cave. I have this little cabaña on the edge of town. Teach me, O twenty-three-oh-seven Mariposa. Teach me!*

Sometimes fasting is a feast. All we had to eat that Thanksgiving was a handful of almonds and a few pieces of dried fruit; but in scarcity we found abundance. After a unique day of meditation, friendship, sunshine, clear running water, and a message inscribed in stone, I went to bed hungry, and full of gratitude.

15

A Wake-Up Call

Richard was a Buddy Holly look-alike right down to the thick black-rimmed glasses and slicked-back hair. I'm still not sure if he was trying to kill me or just put me temporarily out of commission that December night in the nut house. Either way, he wouldn't have cared as long as he got away with his crimes. Even without Richard's help, I was doing a good enough job of self-destruction.

It must have been around early December, that first fall on Mariposa, when Rich appeared at the nut house as a new hire. He needed a place to live so we let him crash with us for a couple of weeks before he absconded.

On the night in question, some trusty little white pills got me sped up enough to finish most of my work, feeding nuts to the shelling room, by 2:30 a.m. With five hours to go before quitting time and no supervisors ever on night shift, I might as well smoke a doobie and drop some mescaline.

In a way, it didn't matter if I took the drugs. Sheer exhaustion had been producing a steady stream of hallucinations whether I was under the influence or not. For example, one night, sober as a church mouse, I stopped my van at a dark intersection. I saw a little white terrier crossing the intersection. A mailbox on the corner stretched out like a slinky, opened its "mouth" and gobbled up the poor little doggy. I even heard the "mouth" clang shut.

Rubbing my eyes, I got out of the van to check. There was no dog and no mailbox either. Groovy, man! If only I'd known that these hallucinations, even without benefit of drugs, were an early warning sign of serious illness, I might have cleaned up my act sooner.

SO THERE I WAS, SITTING on the forklift at three a.m., stoned on peyote and speed and pot, when I received a visit from Abe Lincoln. At that hour of the morning, one's brain enters an REM phase, whether awake or asleep, so that must have contributed to the hallucination. My eyes were gazing in the direction of the warehouse wall. The corrugated siding must have been at least three stories tall, more like four, because the almond bins we stacked five-high were four feet square each. That left enough room for a guy to walk around up there in a sea of almonds, but you had to bend over to keep from hitting your head on the rafters.

So I sat on the forklift, enjoying the appearance of galvanized steel undulating like waves on a silver sea, when the wall split open like a piece of paper being torn apart from the top down. I distinctly saw the ragged edges of steel as they curved inward, and beyond them the black of night. From the darkness emerged a thirty foot tall Abe Lincoln dressed in his trademark swallowtail coat, white shirt, black bowtie; and of course the famous stovepipe hat. He had the quintessential Abe Lincoln beard like the one I wore. (On him it looked good, but on me it made me look like a Mennonite beach boy.)

He seemed to be walking down out of the sky at a forty-five degree angle, which made an interesting study in foreshortening.

He looked into my eyes in his deep, dark and kindly Abe Lincoln manner.

"Wow….Hey, Abe," I said, mouth agape.

He kept looking at me abstractedly, but now I could sense he was angry in a smoldering way that made me feel uneasy. Abe wasn't in a mood to talk, I could tell. He didn't like people from the twentieth century distracting him while he was busy walking around at night. Besides, he was bigger than I. He shot me an angry look and then the movie ran in reverse, with Abe backing into the night and the peeled pieces of the warehouse wall zipping back together like a pair of pants.

"Sorry, Abe," I said. "How about a re-run?"

The wall zipped open again and Abe appeared, but this time he stood outside in the dark, peering through the upside-down triangle of an opening. I could see him only from the waist up, but this time I didn't stare; I just studied him obliquely. He seemed to be surveying the tops of the nut bins.

Maybe he was hungry? As soon as I thought that, Abe disappeared again and the corrugated steel zipped shut.

Operating heavy equipment such as a forklift while hallucinating monster-sized Abe Lincolns was not a good idea. I needed to calm down. I decided to take a break.

One of the crew walked by and I had him use the forklift to raise me to the top level of bins. Lying twenty feet up on top of 1,200 pounds of shelled almonds, I burrowed in and covered myself with an insulating layer. Popping a handful into my mouth, I munched and stared at the rafters and their zigzag bracing. With a grin, I mused that it was I, not Abe, who was hungry, and I thought how far out" it was to see Abe in the nut house. It was soothing to watch the liquid shadows shimmering under the ceiling, and to feel the warmth of my insulating layer of almonds while smelling and tasting them.

I drifted off into something like sleep, though I couldn't have slept too hard because of the Dexedrine. All I remember next was my eyes jolting open. The rafters were moving to one side and getting farther away. I felt suddenly seasick. The distant thrum of an engine reached my ears and for a moment I thought I was waking up on a cruise ship in the Mediterranean with Em. But then, snapping to awareness, I thought, oh shit! *Someone operating the forklift is going to dump the nuts and me into the hopper that feeds the sorter.*

When I bolted upright, the box with me in it was lowering to floor level. Over the edge of the bin I could see my pal and temporary roomie, Rich, twisting around to see where he was going as he sped backward. I thought surely he'd see me standing up to my knees in nuts, waving, and hear me shouting, but he stopped only briefly; then, with a goofy grin, he sped forward toward the hopper.

He was doing my job for me, so I knew exactly what was going to happen: zip forward while raising the forks twelve feet; slide the bin into the carriage; release the forks and whip around in a tight back loop to reach the tilt button; push the button that tilts the whole 1,200 pounds of nuts—correction, 1,200 pounds of nuts and one 165 pound nut—into the hopper. And that's exactly what he did. Whether I was yelling or not, or frozen in fear, or if Rich was amused by the slapstick image, or all of the above, he didn't notice; or, it suddenly occurred to me, he knew I was there but didn't care. Knowing Rich, he might even be amused at the brilliance of his felonious intentions.

My choices were limited: survive a twelve-foot jump onto the cement floor, or take the Disneyland ride. Quickly I found out that jumping was impossible because standing up to one's knees in almonds is like being trapped in thick cement slurry. With only one option left, I flattened my body as best I could on top of the nuts to avoid hitting my head on the top front edge of the hopper's mouth. This was no easy feat.

In we went, all those almonds and me.

It was like being thrown hard in judo and landing on steel while being pelted with stones by an angry crowd of a thousand. I can still hear the sound of nuts pinging the sides of the funnel-shaped hopper, and the silence once I was completely covered and smothering and sliding toward the bottom chute that fed the nuts onto a conveyor belt. All I could do was hold my breath and wait.

Once some of the nuts funneled out onto the shaker pan below, a cone of space formed in the middle of the nuts; I wiggled around enough to spread-eagle and to keep my feet from sliding out the narrow end of the chute onto the conveyor belt, a scant eight inches below. But when I tried to climb the smooth stainless steel sides of the funnel, I slid like a spider trying to climb out of a wineglass.

The hopper was almost empty by now, but the opening at the bottom was too close to the shaker pan to get out without being pulverized. Then I realized the next twelve hundred pounds of nuts on top of my head could be even worse. That's when I started pounding on the sides of the hopper and yelling. Some ladder rungs were welded on the straight upper insides of the hopper, but I couldn't reach the rungs as I kept sliding down the stainless steel funnel. So I pounded and yelled and yelled and pounded and some of the time I stopped to wait and listen.

That's when I started worrying that I might still be in the hopper at seven a.m. when my supervisor came in. After an hour of alternately waiting and pounding, somebody came by and tossed a rope down the hatch to get me out. I don't remember who did this, but one thing I know for sure: it wasn't Rich.

WHEN I GOT HOME AT eight a.m., Rich was there, acting nervous. He didn't mention the life-threatening incident, so I confronted him, but he didn't apologize and he changed the subject. He kept asking what I was going to do that morning. Where would I be? This raised my suspicions that he might be scheming to take some valuables and split, so I went inside to check the forty-five dollars in my dresser drawer. I looked at my crates of precious record albums. I decided I didn't want to hide anything or lock anything up, and I wasn't going to change my plans for the morning on account of Rich's nervousness. I went back outside and told Rich I was going to take a nap, then take Gene out to the trailhead to his new cave.

When I got up, Gene arrived and Rich was still nervously shuffling about. By happenstance, Calhoun and his girlfriend Janet showed up, too, and they wanted to go along for the ride. Since we had no lock on the back door, I urged Rich to come along, but he refused. Reluctantly, I left Rich at the house. When I got home, Rich was gone, and so were several record albums, the forty-five dollars (half a week's pay), and an eighty-dollar pair of Wellington boots of mine that fit him perfectly.

I never saw Rich again, but we located his mother in Oregon, and she said he had come home briefly. Rich had told us he was twenty-one and a Vietnam vet, but she said he was seventeen and he'd never been in the military. She also said he had some warrants out on him for petty theft and grand theft auto, which was why he had left home and come to Chico in the first place, "borrowing" her car to do so. When he came home, she thought she had her car back, but Rich soon took off with it again, and she filed charges, adding another warrant to his resume.

This incident with Rich was a big wake-up call. Shaken, I stopped using drugs, but like a true addict, abstinence lasted less than a month, and it was a case of too little too late. I believe I already had mononucleosis, which I refused to acknowledge.

Throughout December and into January, my health got worse and worse, and I kept having the image that I was a spider swirling in the vortex of a bathtub drain. Several weeks after the bizarre night when I met Abe Lincoln and spent an hour in the nut hopper and got ripped off the next morning, I came really close to keeping an appointment with the Grim Reaper.

16

Christmas in Lafayette

Two Thanksgivings and two Christmases came and went while I lived on Mariposa Avenue.

During the first Christmas, even Gene went home to be with his family. I had two choices. Stay home by myself in a cold, drafty house, or go home to Lafayette, where I could stay warm and be fed. I was cold and tired and hungry and my lungs were starting to rattle. For weeks, my energy had been on a slow downward slide. Shrugging off fatigue, I took Dexedrine to stay up, and smoked marijuana to come down. By November I quit that routine, hoping to get well, but abstinence didn't improve matters. I kept going to work, but my get-up-and-go had got up and gone. A week's paycheck away from starvation, I couldn't afford to take any time off. In the end, after arguing with myself, I swallowed my pride and went home, but I wasn't happy about it. So much for wanting to assert my independence!

Arriving while my father was still at work, I was condemned to sit in the den with Millie. To amuse myself, I thought I'd get a rise out of my stepmother. After asking her how her Thanksgiving had been, I casually dropped a little bomb: "Well, I'm happy everyone had such a nice Thanksgiving. Mine was a bit unique. I spent Thanksgiving in a cave."

Her reaction was one of those times when you say something so far removed from someone's frame of reference, as if you said nothing at all. My little bomb was turning out to be a dud.

We sat for a few minutes watching TV. Suddenly, Millie stopped her knitting and needled me with her eyes. "You had Thanksgiving IN A CAVE?"

"Yep." I proceeded merrily filling in details as if she had asked. "Sunny day…friend lives in a cave…bike ride. run…cave…USDA canned turkey…almonds…."

"You're nuts!" she interrupted. "Wait till your father hears about this! Your nutty father—he's gone nuts too!"

"How's that?"

"Just wait till you see him."

"What do you mean?"

"Just wait till he gets home, and take a look at him. He's gone *troppo*. That's all I have to say!"

After another half hour of uncomfortable silence, I heard my father's car growling up the drive. Soon he came in and sat down in his favorite chair. He was wearing a suit and tie, appropriate to his executive position, but his fringe of wavy salt and pepper hair reached past his ears and well below his collar. As well, he was sporting a full, scruffy beard.

Millie was having a field day. "Just look at your nutty father! And, John, just wait till you hear what your nutty son did for Thanksgiving! You've both gone off the deep end!"

"Father," I said. "You're looking rather *hirsute*. What's the occasion?"

Pointing at Millie, he punned, "It's not *her suit*, it's my suit."

"You know what I mean, Pop."

"Well, I got so goddam tired of all those guys at work—'Dirty hippie this, commie longhair pinko fag that'—I told them *my son has long hair*, but they wouldn't quit, so I said fuck 'em, and let my hair grow."

"Now let them complain!" I said. "After all, you're the Vice President!"

Amid more of Millie's chorus of comments and kibitzing, I told my father about my Thanksgiving in a cave.

"Ah," he said, tilting his head back and half smiling the way he did when he was being noncommittal, which was most of the time.

I wasn't sure how to take either my father's fashion rebellion or his "Ah." Did he approve of my lifestyle? Like most young men, I craved my father's approval. Apparently, he'd heard what I said to him on the day of the Two New Windows a few months previous, about my wanting to get back to the earth; but, he didn't say so explicitly. Looking back, though, now that he's slipped the mortal coil, for him to say he approved of my lifestyle would be a bridge too far, especially in Millie's presence, but I can still picture him with his long hair and scraggly beard, tilting his head back and saying, "Ah."

How cool was that? My father, the hipster!

17

Tomatoes in the Park

"Not what we have, but what we enjoy, constitutes our abundance."
Anonymous

The evening of January 1, 1971, I sat alone in the kitchen, perched on a produce crate. The night before, New Year's Eve, Janie had come over to celebrate. The veil of privacy shall be drawn over that night, but let's just say it involved bubble bath, massage oil, pot and peyote, and we were awake in the bedroom 'til dawn's early light. If we weren't in love before that night, now we were.

Janie left at noon, and I slept till after dark. Now I sat in the kitchen feeling content but strung out. (Little did I know that two weeks later I was going to collapse on someone's front lawn when I was out for a run.) Meanwhile, I sat on the crate in the middle of the kitchen listening to the rain, feeling weary and unmotivated to go out or call anyone. Three days worth of rain seemed to be tapering off a bit, and the occasional splat reminded me that inside was the place to be.

There was nothing to do, no books to read. Janie? *Who knows where she is or with whom tonight? I don't ask, and she doesn't tell. Jim, Barney, Gene? Nowhere in sight. Might as well sit here like a ghost on a bench talking with other ghosts, but damn, I'm hungry and I'm broke.* On top of the dresser sat a dime and a penny, all I had until payday—or until I collected my first unemployment check after the seasonal layoff; I can't remember which. The green refrigerator was as empty as my gut. The orange refrigerator held half a cube of butter, some salad dressing, one leaf of wilted romaine, and one egg.

I sat thinking, *this is the life I have chosen for the present, a life of voluntary poverty and consciously selected emptiness. This night, this nothingness, this life, won't last forever. Might as well sit and listen to the plinking drops and at least enjoy the fact that nothing bad is happening. But the gnawing in my gut—now, that's bugging me. There must be something to eat in the garden.* But before the rain started, I'd stripped the garden and turned over the soil to compost all winter. *Damn. The tomato vine? Stripped it too, but that was a couple of weeks ago. But wait—just on the other side of the kitchen window, only a few feet away, a mouthwatering treasure might be hiding.*

I didn't want to get my hopes too high, so I sat and meditated on the nothingness and the emptiness and let go of the outcome of a potential tomato search.

Finally, I couldn't resist going out to look. Stepping off the back porch into darkness and sporadic sprinkles, my raggedy running shoes sought traction in the mud, and slowly I rounded the corner of the house. The light through the kitchen window blinded me, so I felt my way back inside to shut off the light. Outside again, one hand on the side of the house oriented me as I shuffled sideways in the mud and waved my other arm around, feeling for signs of life. *There. Vegetation.* Squatting, I spread my arms in a hug position, and wrapped around two big wet tomato bushes.

Okay, visualize the biggest, juiciest, freshest ripe tomato you've ever known, and you shall find it. All you have to do is reach in and it will be there, ready to give its life to satisfy your hunger.

Momentarily, the pessimist in me tried to hold sway: *There will be no tomatoes, you fool. It's just the hunger that's causing your deranged fantasy as you squat here in the mud in pitch dark with rain falling on your silly blond head. If there are any tomatoes, they will be small and green and hard.*

But the optimist returned: *Okay, then, I'll have fried green tomatoes! But I can do better than that! Visualize the biggest, juiciest....* Slowly, so as not to damage the vine, my hands found the base of the plant and followed their way up its contours. Nothing. *Now, if I were a tomato, the juiciest, firmest, ripest tomato ever known to man, where would I be hiding right now? Inside! Inside the vine just as I was hiding inside the house this glorious night of my gloriously empty young life, the earthen vessel of my body awaiting fullness, conserving energy, maturing slowly but surely. Reach in, into the vine, and find your treasure!*

Left hand in, right hand in, slowly, slowly. Something cool and round and bigger than my fist met the palm of my left hand. *Can this be a tomato? Yes! It's too good to be true!* My right hand met another cool globe. I squatted there in the dark, rain falling on my golden godlike mane, caring not that I was wet and muddy and weary. Squatting alone in the dark, I only felt the cool roundness of earth's goodness resting in each hand.

Abundance is mine! Pessimist, go away. You shall not be heard from again this evening. I will call you when a skeptic is needed. For now I shall squat here feeling these treasures, and know that abundance is mine in life if I simply expect the best, work patiently, and reach for it.

Suddenly, a burst of prescient knowledge came to me. *Some day, my father and my brother and I will have a reunion. Even if it takes thirty years, it will happen, but first my stepmother has to be out of the way, and the only time that woman will ever get out of the way is when she dies! I can always hope that she'll die sooner, but no, I shouldn't wish death upon anyone. She'll get hers in the end, but I predict that old "tomato" will live to a ripe old age, and when she dies our father will want his sons back, and we'll be bloody rich, my brother and I, because we'll be reunited, and when it's his turn to die, our father will leave us each a pile of booty! The future is beyond my control. I can only wait and hope. Meanwhile, I have these rich and glorious tomatoes!*

A gentle twist will tell if each tomato is ripe or green. Ripe will fall off the stem, green will cling. Gentle twist, left hand, oh my god, a ripe one! Gentle twist, right hand, a green one. *Be happy with just one.*

Withdrawing one hand full and the other empty, and retracing my steps, I stepped back in the house. Closing my eyes against sudden brightness, I flipped the light switch, and with delicious anticipation awaited the first sight of my treasure. *It must be golden.* Slowly I opened my eyes. There, resting in my left hand next to my heart, a glowing red tomato with translucent skin.

What followed was a feast as delicious as a slow, comfortable screw. In fact, it seems like a continuation of the previous night's pleasure. With deliberate slowness, I sliced wedges on a salad plate, arranged them in a starburst pattern, sprinkled sea salt, sat up straight and ate like a prince with a fork and a knife. Before placing each piece in my mouth, I enjoyed its scent. Closing my eyes, I remembered all the happy days of gardening in the fall: turning over the soil and breaking the clods; plowing in the compost; sculpting the furrows; planting the seeds; watching the slow dance of shoots sprouting, pushing up, up, the soil splitting open, little caplets of earth being shoved upward and falling off; chasing away the bugs and the gophers; the sensory feast of sights and scents;

and I remembered the many simple and joyous meals fed to my Mariposa family.

And now dessert. I wondered, *shall I pick another one or save it for later?* Back outside, to my delight, I found tomato after tomato, but they didn't yield to a gentle twist. *They must be green.* A week's supply until payday! With a strong tug, I picked one fried green tomato for dessert.

Back in the kitchen, I cracked the one egg from the refrigerator to batter the green slices, frying gently. I've never tasted anything so good before or since, with the exception of the red tomato that fed me just before the green one. *Fried green tomatoes Monday through Thursday, and some red ones too. More tomatoes await my pleasure. They are hiding inside the vine, gathering energy, growing slowly, reminding me to expect the best and appreciate the simplest treasures.*

Who knows what any of the rest of the Mariposa crew did that night? For all I know, Janie might have been getting it on with Calhoun. Should I be jealous? No, because I had my solitary, rainy winter's night of tomatoes in the dark.

It was a night of abundance I'll never forget, even if I win the lottery.

18

Fried Green Tomato Blues

"That's what the blues is. It's truth. The thing about the blues, and the point of the blues, is in sharing that experience. You can laugh about it, you can talk about it, and you can cry about it, you know, that's what blues is. Quite frankly, that's the purpose of music, in my opinion."

Robben Ford

Not long after the night of tomatoes in the dark, I got to thinking, *what the hell am I doing here on Mariposa? What will I do with the insights and understandings that were gifted to me by the tomatoes in the dark?* While cooking up some fried green tomatoes to share with Jim, I asked him what he thought, and here's what he said: "I don't know what we're doing here, but we're getting ready for something!"

"Getting ready for what, for instance?"

"I don't know, but we're getting ready for something."

The tomatoes sizzled and I gave that some thought. Knowing I couldn't pry a more detailed response out of him, and not wanting anything forced, I served up the tomatoes. After some reverent munching punctuated by caveman grunts and moans of appreciation, I related my tale of Tomatoes in the Dark in its entirety.

"What do you think it all means, Jim?"

"I still say we're getting ready for something."

"Let's be specific, then," I said. "How about yoga?

We've learned yoga, and that can help us stay healthy later in life. We've learned to meditate, also a healthy practice. We've learned to survive on next to nothing: a twenty-five pound bag of brown rice, a dozen eggs, a stick of butter, some miso and soy sauce, five bucks a week; eat from the garden for free, and feed a whole lot of hangers-on to boot. These skills might serve us well later in life. Is that the kind of thing you're talking about?"

"Could be, but I think we're going to find out, that's for sure."

"What if I become a millionaire? Will our vows of voluntary poverty be all for naught? Will I continue to embrace the simple lifestyle?"

"Did you say you had a million dollars? 'Cuz I'd sure like to see some of it. Right now I'll have to settle for these here fried green tomatoes. You got any more?"

Looking toward the window where the vines grew next to the house, I replied, "I can almost *hear* them growing right now, but we'll have to wait. Rationing is in effect until payday."

"Waiting for Godot. Waiting for tomatoes to grow. It's all the same to me."

"Yeah, theatre of the absurd! Meanwhile, I've got an idea for a song."

"What's that?"

"The Fried Green Tomato Blues."

"What's the first line?"

Then our conversation turned to a spoofy blues, as our conversations often did. We alternated lines, making them up on the spot.

Bix: *Here I sit, waiting for Godot*
Jim: *Waiting for tomatoes to grow*
Bix: *I can hear them singin' on the vine*
Jim: *They're sayin', Come to me baby, because you're so damn fine!*
Bix: *Now don't you gripe, wait till I'm ripe.*
Jim: *And someday you'll be mine.*
Bix: *Now patience is a virtue.*
Jim: *Just watch them tomatoes grow. Bix: But I can't wait, for heaven's sake*
Jim: Fried green tomatoes is all I know!
Bix: *Cuz I'm hungry, yeah, hungry all the time.*
Jim: *So fix me up a batch o' them fried green tomatoes*
Bix: *Yeah, baby, everything's gonna be fine.*

Jim reached over and picked up his guitar, started strumming a blues rhythm line. We ran through the song again with his guitar accompaniment, and spontaneously added a closer:

Together: *Fried green tomatoes, uh huh. Fried green tomatoes, oh yeah. Fried green tomatoes is all we kno-o-ow. Just watch and wait.*
[strum, strum]
Just watch and wait. [strum, strum, fade]
Oh, yeah, baby, just watch and wait. [fade to silence]

"What the hell *are* we doing here, Jim?"

"I don't know, but…."

"….I know. We're getting ready for something."

And so we sat, eating our fried green tomatoes and singing and playing throughout the afternoon.

19

Banana Bread Woman

Discovery of the tomatoes happened on a Sunday night. I could survive on tomatoes until Friday when I had some money coming in, but why was I so stony broke amid such opulence? My weekly take home pay was $85. At $75 per month, split three ways, it only took six hours work per month to pay the rent. Grocery staples cost about $5 per week, utilities some negligible amount. Perhaps the twenty-five pound bag of organically grown brown rice had taken on some additions left by the mouse family, causing the brown rice to look a lot like "wild" rice. Most likely the fact that every week I stuffed the entire amount of my paycheck into my pocket, to spend at will, had something to do with my lack of groceries.

Whatever the reason, by the time Banana Bread Woman knocked on our door, on the fourth day of my fried green tomato fest, I swore that when I grew up, I would have a job that provided vacations, money, food, shelter and transportation all at the same time. My Step Van was parked out back, but at twenty-five cents a gallon, who had money for gas? Voluntary poverty wasn't nearly as fun as I thought it would be. This lifestyle couldn't go on forever, but for now my miseries and my joys matched the *chiaroscuro* of my inner landscape.

There I sat, contemplating my situation, when I heard a knock on the back door. I was expecting Betsy, but this was her first visit to the house, so she didn't know the protocol: Knock and walk in.

Strangers—such as Fuller Brush salesmen, Mormons and Jehovah's Witnesses, The Woman with No Name, and Barney's brother Louie—knocked on the front door.

I opened the back door. Sure enough, it was Betsy, my good friend and godsend, holding a loaf of freshly baked banana bread wrapped in tinfoil.

I first met Betsy at the end of my sophomore year in college. She was one of the Chico State students in the same group as I, going abroad to study in Spain. We spent a year studying at the University of Granada with twenty-three other students from California state colleges. When Em abandoned me, Betsy was there to help me pick up the pieces.

"Banana Bread Woman, come in!"

"Call me by my real name."

"Okay: Betsy. Why didn't you knock and walk in like I told you on the phone?"

"Is everyone decent?"

"I'm a decent guy most of the time, and besides that, I'm fully clothed. Such a shame! Come on in."

"Is Janie here? If so, I'll come back another time."

She stepped up into the kitchen. A concerted effort toward civility barred me from grabbing the banana bread from her hands and wolfing it down.

"Have a seat, dear Betsy." I offered her Gene's tripod stool with the leather seat.

To sit on Gene's chair, you had to straddle it like a saddle. "That doesn't seem very ladylike," she protested.

Betsy. Dear Betsy. Straight as an arrow. Neatly coiffed, short auburn hair brushed back. Hers was a sort of mousy but nice-looking face with happy, attentive green eyes that spoke of a no-

nonsense approach to life. Short, maybe five feet two, with a thin, attractive upper body and a sturdy, attractive lower body that somehow didn't match the upper. It was as if God fished around in the parts bin and mistakenly put together the upper body of a thin person and the lower body of a sturdy woman. The overall effect, though, was fetching, given her honest and caring personality—and her banana bread. Moreover, she was the only non-hipster woman who frequented the house. The contrast was remarkable and refreshing.

"Okay, I'll trade you," I said, and offered her the produce crate. She sat down. "What's up with you these days?" I was trying to keep my eyes off the bundle in her hands.

"I'm still teaching junior high in Oroville, but I can't stand it, so I'm going back to San Jose."

I felt a vacuum sucking the wind out of me. "When?"

"Not right away."

I felt relieved, somewhat. "When?"

"My mother teaches kindergarten down there. I've always wanted to teach kindergarten, like my mother, and I can't stand the seventh graders I'm teaching in Oroville. My mother thinks I can get a job in her district. If it doesn't work out next school year, I'll try for a job in elementary in Oroville, and go home to San Jose the following year. That brings up what I came over about."

"Banana bread?" By now I was salivating, and thinking about the cube of butter in the orange refrigerator.

"We'll get to that in a minute. What are your plans for next year?"

"Next year? I haven't thought beyond my paycheck tomorrow, and that bundle you have in your hands. Did you bring that for me, or do you have another stop after this visit?"

"Now let's not be in such a hurry. I baked the banana bread this morning for you and the guys, but first, I want to know what your plans are for next year."

"Betsy, I'm sorry, but I have to admit I'm so goddam hungry, I can't think that far ahead. How about if we open your gift and enjoy some? Then I'll be in a better mind to tell you my thoughts about my non-existent future."

"Okay, okay then. Here," proffering the loaf, "but only a slice or two. Save some for the other guys."

I took it in a gentlemanly manner, slowly peeled back the foil, and held the loaf's freshly baked warmth to my cheek.

"You can't eat it that way!"

Continuing my sensory exploration, I held the loaf to my nose, and took some deep whiffs. In its warm, sweet goodness, I could feel Betsy's love.

"It's fresh, not stale," she complained.

I explained that sniffing was part of the sensual enjoyment of my food. Jim had started the tradition. Everyone who shared a meal with us at the house learned to sniff their food before eating.

"That might be okay with your other friends, but let's have some manners."

"Okay, Betsy." But I couldn't control myself. I bit a big chunk off the corner of the loaf.

"Not like that! I brought that to share, not for you to gobble down."

"I'm sorry, Betsy." I put the loaf down. "Let me explain." I told her about my financial condition and the state of my larder.

"Okay, then, you can eat most of it, but I'm having some, sliced, and leave a slice each for Jim and Mike. You can have the rest, but eat it like a human being."

"Betsy, you're weird by my standards. You're weird, because anyone normal is weird, and I've never been normal, at least not since 1958, and I've never known anyone as normal as you, and that *is* weird! You're so good, and so normal, and so wholesome and warm like this here loaf of freshly baked banana bread, I love you dearly." And I gave her a hug, which she received somewhat formally. Apparently she was still feeling maternal about my manners.

"I'm sorry about my etiquette. Let's enjoy some banana bread. Then I'll answer your questions about future plans."

Gratefully, I sliced three pieces, one for Betsy and a thin one each for Jim and Mike. Then I cut slabs and slathered them with butter from the orange refrigerator, and ate the rest of the loaf, consuming a quarter pound of butter in the process. I pictured myself as a male lion with a golden mane, enjoying the lion's share.

Hunger quashed, I said, "Life is short. First we have dessert; now, the main course. Have you ever tried fried green tomatoes?"

She hadn't.

We made small talk while I sliced the tomatoes, dipped them in egg and flour, and fried them. While we enjoyed the tomatoes, which to her surprise she liked, I gave Betsy a condensed version of my epiphany on the night of tomatoes in the dark, leading up to my current situation (leaving out the sensory details and metaphysical meanderings which Jim enjoyed); how I knew I would move on from Mariposa someday, but my crystal ball showed only vague images of the future; how I felt aimless and desperate and happy all at the same time, but I had no idea of what my next move would be.

Then I asked her advice.

"You need to get out of here. Get away from this lifestyle or you'll get a sickness that will kill you, or you'll be in jail and, when you get out, you'll have a criminal record and you'll never be allowed to teach."

Betsy had a way of making things plain and clear. She has always been a straight shooter—"the genuine article," my mother called her. Among all my ethereal and stoned and stalled friends, she was a breath of fresh air, a vision of clarity, which I nonetheless resisted. If I did what she said, I'd have to do the imponderable: have a plan, and be responsible; yet, the seeds of change were blowing in the wind.

Not wanting to add fuel to her fire, I didn't tell her how I'd been feeling weak and run down for several weeks already. Instead, I said, "Betsy, I think you might be exaggerating a bit about the legal implications. I'm not a drug dealer. I just smoke pot and occasionally take hallucinogenics." I didn't mention the Dexedrine I'd been taking either. "But you're right. I'm stalled-out here. I'm not sure I'm willing to give this up, but what shall I do?"

"Go back to school and get your teaching credential. You always wanted to teach anyway, didn't you? What are you doing here? That brings up why I came over. I thought maybe when I move back to Cupertino, you could get a teaching job down there."

"And live with you?"

"That wasn't what I was suggesting, but if that worked out, after a lot of talking about our relationship, that could be arranged. Given that I would be living near my parents, I would prefer to be married."

"Betsy, are you proposing marriage to me?"

"That would be in the realm of possibility, but first get your credential, get out of this place, and get a job."

"Dear Betsy, you're too good for me. I don't deserve you. You don't deserve me. I'm too wounded and messed up. Surely that's why Em left me for Dennis before we graduated. She had two choices: me, with my screwed up dark past and my sick, fractured family; or, Dennis, the straight arrow Chico farm boy from a "normal" nuclear family…" I couldn't resist adding an aside about Dennis: "…the blockheaded, begoggled bastard! Oh well, I'm not resentful. Just look at the life I'm living right here in this soul kitchen."

I jumped up off the tripod stool. Dancing, I mimed holding a microphone while I broke into a bad rendition of an Albert Collins song:

Now what we got
Right here in the kitchen?
It's soul food! Soul food!

"Your banana bread is my kind of soul food, thank you, Betsy; and you're my kind of soul food.

Trouble is, Janie, my exotic and sexy main squeeze, is my soul food as well."

"You'll have to get rid of her, or it won't work with you and me. I won't put up with that."

"Can we consummate our marriage now? I have a queen size bed and clean sheets. That way we can enjoy the benefits of marriage without actually going through with it. Then we won't have to go through the misery of divorce."

"Think about what I said."

Betsy gave me a lot to think about that day. I knew my Mariposa days would come to an end at some point, but how, and when? The answers would reveal themselves gradually. Essentially, Betsy had given me the key to unlock the door to my future. After our talk, my Mariposa time, in effect, ended even as it had barely begun. The rest was denouement, a playing out of Gothic beauty and decay leading to a near-death illness which forced me to make a decision—to live or to die; to stagnate, or to pick up and move on—followed by lengthy recuperation and months of hang-loose joy. It was time to move toward the seemingly lesser evil of an unknown future in the teaching profession, but that was a year and a half away. There was still a lot of cooking to do in the soul kitchen that was 2307 Mariposa Avenue.

20

Womb of Fear

"You won't be able to be free of feeling alone until you look death right in the face. That sounds like romantic crap until you go right up into the ass of death, till you find a womb of fear, and then maybe, maybe you'll be able to find [the place where you no longer feel alone]"

Marlon Brando's character,
Last Tango in Paris

I felt as if a team of mosquitoes had been working in shifts, slowly but steadily sucking away my lifeblood. Even though I'd quit drugs for a month after the night I met Abe Lincoln, and Richard dumped me into the giant funnel, it was a case of too little, too late. The New Year's Eve marathon with Janie hadn't helped, either.

You could say my resistance was down; I ignored the symptoms and became ill; end of report. That would be a simple and valid explanation. However, throughout the fall and winter, ever looming in the background was a sense that I had an appointment with Death. A decade's worth of suppressed grief and accumulated angst was backed up in me like a bad traffic jam. I was trying to outrun my grief, but the harder I ran, the more it caught up with me.

In moving to 2307, I opened Pandora's Box and all my demons came flying out in my face: habitual pessimism; morbid preoccupation with death; stored resentments toward my father and stepmother; suppressed anger, and my deep and abiding fear of anger itself; lack of impulse control; unreleased sorrow over the dissolution of my family of origin and the death of my brother; and my stubborn refusal to accept that my college sweetheart and rescuer, Em, had broken up with me two years earlier. The yearning for Em got all balled up with every other yearning I'd ever known—the yearning to recover my lost family, my deceased brother, my mentally ill mother, my imprisoned brother, my unavailable father, my lost innocence, my lost hope. If all these other yearnings were a steadily smoldering fire of longing, Em's departure was the accelerant of a blaze across my field of dreams. That first fall and winter on Mariposa, it was too much to deal with all at once. I thought medicating myself with pot, psychedelics, Dexedrine, and abundant sex would help slay my dragons.

Despite depression and worries about possibly being drafted into the army, I can't say I wasn't enjoying myself with Janie and Helen; with fixing up the house; with getting to know Jim and growing closer to my brother and mother; visiting Gene in his cave; being amused by the characters who frequented the house; and just hanging loose. On the surface, everything at 2307 seemed to be copasetic, but underneath my heady experiment in paganism ran a cold current of fear.

In my own Hero's Journey, I was about to join the battle for my life.

You could say a good deal of denial was at work in my steady decline. Whatever denial I hadn't learned from father or mother or stepmother, I supplied on my own, based on their template. Denial was the disease that ate my family from the inside out, chewed us up and spat us out, and it was about to do the same to me. Ignoring my symptoms, I pressed on, refusing to go to the doctor. Thinking to 'purify my system', I went on a fast. It was the dietary equivalent of medieval bloodletting. On the third day of the fast, feeling very weak, I thought a five-mile run would stir up some energy. Instead, at the three-mile mark, I collapsed and blacked out on someone's front lawn. The homeowner kindly collected me and dropped me at 2307, asking, "Are you sure you don't want to go to the emergency room?"

The next day, I temporarily set aside the baleful influence of my Christian Science background and went to the doctor. Going to the doctor was a good, though belated, decision; the doctor I selected, a very bad choice.

A VISIT TO DOCTOR HIPPOCRATES, THE "HIPPIE-CRIT"

The doctor came into the room just long enough to exclaim, "Oh no, not another one of *you people!"* and he walked out.

I was bewildered, but I soon realized that "you people" meant hippies, and he wasn't going to treat me. I felt like a black man being shooed away from the whites' drinking fountain.

After a long wait, during which I sprawled on the treatment table feeling like I was going to die, the nurse came back in and told me I could leave.

I told her, "The doctor hasn't treated me yet. If he doesn't come back in and help me, and if I ever feel well enough again, I'm going to come back and kick his ass. And if I don't get well and I die right here, I'm still coming back to kick his ass! Now you go tell him I said so." I remember being surprised that I screwed up enough energy to say that, but I was fighting for my life.

I lay there looking at a picture of a sword and serpent on the wall. I knew it meant something, but I couldn't remember what.

The doctor burst into the room. "What's going on here?"

There were many things I wanted to say to him, but I had difficulty forming complete thoughts. All I could think to say was, "What's that?"

"What?"

I pointed. "On the wall...serpent…sword."

"Oh, that. It's the symbol of Hippocrates."

"Meaning?"

"*'Physician, do no harm.'* It's an oath every doctor takes."

In my addled condition, I couldn't quite form the word I was looking for: *Hypocrite!* Instead, I said, "Liar."

"What do you mean?"

Again it took every ounce of energy I had to say, "You will do me harm if you don't treat me."

Abruptly, he said, "I'll send in a prescription with my nurse," and he left the room. That was as close as I ever got to a diagnosis.

I never saw him again, but a few years later, I stopped by his office to have a "nice little chat" with him. At the last minute, I left the baseball bat in the car. The same nurse who had helped me was now working for a different doctor in the same office. She said that my Dr. So-and-So had died a couple of years before. According to the nurse, at the time the doctor treated me so poorly, he had just been diagnosed with terminal cancer.

AT THE PHARMACY

At the pharmacy, I found out the doctor had prescribed antibiotics. My ill-advised penchant for natural healing returned, and I gave the pharmacist a lecture. "I'm not taking antibiotics because they're not a *natural* remedy. Don't you have any *natural* remedies?"

"Do you want the prescription or not?" she asked.

"Well, I don't think so. Listen to the word: 'anti' means against. 'Biotic' means life. Therefore, antibiotics are 'against life'." I was about to faint as I said this.

"Well, it's your choice. Do you want it or not?"

Refusing the prescription, which would have cost me a week's wages, I bought a vaporizer that the doctor's nurse had recommended. Vapor was natural, after all.

The delay in my treatment put me over the line from bronchitis to walking pneumonia to double pneumonia. It didn't help that I had mononucleosis and yellow jaundice as well (something I figured out later).

BACK AT THE RANCH

At home, not having enough energy to set up the vaporizer, I flopped on the bed under my one flimsy blanket. I sweated and shook and shivered feverishly for who knows how long, perhaps a day or two, and at some point Jim called Betsy and she came to the rescue.

She sat by the bed and asked, "What's going on?"

Between coughing and gasping for air, and resting from the exertion of talking, I told her about the weeks of declining energy; how I'd tried to shrug it off; about the fasting, running, and collapsing on someone's lawn; about my visit to the doctor and his reluctance to treat me; and, about the pharmacist and my refusal to take antibiotics. I didn't mention feeling depressed and suicidal. That would have taken too many words, and I didn't want Betsy to say, "I told you so."

BETSY TO THE RESCUE

Betsy asked questions and listened. Then she gave me the ultimatum that saved my life. "You're going to die here if you don't get treated. You have exactly two choices. Either I take you to the hospital or I take you to your parents' house in Lafayette and you go to the doctor there."

My medical insurance had expired. Who needed medical insurance anyway? "Take me to Lafayette."

Betsy got some broth into me and came back in the morning with some scones she had baked.

"Shall we call your parents first?" she asked.

"No. My stepmother will tell me not to come. There's no other choice. Once I'm there, I'm not leaving. She'll like it or lump it."

"When you go to the doctor, who will pay for it?" Betsy's question sent me into a flashback. I had heard those words from Millie before: *"Who will pay for it?"*

"WHO WILL PAY FOR IT?" Millie had said when I was fourteen and I asked her to send me to a psychiatrist or psychotherapist. I was hurting and confused by all the changes involved in my family's breakup, and unhappy with living in Lafayette with her and her kids. I knew I needed the kind of counseling my brother Tim was getting in the group home; the kind of help my mother was getting in the mental hospital. Millie told me she wasn't going to pay for any such thing, and my Dad wasn't going to, either (meaning she wasn't even going to broach the subject with him and I'd better not, either). She said I'd better just straighten up and fly right.

Not long after that, in an attempt to self-medicate, I got caught stealing a bottle of peach brandy from the supermarket, and received a severe beating from my father (mentioned previously). I couldn't sit down for a week. The closely spaced welts covering my shoulders to my thighs lasted longer.

"WHO WILL PAY FOR IT?" Betsy asked again.

"Wait," I said. "I'm thinking," and I drifted into other remembrances of times when Millie had promised to pay me for work performed, then reneged on her offer. One of those times, I got poison oak so badly from clearing brush behind the house that my eyes swelled shut and my face swelled to the size of a basketball. She refused to take me to the doctor even though my father went every time he got the itch, and a cortisone shot fixed him up within hours. The case of poison oak kept me out of school for a week. Later, she refused to pay me the hourly wage she had promised for the work I had done, saying, "You didn't finish the job."

"EARTH CALLING BIX!" SAID BETSY.

"Sorry, Betsy... Millie will pay the doctor."

"What makes you think she'll be so generous?" Betsy had Millie's number.

"Because, Betsy—don't ask me to explain right now—Millie owes me."

"Okay," she ordered. "Get up and get yourself together and let's go."

THE TRIP TO LAFAYETTE

During the three-hour trip to Lafayette in Betsy's new Ford Falcon, I slept, waking only when the car stopped at the familiar cul-de-sac in the hills above Lafayette. The steep driveway had a 100-degree turn halfway up. Betsy made me get out and drive the rest of the way up to the house.

Millie was not happy to see either of us. She gave us the expected lecture about calling first, and, "Don't ever show up sick at someone's house." Since these words were expected, they didn't bother me. I went directly to bed where I could hear most of the balance of the conversation between Millie and Betsy.

BETSY SHOWS HER METTLE

I was hoping Millie wouldn't treat Betsy the way she had treated my fiancée Em the one and only time she had come to the house to wait for her father to pick her up. I had hidden Em in my bedroom, hoping Millie wouldn't interact with her. When Millie happened into the bedroom, she said to Em, "Who the hell are you, and what are you doing here? *Are you trying to steal my mother's jewels?* Get out of here before I call the cops!"

When Millie tried to get Betsy to take me to her parents' house in San Jose, Betsy, dear sweet Betsy, stood her ground against my stepmother. Even in my worn out state, the request seemed surreal: having just told me never to show up unannounced at anyone's house, now she wanted me to do exactly that to Betsy's parents.

"Bix is very sick," said Betsy. "He needs to see a doctor soon."

"Then why don't you take him to *your* doctor?"

Betsy did not take the bait. "My brother will be home this weekend, and the beds are all full," she said. "Here's my phone number in San Jose," she said, and left.

I WON'T TELL YOU HOW ILL I BECAME

When you've been ill, you probably want to give a detailed description of your symptoms to anyone who will listen. No one wants to hear the gruesome details, so here are just a few highlights. I lay near death in my father's house for two weeks, spitting up gallons of sputum into two plastic buckets. In order to empty the buckets, I slithered on my belly across the bedroom and hallway, pushing the buckets ahead of me to empty them into the toilet. I was so weak, a round trip to the bathroom and back took a half hour to an hour per bucket.

Even after those two weeks in Lafayette, back in Chico it took four weeks in bed before I could stumble as far as the bathroom; three months before I could ride my bicycle half a mile, or walk a quarter mile, without stopping to rest; and a year before I could jog a slow mile. A year after the onset, I still needed twelve to fourteen hours a day of sleep. No, I won't catalog my symptoms. Nobody wants to hear about that; but I do want to relate the surreal dreams and hallucinations I had, and the redemption that came about from a life-changing descent into hell.

IN DELIRIUM

I stayed in bed in my old room in Lafayette for two weeks. All sense of time disappeared as delirium took over. However, some waypoints I do remember.

My stepbrother Mark came into my room looking for a book and was as surprised to find me there as I was to see him. He had just returned from Vietnam. To the chagrin of his mother, he was at loose ends and needed a place to stay.

To Mark I voiced a sense of confusion that my father wasn't around. Mark explained that Dad was away on business—Belgium or such—and he'd be back soon.

When my father did show up, I was invited to dine with him and Millie in the den. I had eaten hardly anything for two or three days except for the scones Betsy had made and half a sandwich Mark shared with me. Barely able to sit up, my head hung over the plate of food. "Meat," I said, unappreciatively. "Red meat. I don't eat red meat."

"You and your vegetarian crap!" said Millie.

Somehow I felt stronger and safer in my father's presence since I'd had that passionate talk with him six months before, when I picked up the two new windows. Back then, I'd gotten angry at Millie and flipped her two birds for the price of one, but I refrained from saying the "F" word.

Now, for the first and only time in my life, I exclaimed to Millie, "*Fuck you!*" It felt pretty good to say that, downright cleansing. I knew I had just cancelled my meal ticket for the remainder of my stay, but I didn't care. I'd lost my appetite for the kind of "nutrition" Millie had to offer. I'd lost my appetite for putting up with her bullshit, her betrayal, and her verbal abuse. I'd lost my appetite for her approval as well. I was my own man now, and Millie could go play leapfrog in the asparagus patch. Shoving in potatoes and some kind of vegetable with my fingers, because eating with a fork was too slow, I apologized to my father for disrespecting his wife and for eating with my fingers, excused myself, and went back to bed. My father left the next day for England.

In two weeks I lost 18% of my body weight; but, cussing out Millie, I felt like I'd dropped a thousand pound burden off my shoulders.

MY STEPBROTHER COMES TO MY RESCUE

During the whole time I was ill in Lafayette, my stepmother never checked on me nor offered any assistance. My father was gone most of the time, but when he was there, I have a vague recollection of his walking into the room, exclaiming, "Sheesh, it smells like a sick room in here!" and walking out. (I remember thinking, *if my stepbrother wasn't here checking on me, how long would it take for the smell of my corpse to attract the attention of my parents?)*

Betsy wasn't my only angel of saving grace. If it hadn't been for Mark, I don't think I would have survived the illness. He took my temperature—105°. Many people die at 106°. He brought water and some bits of food, though not much because he was nearly as broke as I was and he wasn't sharing meals at the family table, either. He took me to the doctor, the same one I had wanted to go to when I'd had the poison oak years before. (In this, I sensed a moral victory over the prior grievance, and I felt no shame in having the doctor send Millie the bill.)

The doctor took one look at me lying on the table in his treatment room, and said, "I know what you have, and you should be in the hospital." Explaining that I couldn't afford it and I hadn't yet taken any medications, I asserted that I'd go later if I got worse, and asked if he couldn't give me some drugs first to see if they worked.

Mark, gods bless him, picked up my prescriptions and made sure I took them: antibiotics, which I took this time, and a powerful decongestant.

When I thanked Mark profusely, he shrugged it off, saying, "Oh, that's okay, it's just what any reasonably decent human being would do for another."

"Thank you, Mark, because your mother hasn't been helping me at all."

"That's because my mother's not a reasonably decent human being. In fact, my mother's not a human being," he said.

DREAMS AND HALLUCINATIONS

The doctor warned me strongly not to take more than one

decongestant a day, so of course the first day I took two. That's when the flood of mucus, the hallucinations, and wild dreams began.

Whether I was asleep or awake didn't seem to matter. The dreams and hallucinations blended one into the other. I lost track of all sense of time, and I couldn't tell if it was day or night, or if my eyes were open or closed. Combined with the dizzying effect of pneumonia, an intense vertigo and fevered delirium took possession of my mind and body for who knows how long? A week? Ten days? Slipping out of time-bound awareness, I spun in a vortex of darkness, feelingas if I was about to be sucked into the void.

DREAM SEQUENCE

Wild dreams ran as continuous loops, round and round. The odd thing in all these dreams was that I became at once a participant and a neutral, lucid observer. Hovering over the bed in out-of-body experiences, I could simultaneously see a young man's body on the bed and watch his dreams dispassionately, like movies projected on a screen. That must explain why I can remember the dreams so clearly today. They were at once terrifying, amusing and edifying.

In the dreams, I faced the Grim Reaper (let's call him "G.R.") who appeared as the archetypal skeleton dressed in a long robe and carrying a scythe. His right hand man, the Pale Rider of the Apocalypse himself, was seen in the dream as my sadistic brother Jon, who looked like G.R.'s twin. In the dream I remarked, "So that's what happened to Brother Jon after he died. He's Death's right hand man. It suits him."

Escaping the scythe, I found myself in a hall of mirrors where

I saw my face reflected as various people I knew. Looking in one mirror, I saw G.R. and Brother Jonny eagerly looking over my shoulder. Escaping through a door at one end of the gallery, I entered a tunnel where the light at the end invited me to step into eternity. When I realized I could choose to step into the light, out of this life, I knew the step would be final, and I kept turning back, only to meet G.R. and Jonny in the hall of mirrors; and the cycle of dreams played over and over again with fractal variations and permutations and spinning mandalas thrown in for good measure. I was endlessly facing my fear of death, and death itself, and trying to escape it.

LUCID IMAGININGS

After some days, I periodically became lucid enough to realize I could put an end to my misery by drowning in the family pool. Fearing I might complete the act while sleepwalking, I remained awake as much as possible. Lack of sleep in turn prolonged my delirium.

I was sorely tempted by the sweet release that death would bring, yet afraid that I might actually do myself in. One thought held me back: *If I die, it will be irrevocable.* As days went by, I thought ironically, *if I drown, no one will miss me. I won't be around to pity myself anymore, and self-pity has its payoffs!* At the time, I liked this dark humor. It seemed like a sign that I was starting to feel well enough to think something was funny.

You could say I confronted Death and decided not to go there.

THE FLYING CARPETS OF ALI BABA

But the hallucinations weren't over yet. After perhaps nine days, as a modicum of health returned, that which had previously played out as dreams now shaded into a series of waking hallucinations.

Lying on my right side in semi-darkness with the shades drawn, I could see the set of bookshelves attached to the opposite wall. At one point, idly staring at the books, I recognized one of my favorites that I used to read frequently, *A Thousand and One Nights*. Suddenly it stretched out like a Slinky toy and hovered above the other books on the shelf. The 'book' undulated like sea waves and turned into a miniature flying carpet complete with a fez-wearing genie sitting cross-legged on top. The magic carpet then sped off in a blur and disappeared, leaving an empty place on the bookshelf!

What happened next, you might guess.

The entire sequence of Slinky, magic carpet, and fez-wearing genie speeding off in a blur repeated itself with the next book on the shelf, leaving another blank space, book after book until the entire shelf was empty! Just to make sure I wasn't seeing things, I rubbed my eyes and blinked and looked at the shelves again. They still looked empty. Just as I was wondering if the bookshelves would fly away as well, Ali Baba brought all the books back one by one, refilling the shelves like a movie running in reverse.

"Wow, the flying carpet of Ali Baba!"

As I mouthed the words, a small but significant shift occurred: I felt a sense of hope that would grow in the coming days. At least this hallucination was entertaining. It wasn't Death awaiting me at the end of a tunnel, nor was it the freaky hall of mirrors, nor was I drowning in the family pool. The medication was working; I could breathe again. A sense of time returned and I could tell the difference between night and day.

The mental exercise of choreographing the hallucinations kept away the nightmares. I thought if I could keep the hallucinations going with a thousand and one variations, I would forestall death just as Scheherazade had told a thousand and one stories on a thousand and one nights to postpone her execution by King Shahryar. With that thought came a burst of hope. As long as I had my wits about me, and my imagination, Death might spare me.

At some point, the Ali Baba hallucinations were no longer sustainable. I missed my magical little friend, but his absence was a good sign: I was getting well. To pass the time without Ali Baba, I devised a project, to remember all I could about *A Thousand and One Nights*. Each remembered detail was a reward that proved my head was working again. As health began to return day by day, I said a fervent prayer that, like Scheherazade, my life would become a thousand and one stories and I would live long enough to tell them all.

CASEY JONES

One morning—I must have been in bed in Lafayette about ten days—Mark came in, opened the blinds and turned on the stereo. "You're getting well now, so wake your sorry ass up and enjoy the day," he said, and left the room.

I woke up slowly with the sun shining on my third eye, realizing the dreams and hallucinations were all gone. I lay there listening to the Grateful Dead singing:

Driving that train,
High on cocaine,
Casey Jones you'd better
Watch your speed.

The song had just debuted on the radio that day, and they played it over and over. After half an hour or more of repeats, I thought maybe the record was stuck, but the announcer came on and said they'd had many listeners calling to request encores. I enjoyed every repetition because the words spoke to me directly. I knew I'd been driving too hard and fast, running on empty. I knew the "speed", or Dexedrine that I'd been taking had been partly responsible for making me so ill. Wanting to avoid a relapse, I understood that the mental habits which had taken me to the edge of the abyss had to change.

LETTING GO OF THE PAST

With my mind now clearer, I stayed in Lafayette another four days, assessing my situation.

Lying there in bed on one of those lucid days, I spotted some volumes of Proust that I knew my stepmother had enjoyed. I thought anyone who read *Remembrance of Things Past* couldn't be all bad. *Maybe*, I thought, *I will write my own remembrances someday. If so, what do I want them to sound like, whining and angst ridden, or full of high adventure, humor, love and forgiveness?* I thought I might never *forget* my resentments toward Millie, but I could at least *forgive*. In fact, I realized I *must* forgive, or grief and fear and mean people would continue to own me.

Right then and there I decided to make friends with my adversities; to release the binding influence of the past. I realized that if I didn't, I would be forever angry, and anger can be so unhealthy as to be life-threatening. On some level I knew that resilience was the only way I would outlive my angst. From the present-day perspective, that sounds simple and obvious, but for a young man whose emotions were bound and gagged, whose fears ruled his behavior, releasing the past was a huge revelation, and a lifesaver. The near death experience was like Roto Rooter for the soul.

Old mental habits die hard, but in the remaining days in Lafayette and in the months to come, each day when I woke up I celebrated another day of cheating Death. I reminded myself to live in the present, to quit using the lens of the past to project dire outcomes on the future. Not only was my new outlook mentally healthy; I was certain it was necessary for my survival. During recuperation, my four oft repeated commandments to myself were:

> *1) Wake up from the bad dream!*
> *2) Pay attention!*
> *3) Live in the present!*
> *4) Quit your Stinkin' Thinkin', and apply the antidote!*

In this way, much of the trauma and drama of the past began to flake away. However, mental wellness doesn't always come as a grand epiphany. Sometimes growth is incremental, and the battle against bad mental habits is like swimming upstream in a flood. If only I'd known then what I know now, I'd have been perfectly repaired overnight and there would be no story of recovery to tell. In an ideal world, my family would have been an episode of "Ozzie and Harriet" or the "Brady Bunch." But that would have been a different life, someone else's, not my own.

A funny thing happened on the way to adulthood. My spirit went into solitary confinement. Before beginning to overcome spiritual amnesia, I had to "go right up into the ass of Death" and face my worst fears. During the weeks of delirium and recovery, I entered a womb of fear, and emerged physically devastated but spiritually reborn. Where fear had previously ruled my life, now hope had taken its place.

TO EVERY SEASON, TURN, TURN

With the early February sun shining in the window, and birds singing in the trees, I was eager to return to 2307 Mariposa Avenue and get on with life.

2307 Mariposa Avenue, I thought, will be an emotional clearinghouse. It will be a grand experiment in the soul kitchen of the Human Potential Movement! I'm going to get my doctorate in Self-Expression! I'm going to live a thousand and one stories, and have a thousand and one stories to tell! I'm going home. Gonna get to feelin' better; make love with Janie; quit singin' the blues! Gonna make a home for myself and the family of my choosing; get back to my roots by planting a garden; gonna plant a good crop and reap what I sow!

21

Meanwhile, Back at the Ranch

"In the midst of winter I found there was in me an invincible summer."
Albert Camus,
The Stranger

When Mark took me back to Chico after my two weeks in Lafayette, Janie was nowhere in sight. She didn't call. She didn't come over. She didn't send any messages or make any inquiries about my well-being. Did she even know I was sick? Perhaps she thought I'd run off with someone else. I was still too weak to get up and use the phone.

Six weeks went by in a haze. I slept twenty hours or more per day, but this shaded down to sixteen. (Nine months later I still required fourteen hours per day.) My first time walking (not crawling) to the bathroom was cause for celebration; sitting up in bed, reading a book for a half hour, a major victory. During this time, Janie made herself scarce, and I was going to find out why.

BANANA BREAD WOMAN: REPRISE

And who was there holding my hand and taking care of me? If you guessed Betsy, you guessed right. She brought her famous banana bread, plus an occasional variation on the theme such as zucchini bread or scones or cookies. She made sure I took my medication and she forced chicken broth down me. She read aloud to me, and we discussed books, and we played endless games of Scrabble, which frustrated her no end because I had all day to study the dictionary. She soaked washcloths in hot water and laid them across my forehead. She worked all this around her busy and exhausting teaching schedule.

After several weeks, with atrophied muscles I wobbled to the phone and begged Janie to come over. My libido was returning, and I wanted her special brand of attention. She gave it to me, along with gonorrhea. As I took yet another round of antibiotics, I wondered where she'd been, and with whom. When I confronted her with the fact, she tried to wiggle out of it, saying she hadn't been with anyone. She must have thought I'd be dumb enough to believe her. Later, she admitted it was some guy named Randy who worked at Sambo's Restaurant. She said he could pour coffee from three feet in the air without spilling a drop, and that excited her.

Even though we stayed together another year and a half, that was the beginning of the end of Janie and me.

"You know what?" I said, "I don't blame you for getting it on with someone while I was too sick to take care of your needs, but my health is already compromised, and now you give me this. Have you ever heard of condoms?"

"Well, yeah, but, you know, we took this mescaline, and one thing led to another, and we got it on for hours."

"Spare me the details. Here's what really bugs me: You lied to me. Now I can't trust you anymore."

Despite my righteous indignation, I had to admit that our arrangement to that point had been pretty loose and based on a sort of Free Love double standard—don't ask, don't tell—but I had started to become fond of Janie. I went on to tell her she couldn't have it both ways. She resisted, and I held my ground. "It's me, or him. You can't have both." It remained to be seen how that played out. I was ready to make a commitment, but not on a one-way street. Janie was the woman I wanted that I shouldn't have;

Betsy, the woman I didn't want that I should have. One was a love goddess; the other, a good solid citizen, compassionate and caring. In my mind there was no resolution of this dichotomy, but it was clear I was more attracted to sex than good sense. Somehow, I was still stuck with the cruel notion that Betsy was the consolation prize for my erstwhile Em. I respected Betsy but I loved her mostly in a brotherly way. For Janie, I had a passion that surpassed understanding.

REALIZATIONS

Back at the Ranch, I had lots of time to think and problem-solve. It was as if I'd been struck by lightning, and I had to learn to reorganize the workings of my brain. While my body was pretty useless, retraining my mind became my best medicine.

Lying in my bed of getting-wellness, I decided to continue the project begun the last few days in Lafayette, where I'd made a mental chart of Remembrances, Grievances, and Plans of Action. Among other edifying thoughts came a fundamental realization: You can't have it both ways! You can't be faithful to someone while having a fling with someone else. (This explains why I had the backbone to speak up to Janie as I did.) You can't have a death wish and be fully engaged in life. You can't hold onto resentments and be happy. If ambivalence is your stock in trade, you'll never be mentally well. If I wanted to be healthy and thrive, I would have to learn to let go and move on.

Letting go was easier said than done. Several issues hung fire, but one in particular comes to mind: The grief over Em, which at times became an obsession. The issue of her departure plagued me for longer than I'd like to admit, two decades or more.

My reluctance to move on became a talisman of longing and self-pity, especially in times when I felt lonely, depressed or bereft. Mourning her loss became an indulgence in melancholy that served as a way to feel something, to feel anything, because often I believed myself a victim and allowed myself no joy.

It took many years to come to a point of complete acceptance, but lying there in my sickbed in Chico, the best I could do was to apply what I'd learned about not having it both ways: *You can't hang on to Em, and be fully in love with Janie. Make a choice. Decide.* But a stubborn part of me still wouldn't let go. Intuitively, I had a sense that this tendency was going to cause problems in the future, and it did. Still, despite my doubts and dips into depression, growing in me was an invincible summer.

Having almost completely imploded, I entered a state of grace and acceptance. Every day became a feast of joy. As long as I wasn't reading about myself in the obituaries, everything would be okay.

SIRLOIN SALVATION

One day the familiar putt-putt of Barney's Harley passed my bedroom window at midday and semi-circled the house. The engine shut off, and he came in.

Even without the motorcycle I'd have known it was Barney. Lying in bed for a couple of weeks since returning from Lafayette had taught me the footfall and door opening style of each person who came to the house. Martial artist that he was, Barney walked like a cat, silent feet hitting the back porch. The sound of the door opening was limited to the squeaky handle, but even that was quieter than most.

I knew what he was up to at the moment. One or two cat leaps across the kitchen, and he was standing in front of the stove, reaching for the bottle of Trappey's Hot Sauce on the shelf. By now he must have completed his Trappey's routine. What was he doing in there? Again, no footfalls, and then suddenly he was in my room at the head of the bed.

"What the hell are you doing in bed at this hour? Get your lazy ass up!" he said in his usual friendly manner.

"Haven't you heard? I've been really sick."

"That's no excuse. Now get up. We're getting you out of the house to go for a ride."

At the time I hardly knew Barney so his behavior was a little annoying, but his well-intentioned attitude was infectious. Suddenly I almost felt that I could get up and hop on the back of the Harley and go tooling around the park, but ignoring my symptoms was part of what had put me down for the count in the first place. It took some convincing, but he relented on the bike ride when I related my most recent adventures in the land of delirium. He seemed to get what I was saying when I told him that the mere act of getting up to use the toilet, just feet away from my bed, exhausted me.

Just as Betsy had done before she took me to Lafayette, Barney sat on the stool next to my bed, asked questions and listened, assessing the situation. "Have you had anything to eat?"

"Not much. Brown rice. Veggies."

"Are you hungry?"

"Yes and no. I eat till I'm full, but nothing satisfies me."

He thought a little, and made a decision. "All right, do you have a couple of bucks?"

"What for? If I had any money right now, I wouldn't loan it to you. I can't afford to give it away."

"It doesn't matter. If you have a couple of bucks, fine. If not, I've got a couple bucks."

Again I asked, "What for?"

"I'm not telling you because you're not going to like this, but I'm going to the store and get you something and I'm coming back and I'm going to fix it for you and you're going to eat it and you're not going to complain and you're going to like it." That was the way Barney talked, real fast, with no periods, just lots of 'ands'.

At this point I'd eaten almost nothing but brown rice and veggies for months, and not much of that. It showed in my skeletal frame. Still, I was suspicious. "What are you going to get?"

"I'm not telling you because…." And he repeated his short speech. Then he asked me if I liked mushrooms, and I said yes, vegetarians eat mushrooms.

"Okay," I said. "There's a couple of dollars in my dresser drawer."

He got it. Before he left, he reasserted, "You're going to eat it and you're not going to complain and you're going to like it."

The Harley thrummed and faded in the direction of Longfellow Shopping Center. Ten minutes later he was back, rummaging around in the kitchen. Soon I heard a sizzling sound.

He came into the room. "It's almost ready. Remember, you're not going to complain and you're going to like it and you're going to eat all of it because it was expensive and if you don't I'm going to shove it down your throat."

What he brought me filled the whole plate: a steaming one and a half pound sirloin steak smothered in a pound of sautéed mushrooms. Sitting up took a lot of effort.

"C'mon, sit your ass up, your food's getting cold!"

With much concentration, I finally got propped up against the headboard. Barney threw a towel in my lap. "Here, have a towel that I got from the bathroom because you don't have any napkins in the kitchen."

"Who needs a napkin when I usually eat with my fingers like a Vietnamese peasant?"

I must have been staring at the steaming steak and mushrooms as if it were some foreign object because Barney barked another command to make me start the feast.

I started in on the mushrooms and kept going on them.

"Take a bite of the goddam steak! That's sirloin steak, boy, and it'll do you good."

"But Barney, I always eat one thing at a time. First the mushrooms…."

"Then eat the steak first! C'mon, goddammit, I told you, you're going to eat it. I didn't come over here and go to the store and come back here and fix you an expensive steak so's you could eat it cold."

"All right, all right then, I'll take a bite." The first slice revealed a piece of meat cooked medium rare, hot all the way through but pink in the middle.

"Is it cooked right, the way you like it?"

"Just the way I like…." I caught myself. I wasn't supposed to say I liked red meat. Revising the sentence, I said, "Just the way I used to like it, when I ate red meat."

"Well, you're eating red meat now, and you'd better like it because that's prime USDA, straight from the steer."

I took the first bite; closed my eyes; lay my head back on the pillow and chewed forty times till the meat turned to liquid. A couple more bites like that, and I swear the stored solar energy of 100,000 grains of wheat was mainlined into my system. If my body's battery had been on discharge for several months, now it felt like someone had plugged me into quick charge. As soon as each bite reached my stomach, energy radiated in all directions through my whole body, out to my extremities. My scalp tightened, my hair stood on end, my nostrils flared, and my ears flexed. Every square inch of my skin was tingling, and little chimes were ringing in my ears. Frances Moore Lappé and her *Diet for a Small Planet* be damned! Never in my life had I tasted anything so good, nor received so much energy from it.

Barney kept asking me if it was okay, but I was so "into it" that I was speechless. I made him sit and wait and watch while I consumed the whole steak and the rest of the pound of mushrooms with my eyes closed. It must have taken half an hour. Only then did I take a break. I wanted to use words like "exalted" and "godlike," but no words were adequate. Instead, I just nodded like one of those toy dog nodders you see in peoples' rear car windows, with a big grin on my face, saying *good* and *thank you* over and over, interspersed with caveman noises and *wow, oh man, wow.*

When I recovered enough to speak intelligibly, I said, "Damn, Barney, you were right. I hate to admit it, but I needed that. You got any more of that stuff?"

"That's all for today, but I'll see what I can do tomorrow if I can rustle up a couple more bucks."

Listening to Barney's putt-putt going down the street, I slid back under the covers and lay there feeling the energy pulsing into my body. for what seemed like forever. Then I slept for twelve hours.

Barney came back the next day with some more sirloin salvation, and the next. Then he told me if I wanted any more, I was going to have to get up off my lazy sick ass and go to the market myself.

I wasn't sure I could get there under my own steam, but it became a goal, a reason for living. Meanwhile, Betsy and Jim fetched for me, and I had sirloin steak with sautéed mushrooms four or five times in two weeks.

The day came when I was ready to venture forth on my own. The mental preparation was like getting ready for a marathon. On the way to the store, which was a quarter of a mile from the house, I pushed my bike. Too weak and wobbly to ride, I needed the bike for its basket because I wasn't strong enough to carry a small bag of groceries back to the house. Somebody could have fetched for me but, no, Barney said I was going to have to get up off my lazy ass, and by the gods I was going to do it. So I pushed the bike and stopped eight times to lie down on the well-trimmed grass of tract houses along the way.

After buying groceries, I rested, stretched out on the gum-splotched cement next to a post where my bike was locked. The cement felt cool and good. Several people stopped to ask if I was okay. Then I pushed the bike and stopped eight more times on the way back to the house. I put the steak in the orange refrigerator. The round trip of half a mile took me two hours. "A quarter of a mile per hour, like my old friend the tortoise, of tortoise and hare fame," I thought. Too fatigued to prepare the food, I went to bed and slept soundly for six hours.

At dusk I got up and had a pound of sirloin salvation. Going back to bed, the energy rush from the food kept me awake for an hour. Then I fell asleep for another fourteen, and dreamed about three towheaded boys in 1950's backyard barbeque America, joyously chomping monstrous double cheeseburgers grilled by our father and letting the grease run down our chins after a day of playing war in the back forty, using ketchup for blood.

Overseeing the whole scene in the dream, a Herculean Frances Moore Lappé, wearing my mother's apron, looked out over all of the farms, feedlots, slaughterhouses and barbeques of America, trying to reform us all, saying, "Tsk tsk, so many acres and so much grain produces so little meat," but the three well-fed boys in the dream, and one young, happy, steak-stuffed dreamer lying in bed in a house on Mariposa Avenue, didn't care what the monumental Lappé had to say.

A REASON TO LIVE

"It's the new Mother Nature takin' over,
She's the new splendid lady come to call."
Guess Who

Man cannot live on meat alone.

The daily sirloin steak and mushrooms were giving me enough strength to contemplate planting vegetables. The previous fall I'd planted a "starter" garden, which included the vines of 'Tomatoes in the Dark.' But this year I had bigger ideas.

After reading the Tolkien trilogy twice, and *The Teachings of Don Juan* three times, and studying the dictionary daily, I was starting to go out of my skull with boredom. I was still too weak to do much, but I'd said I was going to live off the fat of the land, and it was time to start making it happen.

With limited energy, I had to plot my moves.

Day One, I literally crawled out to the garden at midday, only to discover the soil was root bound. Tilling it was more work than I could handle lying down (because I could only stand for a minute at a time). That was all for that day. I crawled back in the house, and fell asleep till dark.

Day Two, I crawled back out, but this time I collected a claw hammer from the porch on the way out. I clawed away at the roots but I rapidly became winded.

Day Three, I tried another tack; ran the hose on the hard-packed dirt driveway to soften the soil. My roommates complained, but so what?

Day Four, I crawled out and started clawing away at the driveway. Oddly enough, the hard-packed dirt was friable. At least there were no roots to deal with here.

Forsaking the previous year's garden site and using the hammer and a hand trowel, I constructed two mounds to one side of the driveway in full sunlight. I worked lying down, stopping frequently to rest. Furrows were out of the question because I'd have had to stand up and use a shovel. I planted zucchini on one mound, cantaloupes on the other. I begged everyone not to drive over the mounds. Day by day, I grew stronger. My endurance increased. I slept less each day.

Now I had something to get me out of bed each day: to get up and check the mounds and keep them moist.

The planting must have been complete around mid to late March, because in the early dawn, ten days after planting, I awoke. It was the first day of spring. The air outside my windows glowed a luscious peach. "Today the plants will sprout," I thought. "In fact, I can feel it. It's going to happen any minute. It's time to get up and look, now!"

The gardening activity and sirloin steaks had me strong enough to walk outside. I sat Indian style facing the mounds, and meditated. The sun came up over the horizon and warmed my forehead. I opened my eyes and I was treated to the most extraordinary display in nature I've ever seen.

I knew precisely where I had planted each seed, and as the sun struck the mound in front of me, a crack developed in the soil like a crack in an egg when a chick is trying to hatch. Briefly I considered helping it, but I remembered a time when I was a boy in Van Nuys, I tried to help a chick break out of its shell, and it died. Little chicks, plants and people need to break out of their shells on their own.

Everything happened in slow motion, but in my meditative state, it all seemed to occur like stop-action photography. A little caplet of soil rose up from the fissure as the sprout took its first peek at the world. The caplet tilted up as the germinating seed raised its head. The unfurling sprout waved slowly back and forth, celebrating life and seeking sun. The little caplet of soil fell, and the sprout, fully exposed, danced in earnest like someone in a crowd doing the wave in a baseball stadium. Soon the sprout's mates followed suit, repeating the whole dance. Glued to the spot, I held still for fear of missing the birth of my babies. At some point, still seated, I raised my arms and mimicked the sprouts' dance.

I think I must have stayed there at least two hours till all the seeds sprouted and danced and deployed their first leaves. Then I got too hot and went into the house. I lay on the bed in absolute ecstasy. My plants were being born, and I was being reborn. Having something to look forward to every day—something alive and growing—gave me a reason for living.

The garden expanded in concert with my increasing energy and endurance. By early June, many friends had already enjoyed enormous sweet zucchinis from the first mound, and the cantaloupes—well, they were the best anyone had ever tasted, with thin translucent skin but firm, sweet flesh all the way through. Little by little, I managed to dig up the big garden plot until it covered a thousand square feet. Successive plantings were continuously bursting forth in different stages of growth: radishes, carrots, romaine lettuce, turnips, beets, rhubarb for pie, perennial Swiss chard, pumpkins, watermelons, and okra, not to mention an array of parsley, sage, rosemary, oregano and thyme, and a casual spray of marigolds, zinnias, and morning glories. As well, there was a stand of sweet white corn. And let's not forget the cherry and heirloom tomatoes.

Many people were fed for free from my garden. Every evening our meals were rites of gratitude, especially for me, a gardener on the mend. Gardening became a way of life, a daily celebration, and a reason for living.

THE GOPHERS GET A SWIMMING LESSON

One day I heard a mysterious rattling sound that seemed to come from the corn patch.

Along about mid-July when my cornstalks were head-high and starting to ear, one stalk each day mysteriously fell over until only a few were left. The mystery was solved when I saw a stalk jiggle. It rattled like a *maraca* and started to list. Taking a closer look, at the base of the stalk I saw the unmistakable movement of earth that a gopher makes.

What ensued was all-out war.

Finding the freshest mound of earth, I dug it up, found the tunnel, and flooded it with the hose. To my dismay, water started flooding the squash mounds forty feet away. The little buggers had been working the main garden, and digging a commuter tunnel to my beloved squash mounds that I'd planted with such great effort when I was ill. No way were those gophers going to get away with that bullshit! With the shovel, I exposed the other end of the tunnel and shut off the hose.

At this point, I still got tired easily, so I began to worry that all the digging might tucker me out, but anger was good for me. It got my adrenaline going. I got so steamed at the gophers, I set out to dig up the whole forty feet of their tunnel. Working feverishly in the hot sun, I ran back and forth from one end of their tunnel to the other, sometimes turning on the hose to jam it farther in. Every once in a while, I'd see a little head pop up, and I'd sprint to that end of the hole hoping to do the gopher some harm, but the little guy was too quick.

Half an hour of cursing and sweating and huffing and puffing hard made me think of the Big Bad Wolf, so between huffing and puffing I shouted, "I'll dig…and I'll flood…and I'll huff and I'll…puff…and I'll blow…your house…down!" but I didn't have to because turning the hose back on flushed one of them out. The little guy popped out of his tunnel. There I stood, shovel in hand, sweat dripping off the end of my nose, poised directly over the exposed gopher.

In one swift move I could have sliced him in two, but then a weird thought occurred to me: "I'm a pacifist, a conscientious objector. I can't kill a gopher!" And then for a brief moment our roles were reversed. I was the gopher in the trench, and the gopher was standing over me with a shovel. I swear the gopher made eye contact with me, pleading for its life. There was no difference between us. I was him and he was me. Making a bluff stab at the earth in front of the gopher, I let him turn tail and scoot back into his tunnel.

Then I thought of Phil Hanna, my flute teacher's partner. Only a day or two before, he had told me that he and his gal, Susan, got rid of their gophers by meditating and asking them to leave—and they did! In my adrenalinized state, I didn't see how that was going to work for me. Instead, I looked toward the other end of the hole forty feet away and shouted, "That ought to take care of you little bastards for a while! Now take all of your family and relatives and aunts and uncles and cousins and even your grandmother and get out of my garden! Go next door and find something to eat!"

This is a true story: After making war on those nasty little gophers, I had a bountiful harvest and I never had any more trouble with gophers in the garden that year. One day while chatting with the neighbor across the fence, I noticed several gopher mounds in her yard. It looked like a gopher convention. Her lawn was torn to hell.

"I just don't understand," she complained. "I've never had trouble with gophers before this."

"Well," I replied, "I know you'll think this is weird, but I have this goofy friend Phil. He claims...." and I told her about Phil's method of getting rid of gophers. "Go figure," I said.

"That *is* weird," she said. "I don't think that will work for me." Just in case, I hoped she wouldn't take up meditation anytime soon.

I could barely suppress my glee. In fact, I had to hold my hand over my face so that my neighbor wouldn't see me fighting back the laughter. I picked two plums off the tree next to the fence, bit into one (which helped me control my urge to laugh), and offered her the other. I told her I was sorry the gophers were bothering her, but I didn't offer any further advice on how to get rid of them.

photo by Mike Stempe

2307 Mariposa Avenue, Chico, California, circa 1989. The windows are boarded up, but the old place still looks pretty much the same as the day I first saw it.

Three brothers – Jon, Tim, Bix, about 1950

Yours truly, age 11, circa 1957, in a meadow on the eastern side of the Sierras. Early outdoor experiences bonded a love of nature to my soul, a love that carried forth to the Mariposa days of hiking, running, and skinny dipping in Bidwell Park

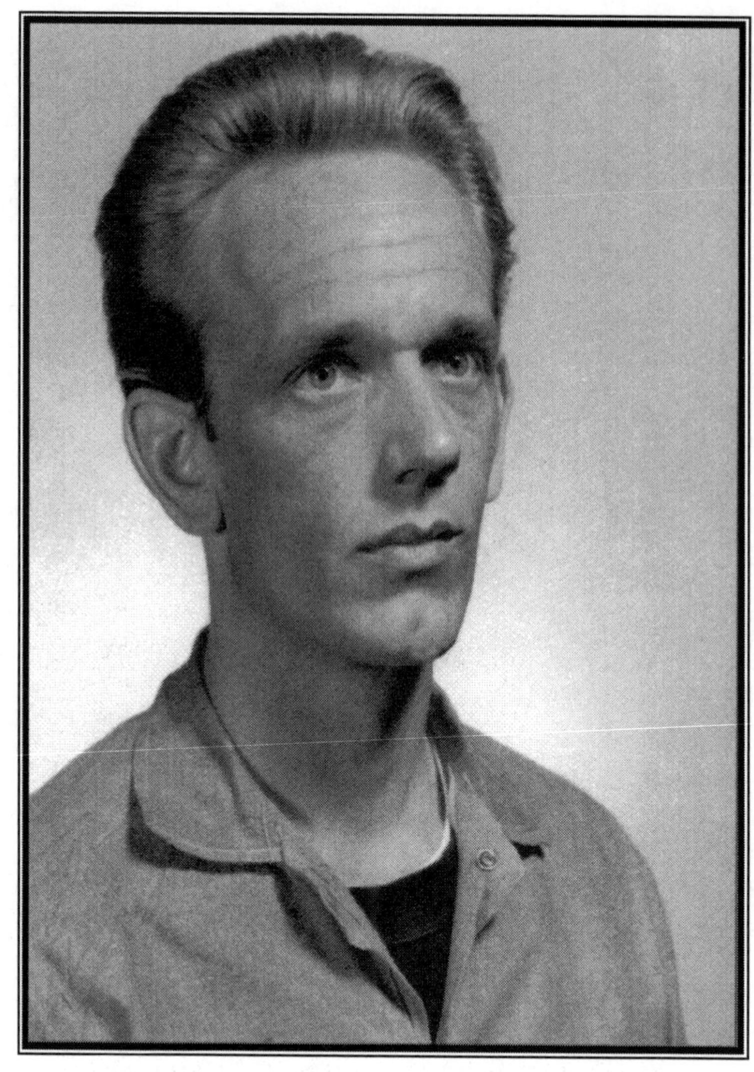

Brother Tim, Vacaville State Prison, circa 1968. He got ten to life, but got out in six on good behavior on Bastille Day, 1969. In this photo, I thought he looked like Don Quixote clad in chambray.

Pfc. Jon Craig Whitcomb upon completing Marine Corps boot camp, circa 1961. Marine training suited him because he loved guns and violence. Jon died in late December of 1962.

At my brother Jon's gravesite

photo by Bud Miller

Flowers from the garden naturally spread under the fruit tree next to the fence: a tranquil place to sit and meditate in my own volunteer English garden.

Janie: The woman I shouldn't have wanted but did.

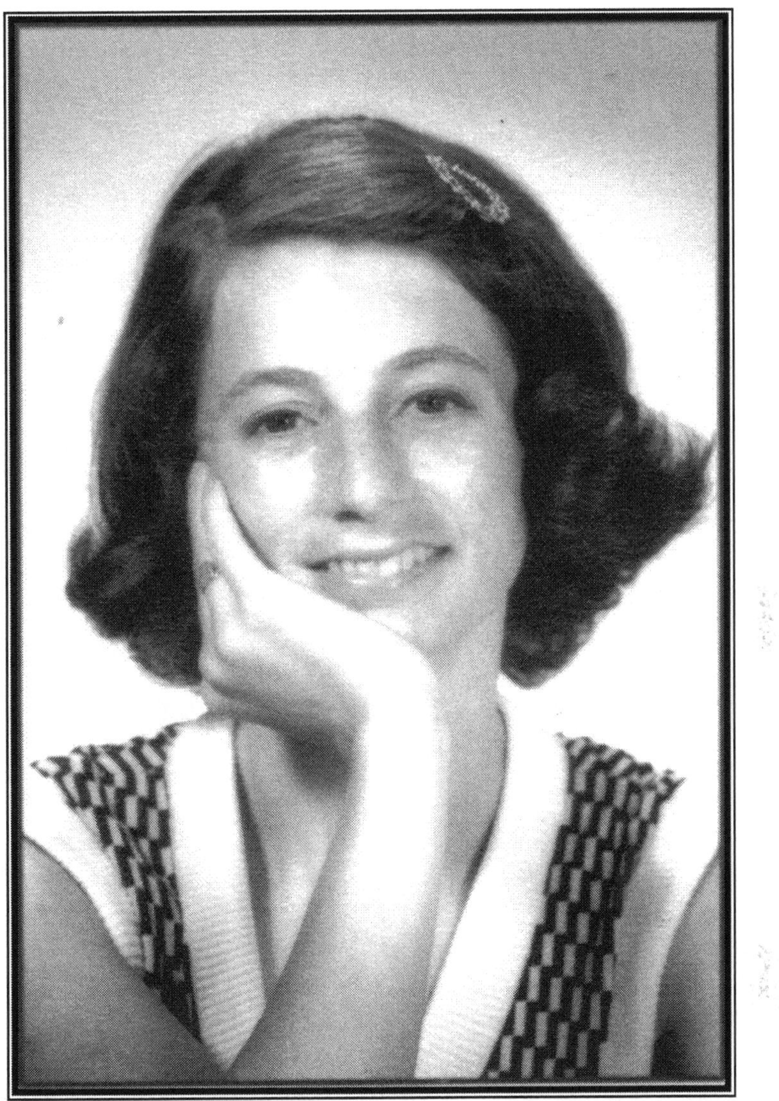

Betsy: The woman I should have wanted but didn't.

During my illness I lost 18% of my body weight.

United Campus Christian Ministry

TELEPHONE AREA CODE 916-342-1211
544 WEST THIRD STREET
CHICO, CALIFORNIA 95926

December 5, 1968

Chairman
Local Board #30
3700 Bevin Avenue
Richmond, California

Re: Bix Whitcomb

Dear Chairman:

Bix approached me recently for assistance in completing his Form 150. I can vouch for his position in the light of that relationship.

I am impressed by his sincerity and his deeply held conviction that participation in the military services would be a violation of his religious beliefs. Though he may not use a great deal of traditional theological language, I am convinced that his convictionsrepresent a deeply held faith which is parallel with a more orthodox belief in God and is not merely a personal moral code.

This young man has thought through his decision very carefully and thoughtfully, and certainly could offer other meaningful service to his country than the military. I would hope that your board would give serious and close attention to Bix's request for a 1-O classification. Thank you very much.

Sincerely yours,

Lorenz Schultz
UCCM Campus Pastor

A Ministry to Chico State College provided by the United Presbyterian, USA, Methodist, United Church of Christ, Disciples of Christ, and Evangelical United Brethren Churches.

While I was still attending Chico State, I got some good draft counseling and applied for Conscientious Objector status. By this means, I was able to stall for three years, using the bureaucracy against itself. Twenty-four years of teaching in public schools was my form of voluntary service.

SELECTIVE SERVICE SYSTEM

LOCAL BOARD NO. 30
CONTRA COSTA COUNTY
3700 NEVIN AVENUE
RICHMOND, CALIFORNIA 94805
(LOCAL BOARD STAMP)

July 15, 1969

IN REPLY, REFER TO:

Selective Service No. 4-30-46-245

Dear Sir:

The Armed Forces Examining and Entrance Station has advised this local board that you failed to report for Physical Examination processing on July 3, 1969 as ordered.

A registrant who fails or neglects to perform any duty required of him under the provisions of the Selective Service Law, is subject to priority induction as a delinquent. So that this local board can determine how to proceed in your case, you are requested to advise the board immediately the reason you failed to report for processing as ordered.

FOR THE LOCAL BOARD

Cindy Vieira

Executive Secretary or Clerk

365 - 8/30/68

Notice to Appear: As early as 1969 I was ordered to appear for a physical. Given the way the war was going, completing the exam would be a death sentence.

Standing between the two redwoods that used to guard our front porch like the Portals to Narnia.

In the early 90's the long tail of fallow land that was 2307 Mariposa was turned into a housing tract. Here Jim gestures as if to say, "Where did it all go?"

22

"Stop Playing That Piano!"

"I didn't think I was resentful.
I just thought I was a very sensitive
guy with a really good memory."
Tim W.

Before my stepmother married my father, she was all sweetness and light.

Every time my father and I visited her at her house in Westwood next to Beverly Hills, she greeted me enthusiastically and asked me to play the piano. I always looked forward to those visits because she had a baby grand that I loved to play. Compared to the old clunker of an upright I used for my first lessons, playing Millie's piano made me feel like a concert pianist. Before I had both feet inside her door, she always inquired, "What have you been playing lately? What's your latest accomplishment? Oh, please, go play for me. I can hardly wait to hear what you've been working on!" My latest rendition of "*Song of the Volga Boatmen*" or "*Drink to Me Only with Thine Eyes*" would meet with applause and exclamations of praise. When I confided in her that I wanted to be the next Van Cliburn or Oscar Petersen, she gave me her avid vote of confidence. "Oh, yes, you can do it, I just know you can! All you have to do is to keep practicing. Someday you'll play Carnegie Hall!"

I wanted to believe her, and I did, but that was the beginning of the end of my believing anything that woman ever said.

When my father announced that he and Millie were getting married and moving from Los Angeles to the Bay Area "to start life over with a clean slate," he left me in the care of a trusted associate for a few months while he and Millie shopped for a house and got things underway.

Later, after summering with my grandmothers, and spending some illicit time in Van Nuys with my unsupervised older brothers, I was to join the newly blended family, which at that time included my brother Jon. Tim was out of the picture, living in a group home, and was not welcome in Lafayette. The thought of living with Jon was a mixed bag. He was four years older, mean and aggressive. Without Tim to pick on, I worried that Jon might turn on me. Still, he was family, and that was worth something—but the one thing I looked forward to the most was that baby grand piano. The news that we would be living in a four-bedroom house with a swimming pool, on a hillside in a well-to-do area sounded exciting enough, but more thrilling was the baby grand. I just couldn't wait to get my hands on that piano. My very own baby grand piano to practice on every day, and a new mother who would encourage me enthusiastically to play! What could be better, except having my own mother back?

The first words of greeting I received from Millie upon entering the house were, "Where the hell did you get that hair?" What could possibly be wrong with the popular *Pachuco* style of the day? Long hair with "side fenders", a "waterfall" in front, and a "duck's ass" in back, all slicked back and held together with Butch Wax and pomade—I looked like Edd Byrnes, the star of *77 Sunset Strip*. I was cool, man. Grease was the word.

"You're getting a haircut now!" she ordered, "And your brother is going to take you to get it!"

Reluctantly, we got into the lavender 1960 Ford Fairlane convertible and drove to downtown Lafayette. On the way there, I asked my brother how things were going in the new place. "I've been here a couple of weeks and it's do this, do that. Dig the flowerbed, rake the driveway. Man, I've already had a job and my own apartment for a year, and now this. I can't stand the bitch. If I want to take orders, I'll join the Marines. In fact, that's what I'm going to do."

At the barbershop, I got my second favorite haircut, a flattop. When we got back to my new home, where I'd spent a total of five minutes so far, I wanted to take a tour, to see where I would bunk, and get to the piano as soon as possible, but Millie caught us at the door. "You call that a haircut? That's not short enough! Jonny, or whatever your name is, take your brother back down there now!"

He refused.

I would have preferred going with my brother.

Millie apparently felt duty bound to assert her new authority. It must have been difficult for her, taking on a new household and a blended family. At the time, I didn't know that my father had passed the mantle of kid ownership to her. Later when I complained about some of the things Millie was doing, such as the haircut, my father's comment was, "I put Millie in charge of raising the kids. I give her *carte blanche* to do whatever she sees fit." The way he said, "the kids," instead of "you kids" made us sound like foreign objects. That was the end of any appeals to him for democratic treatment. The noose was placed loosely around my neck by my father, and Millie jerked it tight many times in the coming four years before I left for college.

At the barbershop she tried to get the second haircut for free, "Because," she told the barber, "you didn't finish the job." The barber, God bless him, said no pay, no play, so she had to fork over another $1.50 for the desired result, a buzz cut. I felt naked as a sheared poodle, and twice as doggish.

During the short ride back to the house, I tried to figure out what to say to this person who it seemed I'd never met before, but cognitive dissonance had me speechless. Who was this woman who used to be so nice to me? Whatever I might say by way of conversation might be cut off like my hair. Millie, for her part, said nothing. This was an early sample of the silence I came to prefer between us.

Back at the house, I brought my duffel in from the car where I'd left it when Jonny had picked me up at the train station in Oakland earlier in the day, and headed straight to the piano.

Now it was time to play that baby grand! I hadn't had a chance in the three months I'd lived with my father's former secretary; nor when I'd been staying with my grandmothers, or hiking the John Muir Trail from one end to the other and back again; nor when I'd been hanging out with Jon and Tim and The Cossacks, a car club/gang in Van Nuys, getting falling-down drunk with them every day for two weeks as we cruised around in cool cars with loaded guns in our laps, all over L.A. and out to Ventura County, looking for trouble which luckily didn't find us.

However, trouble found them later when the Cossacks crossed Satan's Angels and a gun battle ensued in the foothills. Jon was put up as the leader to settle the dispute *mano a mano* against their leader, and Jon got the ever-loving shit kicked out of him. Millie couldn't have been too well impressed with him or Tim because, in the absence of our mother and father, Jon and Tim showed up at Millie's house shortly after the battle in the hills, Jon having two black eyes, scratches all over his face, and who knows what other injuries. (No wonder she equated my hair style with rebellion and wanted to turn me into a clean-cut kid.)

Finding the piano in the living room, I started playing who knows what—"Chopsticks" or some easy jazz piece I'd learned—and I was looking forward to signing up for the high school band.

"STOP PLAYING THAT PIANO!" That was the second directive I heard from Millie on the day I arrived to live in the Lafayette house. The words were so incongruous; it was as if someone had suddenly turned on the TV with the volume way too loud.

I can still see Millie standing in the doorway between the kitchen and the living room, her hands on her hips, her thumbs pointing forward. The odd impression came to me that if she was being aggressive she shouldn't place her thumbs forward. As well, she didn't have an aggressive stance; her feet were too close together.

"Is someone taking a nap?" I asked. "STOP PLAYING THAT PIANO!"

"Millie, you always ask me to play as soon as I arrive.

What's wrong?"

"STOP PLAYING THAT PIANO!"

"You must have a headache. I'll stop now, and come back later."

"NO, STOP PLAYING THAT PIANO! NEVER PLAY THAT PIANO!"

"What do you mean? I'll come back and play…."

"No, you are NEVER going to play that piano!"

"But I've been waiting six months to play! I could hardly wait to get here and play for you like always. What are you telling me?"

"I'm telling you that you are *never* going to play that piano in this house *ever again* because *I'm in charge now!* You'll do what I say under this roof. Get off that bench now!"

Bewildered and disappointed, I said, "We'll talk about this later," and got up to go unpack.

"There's nothing to talk about," she said.

The next day, Millie took Jonny and Mark and me to the high school to sign up for classes. Back at the house, when the subject of electives came up I said I was signing up for band. An argument ensued.

"Forget it! You're not taking band! You're not smart enough to take music and keep up your other classes."

"I only need to practice a half hour to an hour a day."

"Where are you going to practice?"

"In my room, like always."

"No, you're not."

"Why not?"

"Because nobody wants to listen to that crap!"

"You want me to 'woodshed' it then?" I asked sarcastically.

"You won't play in the woodshed either. That's the end of the discussion. Tomorrow you go to school. Take this with you," handing me the class list, "and don't come back till you've chosen another elective."

"But I don't want to take anything else."

"Why not basket weaving? That's nice and quiet." With those words, my music career ended.

Since there was no negotiating with this woman and my father had passed the baton to her, there wasn't much I could say in self-defense on any issue. That day she took away my music. That day was also the beginning of the end of my self-assertion. Later, she also took away what was left of my family. I became two kinds of animal—one, a docile sheep; the other, an angry bull with a pressure cooker temper. A third part of me, a sort of *Übermeister*, developed to referee arguments between the bull and the sheep.

So Millie's alleged love of music was a ruse all along, to win me over while she was courting my father! As well, she wanted to assert her authority by depriving me of something I loved. And that was only the beginning of such reprisals. I was obliged to live under the same roof with a woman who resented my existence. Two years after moving in with her, I found out the true origin of her resentment. Not long after Jon died, Millie came into my room and made what I call "Her Nuts and Kooks Speech," telling me my Brother Jon was "a nut and a kook" and "better off dead," and that my mother and surviving brother were also "nuts and kooks," and forbidding me to contact them. When I protested that she didn't know anything about my mother, she replied that she knew my mother in high school. Suddenly it became clear to me: In high school, my father had thrown over Millie for my future mother! (Some forty years later, I found out more details from my father: My father's parents and Millie's lived in the same neighborhood; the two families spent a lot of time together; and, it was presumed that the two youngsters would one day marry.) My existence was a constant reminder to Millie that her dreams had been destroyed. On the day of her Nuts and Kooks Speech, she was trying once again to wipe out all traces of my mother and force me into a *de facto* orphan-hood in which she, Millie, would be my rescuer when in fact she was making me the brutalized innocent. When I made the connection between my mother and Millie's ancient jealousy, I remember thinking, "How sophomoric! That was over 25 years ago!" I actually felt sorry for her.

Oddly enough, the Nuts and Kooks speech served to reinforce

a tendency that had already been happening since I began living with Millie, a tendency that later came to be called the Stockholm syndrome, in which the hostage shows signs of loyalty to the hostage-taker. To the extent that I empathized with her, and looked out for my own survival, I came to believe as she did: I shouldn't contact my mother and brother; I was better off without them. Opposing this tendency was the thought, "Only two more years and I'm off to college where I won't have to put up with her anymore"; but, Millie held the purse strings for college money, and this in effect kept me tethered to my victimizer until my last year in school when I was on my own.

A DECADE PASSED BEFORE I found the freedom to pick up an instrument again. Preparing to go to college, I thought of majoring in music, but the Catch 22 was that I had to have four years of high school band to get into the music department.

Life took over. I majored in English and completed a second major in Spanish. Five years went by with no music. I can't say it was all bad. In fact, it was pretty wonderful, having a girlfriend, being on the varsity swimming team, and going to Spain for a year and all, but something was missing.

One short-lived run at piano lessons took place in my last semester at Chico State. The class had several students and several pianos in one room, a setup I disliked. The first time my turn came to play, I could only think how Em had left me, and what a waste the stupid class was, and how everything important had been taken from me—first my family, then music, and now Em—and the notes of the stupid, childish song I was supposed to perform, "Susie, Little Susie," blurred behind my tears. Sadness and rage came together as one. All that time lost, all the music I could have enjoyed. I wanted to beat the crap out of the piano teacher and tip over all the pianos, but I knew I'd be crying while committing these acts, and crying in public would be too embarrassing, not to mention the trouble I'd get in for assaulting the teacher and destroying school property.

Instead, I slammed the lid down over the keyboard, walked out, and never went back. The confusion and rage I had felt toward Millie on the day she told me to "Stop playing that piano" came to a head in that moment, but it was all too bewildering and scary and emotionally charged to deal with at the time, so once again I managed to stuff it all down. I remember sitting on the lawn on campus thinking that cramming down my rage was like forcing a Jack-in-the-box back in its container. I feared someday Jack would jump out when least expected, but until then, I sat on the lid and hoped it wouldn't throw me off.

After the failed piano class, another year or two went by before I found my way to 2307 Mariposa Avenue, and back to music. Getting sick and nearly dying brought me to my senses in more ways than one. Having survived a near death experience, I asked, "What do I really want to do with my life? If today was my last day on this planet, what would I rather be doing?"

In my case, the answer came to me one day while lying in my bed of recuperation on Mariposa Avenue. *I have always wanted to play the flute.* Now I was free to do so. The garden was one reason for living. Music was another. As soon as possible I would begin, and the breathing involved in playing a woodwind instrument would be therapeutic for my still-wheezy lungs.

I thought of the flute as an environmental instrument. I could take it anywhere and play—by the creek, in a culvert, in a meadow, in a cave, on a mountaintop, strolling along a path. My flute spoke to birds, and they answered. Deer would gather around me in a meadow. Sometimes they even came close to lie down and listen and chew their cud. To borrow a line from Lao Tzu, I was "Banging the silent zero, sounding the empty nothing." The flute was an instrument that let me listen to nature and keenly hear every little twitter and burble. I liked to listen as much as play. Sometimes I listened more than I played. When the time and the mood were right, I answered with improvised tunes. Sometimes I practiced long tones, hanging on one note for a full breath, and I even learned continuous circular breathing, which let me sustain a note indefinitely.

With Jim's encouragement, I joined in on tunes when he and Mike practiced. You wouldn't think so, but the flute actually sounds good on "Kansas City"! For a time after the Mariposa days, I played with Jim in a "casuals" band that he formed. We played dances at places like the Elks Club, Knights of Columbus, the Grange, and Portuguese Hall, as well as weddings and class reunions. We had a blast and even made a little money.

For a number of years I pursued my ideal: becoming a classically trained musician able to improvise. I enjoyed the trick playing of Ian Anderson, but my heroes were Hubert Laws and Paul Horn. In the 1980's I got to spend a weekend playing with Paul. We have since kept up a loose and infrequent contact. At some point, life took over and the law of diminishing returns took effect: if you don't practice, you don't get better, and you stop playing. Like Paul says, "You don't have to be a musician. What matters is that whatever you do works for you, and you're passionate about it."

The flute was my friend, my sustaining passion, and another big reason for living. Initially, taking up the flute was yet another way of throwing off the bondage of my stepmother's nullification while claiming my bliss. Later, studying flute became an organizing principle in my life. In later years, my stepmother even enjoyed some of the carols I played at one Christmas or another. At least she didn't tell me I had to go practice in the shed.

23

Pretty Arms

Her name was Sue. She came to the open back door and stood there with her back to the afternoon sun while I stood at the stove with my back to the door, pouring a cup of tea. I didn't know who was behind me, but I reached for another cup and filled it, slowly. I liked her vibe; definitely a feminine feeling to her energy.

At that time of year, the blinding late afternoon sun shone directly in the back door. Before she arrived, the sun had been roasting my backside, but now I could feel her casting a cool, comforting shadow across the kitchen and up to my bare shoulders. When I turned around, all I could see was her silhouette. Even at that, I had to shield my eyes and lower my head against the molten aura that surrounded her. She stood very still and neither of us said a thing. My eyes followed the black cutout of her figure, starting at her feet and working up. From her silhouette, I could discern she was wearing some kind of tall shoes; she had long, slender legs; full but well-proportioned hips gave way to a nicely curved waist. Above her shoulders, an Afro as wide as the door filtered the sun.

"Come on in," I said, "and have a cup of tea."

The Afro made me think she must have African ancestors, but her manner of speech didn't match that impression.

"Is Jerry here?" she asked, in a voice distinctly that of a white woman.

"There's no Jerry here, but come on in, have a cup of tea, and we'll see if we can find who you're looking for." As she stepped inside the door and a little to her left, the sun hit me full in the face and blinded me, despite my shielding hand. The sound of her shoes approached, circled to my right, and I pivoted to face her.

"Sorry, I can't see you. I'm completely blinded by the sun." I moved over one step to my right and dropped my hand. "Have a seat," I said, and squatted on my haunches in front of the stove. In front of me she did likewise.

We sat and waited for my eyes to adjust, and it must have taken a full minute or more before some of her features gradually took shape, then became dark again. Frustrating. "Listen," I said, putting my hands over my eyes, "I'm not trying to shut you out or hide my face; I just need my eyes to adjust." We sat and waited another full minute in pleasant, easy silence. "Okay, let's try again." Spreading my fingers and looking through them, I could see her green eyes looking steadily at me; she had a fair complexion, and light brown hair. When I took my hands away and extended my arms with my elbows resting on my knees, I saw her longish, rectangular face, a little pale, with a tinge of red. Her fine, wavy hair extended like a sunburst mandala wider than her shoulders.

We looked into each other's eyes. Nods and smiles passed back and forth like looking in a mirror. We looked each other up and down. We liked what we saw. This went on for several minutes. So much non-verbal communication was going on, we could have started our own mime troupe or psychic hotline.

Finally, she tilted forward onto her knees and placed her hands on my shoulders. "Pretty arms," she said.

Her words went into my core and spread outward like warm molasses. "Pretty arms," I echoed.

"Pretty arms," she repeated, smiling, stroking the length of my arms. All I could think was that I never felt so handsome and beautiful in my entire life.

After a while she stopped stroking and we held hands. I squeezed hers, got up and got the tea. It was still hot. I handed her a cup and sat down cross-legged with my cup. She sat cross-legged too. We sipped the tea in silence for several minutes. Goldilocks tea: just the right temperature.

We clicked our cups in a toast. "Thanks for coming over," I said. "How's the tea?"

"Good."

We finished our tea. I offered her another cup and she declined, so I stood to put our cups back on the stove and knelt down close in front of her. Reaching out with both hands, I traced the margin of a lavender aura that surrounded her light brown Afro.

"Pretty hair…."

OKAY, IT'S NOT WHAT YOU think. The Pretty Arms lady and I did not "get it on" that afternoon. I stroked her aura and that was it. Well, I did stroke her flossy giant Afro and told her it was pretty. I did stroke her arms and tell her they were pretty as well, and we hugged, but that was all. Honest. I admit I was thinking, just for one moment, of other parts of her I'd like to stroke, and parts of me I'd like her to explore, but somehow it seemed that sex would spoil the magic of the moment.

She stayed and we kept wordlessly stroking each other's "pretty" aura and "pretty" hair and "pretty" shoulders and "pretty" face and holding hands and drinking tea and hardly saying anything. I told her my name and she said it was pretty and I asked what hers was and she said, "Sue" and I told her that was pretty too, and she left out the back door the way she came, with the sun below the horizon.

24

Sequel to Pretty Arms

The next time I saw Sue, she fell out the back door of a 1960 Chevy Impala parked in back of the house. That night some guys had brought her over expecting to "party," back when I still thought it strange that "party" had become a verb. I didn't like their vibes, I felt protective toward Sue, and I sent them packing. "You're not welcome here. We don't do alcohol or pills or hard drugs. We'll keep her and sober her up but you're down the road. Now get out of here." Sue stumbled into the house, where she weaved like a drunken sailor on the deck of a ship in stormy seas, with Mike and Jim and Barney and me standing watch.

She was beyond inebriated. Later I found out she had a habit of mixing Quaaludes and alcohol. She was a downer queen. We got some coffee into her, and took turns supporting her and walking her back and forth. When she became lucid enough to speak, I gave her a ride home, following her slurred directions. Luckily, it wasn't too far and only one left turn was involved. I told her to come back when she was sober. She did, and for a time she became one of the family at 2307.

She came back one day when I was out. She and Jim talked. After she had been coming over for a while, visiting with whoever was around, I told Jim the story of Pretty Arms, and said that I didn't know anything else about Sue. Could he fill me in?

"Oh, you didn't know? Until recently, she was a prostitute in San Francisco!"

"Holy f---!"

"She's holy all right, and she might be that other word you said, too, but she quit her prostitute job and now she's back in town."

My curiosity was aroused. The next day she came by and confirmed the story for me. I asked her what her motivation had been. "I was tired of working minimum wage jobs, and I thought, what can I do that I enjoy and make lots of money? The answer was obvious, but I didn't think it would work around here because I know too many people, plus my mother lives here—so I thought 'big city', and Frisco was the obvious choice."

I asked her what her motivation was, beyond money. "Well, I had a goal. I wanted to make enough money to live on for a year, and come back to Chico."

"Did you make the goal?"

"Not quite, but almost."

"Why not?"

"I was doing real well and keeping all the money I made for myself but sometimes it was scary, so I got this pimp to look out for me. He was supposed to screen the clients, but he didn't do a very good job, and he took most of my money. He'd give me an allowance, but that was bullshit because I made the money and he kept it. We got in an argument and he gave me a black eye so I said fuck him and went back on my own, but he kept coming around and bugging me, so I split."

"Do you have enough to live on for a year? That sounds pretty good to me."

"Nine months maybe."

"Long enough to have a baby. Shall we try?"

SOMETIME LATER, SUE WAS HANGING out with the guys in the

living room one evening, and naturally our curiosity got the better of us. We started asking explicit questions that only guys would ask, the answers to which are totally uninteresting in the present, but there was one exchange that Jim and I found especially memorable. Barney, being Barney, asked the most explicit questions.

"What's the biggest cock you've ever seen?" asked Barney.

"Haven't you any shame?" interjected Jim. "Show the woman some respect, and let her tell her story."

Not to be deterred, Barney persisted.

"Thirteen inches," Sue answered readily.

"Longer than a goddam ruler!" exclaimed Barney.

"Who was the owner?" I asked politely.

"A cab driver. He usually got me business, but one day he said he'd take payment in sex, so we went up to this room I rented. I got undressed and when I turned around, there it was, all thirteen inches. I said, 'You're not putting *that* in *me*!" The three other guys thought that was pretty hilarious.

I didn't laugh, but I was impressed with her candor. "What happened next?" Mike asked.

"Well, I took care of him, but not in the way he had in mind."

"How much did he give you for that?" asked Barney. "Like I said, there was no money involved."

"Well, what was the cab fare?" I asked.

"I don't know, not much. Twenty bucks."

"So he stiffed you," I said, enjoying the pun, but thinking better of it, I added, "or I should say, he didn't have a chance to stiff you, ha ha. Was he satisfied with your service?"

"I don't think so. He never brought me any business after that."

That was Sue: plain spoken and honest and unashamed. It was refreshing in a way, having our own local retired prostitute to hang out with. You'd think it would be hard to respect someone who did what she did, but in the manner of the day, we didn't judge her. Like good bodhisattvas, we sat and asked questions, listened, and took in what she said, accepted her for who she was. The San Francisco thing was just a chapter in her life, same as Mariposa was in ours. We were all just trying to get along and find our way in the world, and if that involved a lifestyle experiment, so be it. Sue was at home with us at the house. She was our buddy pal, and more. Still, it seemed odd, knowing this smart, good-looking, funny woman who had allegedly gone astray. A lifetime of puritanical guilt and shame went out the window. Sex was just something people do, like taking a walk or smoking a cigarette. Why had I ascribed so much meaning to it?

Upon reflection at the time, it seemed to me I had been sating myself on sex for three years since Em had split, with an underlying agenda that sex wouldn't mean anything to me; therefore, the pain and frustration of unrequited love with Em would dissolve. To an extent the practice was working, and Sue was an agent of change when change was most needed. With my libido still at low ebb after the illness, and Janie nowhere in sight since she'd brought me her "gift" while I was convalescing, I looked at Sue and thought, why not? I asked her if she'd like to provide me with sexual healing, and she readily consented. That went on for a couple of weeks, but I became quickly bored with it. It all seemed so mechanical and without soul. Sue and I were not a match. Free Love was beginning to feel empty and unsatisfying, like when you need real nutrition but eat a candy bar instead.

Truth be told, I was (pardon the horrible but apropos pun) trying to fill a hole that wasn't fillable; the place in me that wanted enduring and unconditional love; the part of me that looked to sex as a talisman of that love; the part of me that wanted Em back, or the fantasy of whomever Em had been. I hadn't yet learned to love and respect myself enough to stand alone and not be so needy. I relied on external sources for my sense of well-being; my internal guidance system lacked a gyroscope. I thought sex was the magic bullet, and Sue taught me that sex in itself means nothing. It's only what you make of it. Nevertheless, I began to long for Janie's company while doing my best not to pine for the long lost Em. If Janie came back, I would gladly have her and forgive her, and stick by her, but would she do the same for me?

At this point, I began to wonder if Janie might show up. Reminiscent of the scene with Helen, if Janie found Sue and me together, that wouldn't be good. Like a cynical manipulator (I'm sorry, I know this doesn't sound good, but I'm just trying to tell the story the way it was) I thought if I passed Sue off to someone else, that would be the diversion I needed to make way for Janie's return; and that's what I did. The guy in question probably prefers to remain anonymous, but when I asked him how it was with Sue, his only comment was, "Electric milking machine." I had to concur.

When that incident was over and the guy returned to another town two hours away where he lived, I thought, "Why not Jim? He doesn't have a girlfriend at present." And that's how Jim and Sue got lashed up together for a few months. They actually grew fond of each other and had lots of fun together.

The most memorable moment I recall between them occurred one night when Sue and Jim were getting it on in my old bed, which I had moved into the front room for Jim's use. I was trying to sleep in the next room, and they were trying to be quiet, but suddenly I heard Jim exclaim, "*Holy Christ! Did you see that?*"

Mystified, I asked him the next morning what the commotion was all about.

"There we were, getting it on, and I guess we generated a bunch of static electricity because all of a sudden I felt this jolt. Simultaneously I saw these blue sparks fly between our nipples! It was like the energy going back and forth between us got so intense; it just had to produce a shock." Jim got such a kick out of that, recreating the moment became a regular occurrence.

One day Sue stopped showing up at the house. We didn't think much about it at first, but after a time it became apparent she wasn't coming back. Maybe she ran out of money and went back to San Francisco. It doesn't matter.

Years later, Jim ran into her one day in Chico. He said she was dressed for success in a business suit, looking really sharp. She had a good job. She was raising two daughters on her own, and she owned a house not far from 2307.

I will always have the memory of that first day with Sue, but until now I never had a chance to say, "A Farewell to Pretty Arms."

25

We Are Visited by Missionaries

Follow Jim down a trail, and you will learn more about nature than you ever knew before. It wasn't about naming things. It was about opening your senses and noticing the scent of bay leaves, the shape of raccoon tracks, a turtle camouflaged under a cut bank, a rattlesnake in blackberry brambles, and messages carried to our nostrils on the breeze. We were conscious of each step and each breath. A hike with Jim was a form of meditation—you might even get in touch with God. One day at the house, we had some unexpected visitors who shared their views of God with us, and we with them. Not unexpectedly, our views were at odds with each other, but that made it all the more interesting.

No one had knocked on the front door in months, but one day someone did. I slid the hasp and opened the door. There on the porch I saw two clean cut, nice looking young men, late teens, in black business suits, white shirts and black ties. Each wore a nametag on his lapel: "Elder" so and so.

For a moment I puzzled aloud, "Elder than whom?" but this drew no response, so I said, "We don't want any Fuller brushes or anything," and started to close the door.

"Let them in!" Jim said. Jim was always up for company.

Now Jim stood beside me and held the door open. He gave them his famous greeting, "Hey, how have you been? Come on in, set a spell."

They did, and as soon as it became clear they were Mormon missionaries, Jim quickly laid the ground rules. "If we're going to listen to what you have to say, you're going to listen to us as well. If you're here to convert us, there's no point. You might as well leave now. A fair and balanced discussion is in order." They agreed, and sat on the comfy rattan loveseat Mrs. Whitlow had given us.

I figured we were in for a session, so I put on the teakettle.

I'll do my best to summarize what took place in the next two or three hours. Jim made good on his promise to listen. At first I hung back (I was still thinking about Fuller brushes), but eventually I got involved too. We listened carefully to what they had to say, and asked questions.

Jim engaged the young missionaries in an argument whose clever subtleties would have done the Jesuits proud. He didn't tell them they were wrong so much as affirm the goodness of their intentions and suggest they open to an alternative set of views that were, at the core, the same as their beliefs without the claptrap of organized religion. He let them set their own traps and walk into them. For example, when our Mormon visitors asserted that Joseph Smith experienced God directly, Jim said, "Listen to your own words. What you're saying is Joseph Smith experienced God directly, and he wants you to do the same, but now you go through him instead of experiencing God directly." At that point, Jim presented what I call the James Howard Beattie Doctrine of Unlearning. To synopsize:

- You can know God directly through your own experience.
- You don't need a church or a guru or a Messiah; they only get in the way.

- To know God, simply *unlearn* all your societal conditioning. *Unlearn* all you've been taught; let go of all your preconceived notions, and open your senses.
- Having opened your senses, go out in nature and find God in everything you see, taste, touch, smell, and hear. (This, Jim asserted, was why he identified much more strongly with Native Americans and Tarzan than with any church.)
- You are God. I am God. Find God by seeing Him in everyone you meet.

"For example," said Jim, "just look at us here and now. Look where you're sitting, in that loveseat. Do you know how many people have sat in that loveseat in this house and experienced God just from being here? If you were really paying attention, letting go of your preconceived notions, you'd be feeling the vibes coming into you through the cushions, and you'd be ecstatic!"

Then he gave them a complete history of the house and the families who had lived there. He told them how their love had seeped into the framing members of the house; and, he told them about Mrs. Whitlow's gifting us with the very rattan living room set the young missionaries sat upon.

At some point in the discussion, Jim asked them if they had any questions to ask us. The younger one asked, "Are you guys flower children?"

Now I got involved. "Define flower children," I said.

"Do you wear flowers in your hair and take drugs and, you know, do things that only a man and wife should do?"

Now that got me going. "We're not hippies, if that's what you mean. I never have liked that term. It's an invention of the media, and you've been brainwashed to believe certain preconceived ideas. If you were paying attention, the Summer of Love is long over, and the Death of Hippie Parade took place three or four years ago. I like to think we're hip, you know, as in *with it, hip to the scene*? Just because we have long hair doesn't mean we're whatever you think we are. Don't judge a book by its cover. If you insist on calling me something, call me a hipster. That hippie word is an insult."

"As for me," said Jim, "you can call me anything. Just don't call me late to supper!"

With that I went out to the yard and gathered daisies and made four long daisy chains. It probably took half an hour. Linking the ends of each, I made four garlands and came back into the house wearing one. I put one on Jim's head and offered one each to our visitors.

The older Elder accepted his and set it on his knee. The younger Elder readily put his on his head. Since the older one seemed hesitant, I said, "If you put that on your head, it doesn't make you a hippie. Once, it seems like a lifetime ago, I loved someone very much. She was my college sweetheart, and we used to make these daisy chains for each other and wear them on our walks. We weren't hippies. We were just in love with each other and God and life. Now I would be honored if you would join us and wear your crown."

He put it on and I thanked him. "There. That feels pretty good, huh? A crown of daisies, not a crown of thorns! Pardon my language, but to hell with misery! Hell is right here on earth, and so is Heaven. It's all in what you make of it. You choose your attitude and actions. Sin is when you go against the grain of what's good in you. Sin is when you treat others badly. That's what karma's all about, man!"

He nodded assent. I talked about the symbolism of a circle representing wholeness like the daisy chains we wore on our heads. I turned to Jim. "Isn't there a song about a circle being unbroken?"

Jim took the hint and picked up his guitar. Everyone fell silent while Jim tuned up and picked out a few chords. Tentatively at first, then with voices swelling, we sang, "Will the Circle Be Unbroken?" and the Mormons really got into it!

And so we sang and talked and sipped tea and munched crackers long into the afternoon. They left with a promise to return, and they did, several times. On subsequent visits, they came to the back door. Once they even came in casual clothing, and shared a bowl of brown rice the way we liked it with melted butter, miso, tahini, garlic, and soy sauce. Jim encouraged them to smell their food deeply before eating, and chew each bite forty times to enjoy the many subtle flavors. In terms of complementing their sensory education, the younger one even consented to a hand massage, but they both drew the line when I suggested bringing out the peacock feather to stroke their faces.

For a while they didn't show up, and I conjectured to Jim, "They must be pursuing their sensory education out in the park, buck naked, sunning themselves on a rock and worshipping the sun." However, they did show up briefly to thank us and bid us farewell; their mission was through; they were going back home. They said they'd miss us and always remember us, and the feeling was mutual.

Sometime later, maybe a month or two, Jim and I were at home one day when a knock came on the front door. Jehovah's Witnesses....

26

Tales of Geno, the Caveman I Once Knew

THE CAVEMAN COMES TO TOWN

Geno lived in a succession of caves, three to be exact. The first two you already heard about in "Thanksgiving in a Cave". The third one was much larger and more remote.

Geno was living the myth and acting out the rituals of the back-to-the-earth movement. On full moon nights he danced fertility dances to encourage his marijuana crop to grow by imitative magic. He hugged the earth close; called her Mother. Volcanic rock, his bed, supported him like eider down. His bedtime prayer to the earth was, "Teach me."

Prayers and fasting, Yoga postures and dancing, cultivating his crop, bathing in the creek, and stalking wild herbs taught him solitary peace. What visions came to Geno on his vision quest? Was he presented with a vision of healing hands? Is that why he became a chiropractor and a naturopathic M.D.?

Every now and then the caveman put on his boots and his bib overalls and came to town. His need for companionship, loving, and various supplies led him down from his cave in the foothills to a more conventional shelter, my house on Mariposa Avenue, where he could take a hot soak in the lion claw tub, warm his toes between my sheets with Tina, fill up on brown rice and lentils and fresh veggies, and swap tales with the tribe. In short, he used the Ranch as a base of operations. A few days were usually enough to scrounge food for a couple of weeks at the cave. Free supplies of almonds and walnuts came by the pound from Continental Nut where Jim and I worked. Fresh oranges came free for the picking from trees lining the streets of Chico. From the dumpster in back of Safeway he could glean a lot of not-too-damaged edibles.

Sometimes in the evenings we celebrated the wild brave's return by breaking out the instruments and amplifiers. (Jim and Mike were forever auditioning drummers and bass players, but their dream of an employable group never quite gelled. Meanwhile, they practiced, and hoped, and we kept ourselves entertained.) The stalwarts of our tribe, as well as stragglers, came over and we'd have jam sessions. Geno the caveman played harmonica while I noodled on my flute. Others joined in on vocals, chopsticks, spoons, washboard and what have you. Before long the joint got to jumpin' while Geno and Tina, Janie and I, Steve and his girlfriend, and Barney with his latest girl, or three, improvised our tribal dances. Since Geno and I had taken Modern Dance, sometimes these dances got, shall we say, pretty interactive?

From time to time, a couple might find privacy in another room—all very discreet, with the exception of Barney who made no bones about excitedly asking Mike for the key to his room out back. I recall one time, the population of the party decreased by four when Barney took three teenage girls out back, or should I say they took him? All three wanted to lose their virginity, and who was Barney not to oblige?

When Geno was ready to return to his cave, he never announced his departure. He'd have his fill of town, and be gone. When he left, the house had a different feel, a different sound to it; empty, cave-like. One time when he had left, I tried to write a poem about his visit, but I came up with only a piece of silly doggerel:

The young brave
(Loved and laid, fed and bathed)
Has returned to his power place, his cave,
To continue his vision quest.
The gift of his presence will be missed
Until once again he seeks to be kissed.
And when he returns,
There will be feasting and dancing
(No fasting for us)
And music and loving and laughter.
We'll break out the amps and get down
Time to get down, time to get down
When Geno the caveman comes to town!

DANCE AT THE GYM

One night someone said there was going to be a dance with live music at the Chico State gym. Geno and I both got excited about going. If there was anything he and I loved to do, it was dance. What happened that night was a once in a lifetime experience.

A local band was playing. I think it was Blue Cheer, who later went on to minor fame and success. At any rate, they were good.

Geno and I rarely danced with anyone unless it was each other or someone hip enough to take a cue spontaneously and join in. Mostly we did free-form wild hippie dancing, but, given our formal training in modern dance, much of what we did was actually stage-worthy. We were like jazz musicians, classically trained, but we specialized in improvisation.

Once the dance got going, I got an image in my mind of *West Side Story*'s 'Dance at the Gym'. Maybe I could get the crowd moving. Everyone was doing the usual one-on-one bebop kind of stuff. I sidled over next to one couple and did a sort of Jungle Book ape dance, part of which involved slapping the floor. To my surprise, the couple took the cue, and imitated me. We started a back and forth "conversation" in movement. Soon two more joined in, then eight, then sixteen. About this time, Geno danced over by me and he and I started taking turns demonstrating movements that more and more dancers imitated. Before long, the whole crowd of one hundred condensed into our corner of the gym. They kept echoing our movements, and you could tell the band was getting into it because they didn't stop and they upped the intensity.

Then Geno and I started to interact with lifts and mock karate movements and slapsticky pratfalls and rolling on the floor, and everyone turned to a partner to imitate or improvise. A few minutes of that, and Geno and I of one accord broke from each other and started getting real close to people, right in their face, moving fast and mixing it up with the crowd, and the whole troupe started zooming around like traffic in Manhattan.

At some point, Geno and I emerged from the crowd and brought the focus back to echo movements. Then I started getting tired, so I ran over to the part of the gym everyone had vacated earlier, and danced in front of the band, thinking everyone would follow, but the crowd was possessed, and they just kept going till the band stopped.

The spell was broken. Everyone filtered back to their original places and resumed their standard kind of dancing as if nothing had ever happened.

The whole thing lasted maybe fifteen, twenty minutes.

WHEN GENO SPEAKS

When Geno speaks, his words skitter about like droplets of water in a hot frying pan. In fact his favorite word is "hot."

Many times I've heard him say, "Hot! Hot! I'm hot! I feel hot!"

His energy is just as intense as his speech. When he sets out to tell you a story, he appears to be all over the map, with no central focus. Everything he says has equal weight and content. He takes you on a journey with lots of side trips through the terrain of his brain, but he always brings you back home where he started. This can be startling and humorous.

Twenty years after I found the house on Mariposa, I was in Honolulu one Christmas visiting Geno. We were riding down the freeway in his Four Runner when I asked him to recall some high points of his cave dwelling days.

Mind you, his narrative was delivered piecemeal while he multi-tasked. In a matter of a few minutes, Geno made three calls on his cellular phone (one to his office, one to his travel agent, and one to his accountant), cussed out two drivers, made several scary lane changes, ate a snack (granola bar and juice), made several interjections about appointments he had and errands he needed to run—and he told me his stories. Of course he was driving way too fast the whole time, and fiddling with the cassette deck until he found a number he liked, which happened to be '*You Want It, You Got It!*' With his timing and coordination, it was no wonder he was a triathlete and a member of the U.S. Olympic race walking team.

Normally such hyperactivity would drive me nuts, but I know this is Geno, and I trust him. He's actually processing everything at hyper speed just like he used to when he was so excited about the possibilities of cave dwelling. When you go for a ride with Geno, don't try to outguess him. He's got it all under control.

After the wild ride on the freeway of Honolulu, I attempted to write down his story word for word, minus the distractions. It is, after all, his story, and he can tell it better than I. It seems to transcribe rather nicely into three tales to which I give the titles, "Three Days in a Loft", "Singin' in the Rain", and "The Sheriff Comes to Call".

THREE DAYS IN A LOFT

One day I gave Geno a ride out to the trailhead to his third and final cave next to Deer Creek, twenty miles north of Chico. Calhoun and a girlfriend of his named Janet came along for the ride. I thought they were going to ride back to town with me, but at the last minute they got out and started following Geno. I thought I might as well join them, but Geno wheeled on me and told me to go back to town.

"What about them?" I asked.

"I told them, too, but I can't stop them," he said, and kept going.

Bewildered, I drove back to town alone only to discover things missing from the house. (This was the same day the felon Rich absconded with my belongings after dumping me in the hopper at the nut house.) That day in Honolulu, I asked Geno to explain what had happened that day with Calhoun and Janet, and to please tell me why I never got to see his cave.

"Oh, yeah, I remember that woman. She and Calhoun followed me as far as a barn where I sometimes rested. I didn't want them to know where the cave was, and I didn't want you to know either. I hadn't shown anyone—not even Tina, because I was growing pot in front of the cave, so I pretended that the barn was my destination and I planned to stay in the loft. I thought maybe they'd get bored or they'd start getting it on and I'd slip away and leave them there, but then I got paranoid. They might follow me, so we hung out there for what, I don't know, two, three days. They hung out at one end of the loft; I hung out at the other. I just wanted to be alone, but they were talking and laughing and they wouldn't be quiet. I just wanted to meditate, so I did. When they got it on, I wasn't excited. I just ignored them and kept meditating. We got up in the morning and it was the same thing, but I didn't like the way Calhoun was treating Janet. You know Calhoun. He was calling her the "b" word and all sorts of stuff. I kept trying to tell him he should be nicer to her. "Finally, she got pissed off and came to my end of the loft. Calhoun got pissed and left. I guess he hitchhiked back to town. I still didn't want anyone to know where the cave was, so we stayed in the loft another day or two just talking and hanging out. She wanted sex but I wasn't that interested. Besides, I felt guilty about Tina. I was missing Tina, but Janet wouldn't let up. She kept coming on to me, so finally I gave in. What was I to do? She had me hot! We got it on quite a bit for another day and night, but I felt guilty and I wasn't into her that much.

"Eventually, I got bored and I really wanted to go to the cave, so I let her follow me. I think maybe that's how I got caught later on. Not that she squealed to the cops, but she might have talked and word might have got around, or maybe it was those boards I took."

SINGIN' IN THE RAIN

I asked Geno, "What boards?" and he was off and running again.

"In the cave I used to get up at three o'clock in the morning and write poetry. I had the cave all set up with a table to write at, and the floor was a floor—really a floor! I took rocks from the stream and hauled them all the way up the hill. It took a lot of trips all the way up that hill—and it was a long way—and I sweated my ass off. I got rocks of all sizes, a lot of small ones, and filled in the uneven places on the floor of the cave. Then I put boards over all that, and it was really a floor."

I asked Geno where he got the boards for the floor and table.

"I wanted a good place to write. Well, the final straw was when it rained one time, and the floor of the cave flooded. That's when I decided to make a floor."

"Where did you get the boards?"

"I got the table and the boards from the same place. I took the boards, one or two at a time, from an old building down the hill. It looked like someone had stayed there a long time before, because there were all sorts of pots and pans and old-fashioned junk lying around.

"At the time, I didn't think anyone would care. I just took the boards, and they made a nice smooth floor. I'd get up at three a.m. and sit and write poetry, or maybe I'd smoke a joint and go walking all over the woods in the dark until daylight. It might be raining, I didn't care! I'd just go walking all night long in the dark, and I'd sing. I'd sing to the trees or the rocks or the river. I didn't know what I was singing, I just made it up. There was nothing else to do. I had a lot of time, all kinds of time. So I'd just sing. I loved it up there so much, I just wanted to sing to the trees and tell them I loved them. Sometimes they'd answer back, too, especially the river. You could hear it singing."

THE SHERIFF COMES TO CALL

I asked Geno why he had suddenly abandoned his cave. All I

knew was that he had appeared at the house one day as usual, but he didn't return to his cave. Why had he stayed in town?

"I had a really nice marijuana patch right in front of the cave. Not too big, about twenty by twenty. I didn't want to sell it or anything. I just liked growing it. It was beautiful. The leaves looked like emeralds. When the moon was full I'd go out and sing to the marijuana to help it grow. Sometimes I'd swear I could see it growing. That made me so damned excited, I couldn't stand it. So I'd sing some more and watch the plants grow.

"Anyway, one day when I woke up in the early morning, I had a funny feeling I should clear out of the cave and not come back for a while. So I went to town. I came back to find all my marijuana plants pulled up and my sweat lodge burned to the ground. It was still smoldering! The county sheriff had nailed his card to a tree.

"Actually, what happened was, I had someone with me. I hardly ever took anyone with me; didn't want anyone to know where it was. Maybe I only took two people ever. I'd been gone about a week, and as we were approaching we saw smoke, so we stopped and waited. I thought something must be wrong. I thought they must be burning the plants, but when we got there the plants were all pulled up and hauled away, and my sweat lodge was still burning. I didn't care so much about the plants, as long as I didn't get caught, but the dirty bastards could have left my sweat lodge alone! But I was lucky. I could have been arrested. We couldn't have missed them by more than an hour."

I asked Geno, "How do you think they found out?
Did someone snitch?"

"Nobody snitched on me. At first I thought maybe someone had, but after a while I got to thinking. It must have been those boards I took. Up until then nobody ever bothered me or came around at all. What must have attracted their attention was all the boards I took off that building to make the floor of my cave. It was all right till one day I was taking a board, and BAM! The whole damned building fell down! I guess that's what pissed them off, whoever owned the place, and they started checking around. They must have called the sheriff.

"I thought I was out in the middle of nowhere, and nobody owned the place, but I think I took one board too many."

GENO'S JUICE CART

After Geno almost got busted, he moved back into town. His cave dwelling days were over, but his determination to make his way in the world as a gleaner-gatherer remained firm. He would merely have to reinvent himself, and he did so with a juice cart.

"Just look around," he said. "If you look closely, you'll see everything is free for the taking. There are fruit trees all over Chico. All I have to do is pick the fruit and make juice, and roast some almonds and walnuts, which you guys will give me from the nut house, and push a cart around. People will buy that stuff from me, and I'll have enough money to live, and I won't have anyone telling me what to do!"

He lived in someone's garage in an alley while he designed his cart, gathered materials, and refined his business plan. He wanted to use the back porch sink at 2307 to clean up after squeezing juice, so he applied for a business license and the health inspector came over and deemed our porch clean enough for Geno's juice.

Good old "hot" Geno was ablaze with activity. He gleaned lots of fruit from various sources, and built a drying rack in the back yard of 2307. He soon discovered that ants liked to crawl up the legs, so he immersed the legs in coffee cans full of water, and covered the drying fruit with mosquito netting top and bottom. Between gleaning and processing, he worked on his cart.

In keeping with what we now call Reduce, Reuse and Recycle, Geno scrounged most of the materials for his cart for free. Think pretzel cart in Manhattan and you'll have a mental picture of the general configuration, but Geno's was much prettier. He built a basic box of plywood and attached an axle and bicycle wheels. Overhead he had an awning, and the whole thing was painted royal blue and decorated with a botanical theme—understated, nothing psychedelic.

On the top surface of the box, he built a hibachi for roasting nuts. Inside the box, if memory serves me, he must have had some kind of storage for jugs of juice and other supplies. He affixed a dowel for a push handle and away he went, all over town and around campus. People took to calling him Johnny Appleseed, but I called him Genie Appleseed, and suggested that would be a good name for his business, but the name never "took".

For a time, the back porch and yard at 2307 became a place of buzzing industry as Geno showed up with sacks of oranges he harvested from the many trees lining the streets of Chico. "Hot! Hot! I'm so excited, I'm hot!" he said, and his enthusiasm seemed as if it would elevate the house like a flying saucer.

GENO'S EPILOGUE

It was probably around this time that Geno met Dr. Cain, and his life took a new direction. Dr. Cain was a chiropractor fifteen miles up Highway 32 in the wooded community of Paradise.

Just before entering the town, there's a Chamber of Commerce sign, still there today, that reads, "You are ascending into Paradise!" Dr. Cain took Geno under his wing, becoming a surrogate father to him. Given Geno's strained relationship with his own father, Dr. Cain was a real blessing to Geno. Sensing Geno's interest in things spiritual and natural, Dr. Cain sponsored his transition from caveman to chiropractor, providing him with a car and tuition to chiropractic school in Portland. Leaving Chico behind, Geno took Tina with him.

With Geno's high level of focus, he completed not only his doctorate in chiropractic but also his degree in Naturopathic Medicine in record time; I think it was three years. Geno readily passed his State Boards in Oregon, California, and Hawaii.

Having secured his first position at a chiropractor's clinic in Salinas, California, Geno went to Hawaii to surf for a couple of weeks before the job started. While he was there he attended a chiropractic conference, and was offered another position on Oahu.

Let's see…start my profession in Hawaii where the weather is beautiful and so are the women and I can surf every day, or start out in Salinas, the depressing gang capital of Northern California?

His choice was obvious. He begged off Salinas, and he still lives on Oahu today.

Tina joined him initially, but sadly they lasted only another year or two. Her departure was a great loss to Geno, given that she was his first and (to that date) greatest love, just as Em had been for me.

When I visited Geno on Oahu in 1990, I came away wondering why someone who had taken vows of poverty and lived in a cave now had seven houses, seven cars, and a huge pile of money in the bank. While I took Mr. Toad's Wild Ride with him on the freeway of Honolulu, Geno multi-tasked: Eating, talking, cussing out other drivers, fiddling with the stereo, talking with a broker on the cell phone about purchasing eight acres on top of a mountain in Aiea Heights above Pearl Harbor, and filling in details about his cave-dwelling days.

What, I wondered, had happened to the lone meditator, the wanderer in the woods who sang to the crystal raindrops? Had he "sold out to the Establishment"? Returning stateside, the more I thought about this question, the answer was plain: Geno was still Geno. When he was a caveman, he wanted to be the best caveman there ever was. Now he was a chiropractor, and he was the most successful one in the islands. He was still full of *joie de vivre*, and man was he "hot"!

P.S. I'm not sure he wants me to publish this. When I told him I was starting work on a book about the Mariposa days he balked, saying it might hurt his practice. I countered, "Geno, who's going to read the damned thing? It's just something for you and friends and family. If I ever get famous and you see me on talk shows, you can say you knew me when I was a hippie living in a shack!"

I haven't seen Geno since 1990. As publication approaches, I think I should give him a call. I'm certain we'll pick up right where we left off.

27

Room with a View (Reprise)

"Now words, I guess it's too late for words.
It's nothin' that you haven't heard.
I'm all out of alibis,
And still too weak to say good-bye."
Jesse Winchester

It must have been around late April, with the garden in bloom and just before my early-May birthday, that I once again sat at my thinking place on the edge of the bed, looking out the windows. I was taking inventory just as I had done several months before, on the day the windows had been installed.

What the hell had the last several months been all about? Living in my van, finding and fixing up the house, reuniting my brother with our father, getting together with Janie, the fling with Helen, the Dexedrine, the long slow slide into a serious illness, a lengthy recuperation (which was still in progress), the goodness and grace of Betsy, the setback with gonorrhea, planting the garden and watching the first sprouts dancing in the early morning sun, taking up the flute, the interlude with Sue—never had so much happened so intensely in such a short period of time. It was time to take stock.

Betsy, I decided, was right. Staying in the Mariposa lifestyle was a dead-end. Sitting at my thinking place, I decided to go back to school and complete my credential. Teaching elementary wasn't exactly what I'd had in mind. Teaching Spanish or English at university held more appeal, but the path to that goal was longer, more complex, and expensive, with no certain outcome. However, one year in the credential program would place me in a paying position on a career path. Meanwhile, what to do? I might as well enjoy a sixteen-month vacation while waiting for admission, depending on if I got accepted this year or the next. It turned out to be a four-month vacation, because I began the student teaching program in the fall.

These were the shining times on Mariposa Avenue. With my health returning stronger day by day, unemployment benefits coming in, and the garden flush with organic food, the months came and went in a glory of running and bicycle riding, skinny dipping, playing my flute, dancing, and making love. The nights were filled with communal meals, live music, friends and acquaintances dropping by, conversation and whatever silly games we might devise.

I'd always heard that laughter was the best medicine, so that day in my thinking place, I made up a game called "Laughing in Advance". It involved laughing first, then saying something funny. Usually, nobody could think of anything funny to say after laughing hard, so we would just laugh some more, and the fact that we were laughing at nothing became the joke! After a while, anything and everything we said was hilarious, no matter how inane. Sometimes our stomach muscles would be sore the next day from so much laughing. This game was kind of like getting the munchies first, then getting stoned, but obviously the game was easier after a few tokes.

While I sat on the edge of the bed, I wondered if Janie would come back and, if so, on what terms. When I first sat in my thinking place several months before, I had invented a new double standard for the Free Love era: don't ask, don't tell, get it on with whoever pleases you but have a steady girlfriend who would keep the same standard. Clearly, that experiment had proved unhealthy and unsatisfactory. If Janie reappeared, would I have the courage to demand a monogamous relationship, or would we drift along, noncommittally? Not wanting to risk the disappointment of another broken relationship, and being compulsively ambivalent, I came up with yet another double standard: I made my own unilateral choice to be monogamous while hoping, but not demanding, that Janie do the same. In this way, in the vernacular of the times, she would be "doing her own thing" while I did mine.

It was, of course, a senseless construct, but it did have an advantage: I could ride the fence and have her to blame if things didn't work out. Such was my nuanced thinking. In those days, a philosophy in vogue was, "If you love someone, set them free, and if they come back to you, it was meant to be."

Calhoun's reply to that was, "That's bullshit. If you love someone, set her free, and if she doesn't come back to you, hunt her down and fuck her and kill her!" Even though he was being facetious, Calhoun took the philosophy to one extreme while I took it to another.

Meanwhile, no matter how many women I put between Em and myself, the hurt would always be there. Only one time in life does first love come along. We may be hurt and disappointed many times, but never so intensely as when first love is lost. There's no wound so deep and difficult to heal. Intuitively, I knew that letting go of Em was the way to stay healthy, but some things are too big to let go of all at once. I still wanted her with the kind of hunger that could never be fed. I was getting stronger, but I was still too weak to say good-bye.

What if Janie came back and chose not to be monogamous? After all, on the day when I challenged her about the source of my gonorrhea, in her own rather mixed-up words Janie remarked, "I thought you said we could be with whoever we wanted, but you and I, we'd be, like, you know, a couple and all that, but we could be with other people if we wanted—as long as we didn't find out about the others."

My own ambivalence was coming back to bite me on the ass. How could I possibly monitor her behavior, and why should I? I decided to leave this fruitless task to the gods. Meanwhile, I would love her one day at a time; but the seed of dissolution had been planted when she shared her little "gift" with me. Bottom line, I didn't really trust her, yet I didn't want to be without her. Such was my ambivalence, my weakness, and my addiction. Clearly, the Helens and Sues of the world did not nurture my soul. Free Love, I decided, wasn't so very free after all.

Just as I was mulling the Em situation and the cost of free love, I heard a car pull up in front of the house. This was a rare occurrence, so I went out to investigate. The car's bumper sticker said, "Ass, gas, or grass—nobody rides for free!"

28

The Best Birthday Ever

If the first several months at Mariposa had been a descent into darkness, the coming times were an ascent into light. Having almost died, I appreciated life more. Many days of joy were in store. To the extent that I'd been miserable those first months at the house, now joy was intensified as health returned, friends gathered 'round, the garden grew, and I beat the Draft. In many ways, we were wealthy beyond measure with no bills to pay, plenty of time off work, and basic needs met.

Janie and I fell in love again on my birthday, May 4. And what better way to end the day than making love till the wee hours? Often we got it on in the morning, too. Then we'd get up and the carousel of delights began all over again.

That birthday in 1971 was a bit unusual, but then, what wasn't unusual in those days? True to form, I invited everyone to the house but made no plans beyond that, except I did have a certain present in mind that I wanted from Janie, something every guy wants on his birthday. After her previous "gift" that caused me to take antibiotics, and the interlude with Sue, I wanted to make things good with us again. Having survived pneumonia, jaundice, and mononucleosis, my sap was flowing. Springtime was sighing all along the creek and shining in the bedroom windows. The garden, which I'd begun planting when I could barely crawl, was now bursting with life energy. My mother was in town. I had a baggie of pot and I had sequestered a couple of doses of mescaline for Janie and me.

Janie and I hadn't "had relations" since the little medical problem she had caused. When she came over for the party she seemed nonchalant, and I was wondering about the status of our relationship. I thought our friend Mr. Mescalito might loosen us up a bit.

A handful of friends arrived: Mom, Eugene and Tina. Others were no shows, but Jim and Mike were there. For food and refreshments, I hadn't thought beyond the usual bowl of brown rice. The way I figured, if a cake was to appear, it would simply materialize. It would be a happening. Everyone sat and talked. The mood was quiet and gentle. We ate our rice with chopsticks, but Janie and I went light on the food, wanting the mescaline to take effect. When it started to come on, I invited her to the bedroom.

I knew it was rude of me to abandon my guests, but in my narcissistic way, I wanted all my pleasures at the same time. I wasn't sure how long we'd be in bedroom, but one thing led to another and we were in there who knows how long? Maybe an hour or two. As the mescaline took effect, I could see a lavender aura around Janie's irises. She seemed a little confused, wondering if I still loved her, and I told her I did and all was forgiven. She wanted me then. The only thing providing privacy was the thin door between the bedroom and living room. Periodically, we heard the others get quiet; then, Janie and I got even quieter. Janie bit a pillow and held it over her face to dampen her sounds of pleasure, and I could overhear someone saying, "What are they doing in there?" as if they didn't know.

The mescaline enveloped us in a thousand whirling suns, and our flesh became one. It was like our first time together, only better.

I forgave Janie her infidelity and the little "gift" that came with it. When you love someone, there's no explaining. All borders and boundaries between our beings dissolved and we melded into one glowing ball of light.

Now why do I mention this? Let's not be X-Rated here. This is what happened, and I want you to know about it. After all the miseries of depression, my suicidal tendency, and illness, that night I experienced a moment of absolute perfection. It seemed a little weird, making love while my mother was in the next room, but at the moment of peak ecstasy, something became clear to me in my young and often angst-ridden life. In a flood of joy, no words were adequate to express the sudden realization that overtook my whole being, but a poor rendition might go something like this: *Life is good! If this is what life is all about, bring it on! Sorrow no longer owns me. I am free!* For a young man who had long held a morbid preoccupation with death, and who only months before had almost bought the farm, this moment of bliss was a huge affirmation.

Janie and I came out of the bedroom and, discreetly, nobody asked questions. Gradually, we came down from the mescaline. At 2307 Mariposa Avenue, everyone's gentleness and love blended together like the tropical punch we drank. We were all hanging loose and feeling comfortable. Life fit us like an old soft leather glove.

The party went on, and after a while, a surprise appeared. My mom emerged from the kitchen with a Double Dutch chocolate cake and one candle glowing while everyone sang the birthday song. (I had requested a single candle to represent my new lease on life.) I blew out the candle and wished for a long and happy life for everyone there. I thanked my mother, out loud, for giving birth to me and Tim. Quietly, in a corner of my mind, I thought, whether Janie and I stay together or not, it's all good.

That night after the party was over, Janie and I slept well. In the morning, we made love again, and I said, "Thank you for last night, Janie, and this morning. It's the best birthday present a guy could ever wish for!"

But I had to wonder: Was it just the drugs talking? In regard to Janie, I asked myself, Does a leopard ever change its spots?

29

A Yaqui Way of Family

Who can explain why two souls come together? Against all likelihood, Janie and I were a couple for two and a half years—a college grad with a high school dropout, a newly minted adult, 24 years old, with a 17 year old girl who was still living at home with her parents, a towheaded Caucasian with a black-haired Mexican, a young man who had attended university in Europe and a girl who had never left town.

For all my misgivings about Janie, one of the things I loved about her was her family. Janie's family was simple and good, and very different from my stepfamily. So what if her parents weren't intellectuals? How much good emotionally had the intellectual confines of Lafayette done me? Janie's parents' English was limited, but we got along fine in Spanish. Their formal schooling extended to perhaps the third grade in rural Mexico, but like many immigrants they had a dream. They came north, labored, and managed to buy a home where they raised four children.

Valuing education, Janie's parents gave their children a leg up. The children stood on their shoulders and reached higher than the parents ever could have on their own. Sister Mary became a secretary; Sister Susie, a nurse. For whatever reasons, Johnny and Janie dropped out of high school. Still, a tenth grade education was better than a third. At least it put them within reach of later achievements.

So what if the achievements of Janie and her respective family members weren't what would have been defined as acceptable by my university-educated father and stepmother? Millie didn't say anything about Janie, but I knew what she would say: "What are you doing with *that Mexican girl*? What grade did you say she dropped out in?" Initially, it took me some work to shut off the niggling voice, but, when I contrasted the confines of Lafayette, California, with Janie's family home and the people in it, I was more drawn to her people than my own. Lafayette had been for me a rather posh refugee camp occupied by educated people but lacking in love.

With Janie's family, what you saw was what you got: no covert action, just a lot of unconditional love and acceptance. There, in Janie's family home, I felt welcome, more so than I ever had in the Lafayette house.

When I left Lafayette for college, my stepmother had said, "You kids are like birds in the nest. You're getting too big. At some point, the mother and father bird kick the chicks out of the nest. You're getting the boot. You either fly or you die, and don't expect to come back here to live. You get *x* dollars for college and that's all, and when that's over, don't ever ask for more. And when you come back here to visit, you come as a guest." By contrast, Janie and her brother were still living at home until they were ready to leave, no questions asked and no pressure applied; and I was always welcome.

In certain respects, the family home on West 8th Street bore a resemblance to 2307 Mariposa Avenue. An open door policy was observed day and night. With family and extended family coming and going, one never lacked for companionship, and a pot of beans was always on the stove. *Mamacita* patted balls of flour *masa* into fresh tortillas daily. I tell you, walking into that home and immediately being offered homemade Mexican food was heartwarming. Janie's mother, short and round and sturdy as a fencepost, would fix me a plate. Warmth and love went into the food. Wrap your hands around a warm burrito on a cold winter's day, and you were home where you belonged! By contrast, not once during the years I lived in Lafayette did I ever have a friend over to the house, let alone offer them any food.

In the Lafayette house, I was always walking on eggshells. Here on West 8th Street, I could hang loose, let my guard down, and just be myself. When I went to Lafayette to visit, the first question Millie would ask me was how long was I staying and how soon would I be leaving? At Janie's home, the first words were *bienvenido (welcome)* and *how long can you stay?* The love and simplicity of Janie's family was the way I thought a family should be—the antithesis of life in the Lafayette house

Janie's sister Mary had two little girls, Pee Wee and Felisa. Happily, I became "instant uncle" to those delightful, sweet girls, ages seven and ten. They liked me to read stories to them, but more often we made up stories as I watched them play in the backyard. In my Lafayette family, as well as my family of origin, I had no nieces or nephews. My mother and father were each the only issue of their respective parents, therefore, I had no aunts or uncles either. My stepsiblings had two cousins who had lived near us in Lafayette, but I rejected them out of hand as alien interlopers associated with the misery of living with Millie.

Janie's father was reputedly a full-blooded Yaqui Indian, indigenous to Mexico. A present-day Internet search shows the Yaquis concentrated around Phoenix. Perhaps he came from Arizona, but somehow in my mind I used to have Janie's father as a secondary source to the collective unconscious of Mexico's indigenous peoples. Wide and round, with the solidity of an old bull, his given name was Jesus, but even his children called him Jessie.

Jessie was not a talkative man. It seemed his meaning was conveyed more by what he didn't say than what he did. Quiet and acutely observant, he took in everything going on around the house as he sat at his usual place at the head of the kitchen table. If and when he spoke, he was more likely to ask a question and listen than to offer an opinion. You knew, though, that he was processing everything he took in.

Throughout the Mariposa days, Jim and I had been reading and discussing at length a certain book, *The Teachings of Don Juan: A Yaqui Way of Knowledge*. For those not familiar with the book, the author, Carlos Castañeda, a university professor at UCLA, relates how he allegedly traveled to Mexico and met a mysterious Mexican peasant in a town square. Don Juan was a Yaqui sorcerer and Castañeda became his apprentice, learning to do such things as jumping across a canyon by "extending your rays from your navel" and taking a leap of faith. Peyote was sometimes involved. In my imaginings, Janie's inscrutable father, a Yaqui himself, had stepped right off the pages of Castañeda's novel. In this impression, Jim and I concurred, probably making way too much of the notion, but on some level it seemed to apply.

If Castañeda could suspend disbelief enough to jump a chasm, why couldn't I close the gap between Janie's upbringing and mine, and between our very different educational levels? It seemed to me love was the bridge and the dissolver of differences. I believed we would live on love, and that would be enough.

In short, Janie's family was for me a safe harbor, the down-to-earth answer to my cobbled-together, so-called family in Lafayette. In the end, neither cultural nor educational differences split us up. Instead, it was the age-old issue of trust, or lack thereof.

In the two years Janie and I were together, her family offered comfort and refuge I hadn't known since I was a child. I could peer in their window and remember what it had been like living with my family of origin, in the good times before the crap hit the fan. In this way, Janie and her family became agents of my recovery from spiritual amnesia, and I am still thankful for their love. In the ways in which they were of another culture, and they came from a set of values foreign to mine, they were alien to me. On the other hand, they offered simple caring, which seemed at once familiar and transcendent, as if from a long ago and faraway place—perhaps in ancient Mexico.

30

A Lizard on My Leg

I lay on my back, sideways across the Upper Park trail, with my flute resting on my chest. I fit perfectly there, with my bum in a depression and my head resting on a smooth, flat pillow of rock. A lizard sat on my leg. He had come to listen. His head tilted to one side like that attentive black and white dog listening to the Victrola on old Columbia 78 rpm record labels. The slogan on those old records said, “His Master’s Voice,” and now I felt like my flute must be that voice.

The highest “A” on the flute drew the lizard in the first place. (This is the same frequency at which whales and wolves communicate.) Before he jumped up on my knee, my little mascot had done jerky little pushups, listening from a nearby rock while I improvised a high-pitched lizard song. When I took a break, he ran over and jumped up on my knee, wanting to hear more.

I came out here to be alone for a while before others arrived. I was sick of Calhoun and Janie’s flirtation. Back at the house when I announced I was driving to the Upper Park, Jim said maybe he’d ride his bike up. Calhoun was there but he was obviously waiting to see what Janie would do, and Janie, with sidelong glances at Calhoun, was waiting to see what I would do. She coyly hedged, “Maybe I’ll be along in a while.” Weary of the game, I left, not expecting anyone to show up.

For all I knew, I was lying in the dirt playing music to a lizard while Calhoun and Janie were getting it on in my bed.

I played some more music for the lizard on my leg, and finally Jim came up the trail. Always aware of what's going on in nature, Jim noticed the lizard and stopped. "Well, what have we here? Little guy," speaking to the lizard, "it looks like you've found a friend."

I figured the concert was over so I gestured Jim to come ahead. He did and we sat and talked. The lizard retreated several feet and turned to watch us from his former vantage point on a hot rock. I told Jim of my suspicions and concerns about Janie and Calhoun, and how I didn't want to waste any energy worrying about her because worrying was bad for my health, and I couldn't control her anyway. It was useless to try. In a roundabout way, typical of our manner of speaking in those days, I spiraled in to my main points, which could be summarized as follows.

1. *I'm sick and tired of this Free Love bullshit.*
2. *I'm not sure I'm through with Free Love. I know I'm addicted because the payoff is great. Does that make me a hypocrite? Or am I just another jealous lover practicing the double standard?*
3. *I appreciate your keeping your hands off Janie. Your taking a bath with her is okay, but that's where I draw the line.*
4. *If you value my friendship as I do yours, please resist all advances from my flirtatious little love goddess, because I know for a fact she's attracted to you.*

Jim agreed and promised to hold up his end of the bargain.

Just then we heard laughter, and Calhoun and Janie came up the trail. Calhoun the Clown held forth with his usual sexual insults and innuendoes, which Janie seemed to find hilarious. It had been two hours since I left the house. Did they have time for a quickie? As they drew closer, the lizard scurried even farther away and turned to watch, waiting in vain for one last melody. Janie and Calhoun kept walking and giggling and went around us as if we weren't even there.

"See what I mean?" I asked Jim. "Women may come and lizards may go, but you and I will always be friends."

A sea change occurred on that day. Taking the long view, I thought of an out-of-body experience I had a year and a half before while I lay in bed recuperating from pneumonia on a gray day. Just as I had done back then, now I visualized myself as a red tail hawk hovering over the trail. From a mile up, what was happening didn't seem all that important after all.

"You know what?" I said to Jim. "In ten minutes or ten hours, this bullshit with Janie might still matter to me, but, in ten weeks I'm down the road." I had my teaching credential and a summer job teaching preschool with Betsy, and I would be living with her. Betsy was my ace in the hole. "And ten years from now, Jim, this sure as hell won't matter."

I visualized soaring ever higher till Jim and I and Calhoun and Janie and the lizard disappeared into history like ever-receding specks, along with millions like us across the USA who were living the Free Love ethos and finding it lacking.

The lizard came out of hiding and returned to his rock; and Jim and the lizard enjoyed another little concert. I wondered out loud if lizards ever got jealous; if jealousy was a luxury of the human brain, or hard-wired in our territorial nature.

Jim and I got up and the lizard scooted away. We started walking up the trail. I was with my pal, heading for the swimming hole on a hot day, and nothing else mattered.

Later, though, I got revenge on Calhoun without trying. After skinny dipping, he put on his pants, and they were full of red ants! He jumped around like a puppet on a string, slapping at his legs; a sight I'll never forget. He danced like a naked Ichabod Crane being poked with a cattle prod. Cussing and shouting, "Ouch! Ouch!" Calhoun stripped off his pants and jumped in the creek. When he surfaced he was still shouting and cussing in pain. I sidled over to his pants and nudged them onto the ant hill.

31

Plastic Jesus

"Too many churches And not enough truth."
She's Come Undone
by Guess Who

Hitchhiking home to Chico one day in June of '71, I got dropped off at the intersection of Highways 70 and 99. I was on my way home from the Induction Center in Oakland where I had finally completed all parts of my physical. I was Prime USDA, certain to be classified 1-A very soon. Matters of God and war had been much on my mind, but right now it was just goddamned hot—a hundred and ten degrees in the shade, but, there was no shade in sight. And I wasn't carrying any water. The molten asphalt must have kicked up the temperature by twenty degrees. Nothing to do but wait and hope for a ride in a nice air-conditioned car.

I truly regretted not having any water with me. A person could collapse out here, even a young man in good physical condition. Hoofing the ten miles to town could be more dangerous than hunkering down and waiting.

Trying to feel cooler, I took off my white tank top and wrapped it around my head like a turban. Hardly any cars came, but when they did, I put the shirt back on. Who was going to pick up a bare-chested longhair wearing a turban? Finally I just left it on, hoping to sweat and thereby cool down a little.

After what seemed like an eternity, my ride came.

A new looking light blue Buick wagon pulled over, and I caught up at a lope, conserving energy. I didn't bother with the formality of leaning against the windowsill and asking where the driver was going—the way it's done by hitchhikers so the driver and the prospective rider have a chance to sniff each other over before the rider gets in. Hell with it, maybe he has air conditioning. I hopped in.

"Thank you for stopping. You going to Chico?"

He was a middle-aged man, I guessed about six feet four, weighing in about 250 with a slicked back, thinning salt-and-pepper pompadour; real average, straight looking white dude. Nice car, that's what counted.

"Yes, I'm going to Chico. Where can I take you?"

"Thanks a lot for stopping. Hot as hell out there. A guy could die of heatstroke. You're a godsend." I settled back in the seat as he pulled onto the roadway.

Had I known he really regarded himself as sent from God, I don't think I'd have accepted the ride.

We rode in silence. I was too damned hot to talk much. Out of the corner of my eye, I could see him glancing over. Was he checking me out? Was he a pervert, wanting something in exchange for the ride? Or did he just want to talk? Either way, I wasn't buying. I looked straight ahead, saying nothing. With any luck, we'd be in town before long.

Just then I saw a figurine mounted on the dashboard.

"Where you from?" he asked, making conversation.

"Chico."

"Where exactly?"

Getting personal, I thought.

"Chico. Sorry, I don't feel much like talking. Too thirsty, feeling kinda weak. You got any water in here?"

"No."

"You sure? Juice, anything?"

"Sorry."

"How about air conditioning?"

"I don't like to use it."

"I don't want to be antisocial, but I'm just going to sit here, if you don't mind. You do the talking, I'll listen. Say, what's that figurine you've got there on the dash?"

"Jesus."

Oh damn. A frigging Bible thumper, and Chico is a known Bible Belt town, what with descendants of Midwest farmers and refugees from the Great Depression having settled there to work at farming.

Somehow the sight of the figurine drew me out of my shell.

"At first, I couldn't tell it was supposed to be Jesus. Why do you have Him facing the road? Don't you want Him looking at you, blessing you with that upraised hand?"

"He's watching the road."

"I see. Does Jesus know how to drive, or is He just like an automatic pilot?"

"He watches out for me."

"Well, by God, I don't want to offend you, but that little figurine there does remind me of a song I once heard. Know the one I'm talkin' about? Have you heard it?"

"No. How does it go?"

"Well, here goes." Applying my best country western drawl, I sang:

I don't care if it rains or freezes,
Long as I got my plastic Jesus,
Glued to the dashboard of my car!

This guy had me going now.

"You never heard that song before?"

If he had, he wasn't admitting it.

"No," he said, and asked, "what are your religious beliefs?"

"Hellfire and brimstone, I didn't ask for the Inquisition here. All I asked for was a ride to town."

"I'm just asking a question. What are your religious beliefs?"

"Excuse me, sir, I don't mean to be rude, and I don't want to make you mad so you'll drop me off alongside the road here in the fires of hell on this hot afternoon, me being tired and thirsty and all, and then I'd have to hoof it the rest of the way to town without any water to drink, but didn't your mother ever tell you it's not polite to talk politics or religion with strangers?"

"With Jesus, there are no strangers. Jesus loves you."

"Well, that's a mighty fine situation. Do you preach for a living, Mr…what's your name?"

"Reilly. George Reilly."

We shook hands, and I told him my name: "Bix, but my family calls me Beelzebub."

Like many people, he couldn't get my first name right, and I guessed he didn't want to say "Beelzebub."

"Just call me Mac," I said, thinking of my friend Alyosha who had changed his name to Macorgeati just for the heck of it.

"Okay, Mac, have you accepted Jesus as your personal savior?"

This guy was starting to annoy me.

"Listen, Sir Reilly, if I'd wanted a sermon this afternoon, I'd have hitched a ride to church. Can we just get along here?"

"Jesus tells me my job is to save souls. I'm just doing my job. Have you been saved?"

"No, but I do save Blue Chip Stamps, good at most stores. That's my kind of redemption."

"Jesus says if you're not saved, you'll go to Hell."

"Hell? Look around you. We're already there."

I was starting to warm to the subject.

"For that matter, we're in Heaven too. All depends on your viewpoint. It's all happenin' here and now, man. This is it. You're god and I'm god and everyone we know is god. Sin is when you're not truthful in accordance with your own nature…."

"Man is by nature sinful. That's why we need Jesus to lift us up…."

"Sin? I'll tell you what sin is. It's having bad karma, man. You ever heard about karma?"

"No."

"Karma's like whatever goes around, comes around."

Just then I spotted his Bible on the seat next to me. Placing my hand on the Bible, I continued, "Like it says in the Sermon on the Mount. Do you mind if I open your Bible?"

"Go ahead."

I picked it up and opened it. "Hey, what's all this red ink about?"

"The red ink is Jesus's words."

"Okay, here, I found it."

> *Thou shalt love the Lord thy God*
> *with all thy heart, and with all thy mind,*
> *and with all thy soul."*

"I thought you said you weren't a Christian."

"I didn't say that. You assumed it. What I said was, I didn't want a lecture or a sermon. All I wanted was a ride. I love God, God as I understand him. Not your way, no way."

"Well, are you a Christian?"

"You could say I'm christian with a small 'c'. I accepted Jesus as my personal savior when I was eighteen, but I don't go around talking about it and proselytizing people. It's just a personal thing, the way I treat others."

"Prossa-what?"

"Proselytizing. You know, trying to convert everyone you see, hitchhikers and young blond Adonis longhair sinners, and anyone you can corner into listening to you."

"Were you ever baptized?"

"I go swimming in the creek every day. That's good enough for me."

"Well, the Bible says unless you've been baptized...."

"Speaking of baptism, are you sure you haven't got any water in here? Or maybe some wine? How 'bout some of those little communion wafers? I'm getting awfully hungry."

"That's because your soul is hungry...."

I was beginning to get really agitated.

"You think I don't know the meaning of being crucified? My oldest, first-born brother was murdered by my other, second-born brother. The first-born was mean and cruel, and enjoyed hurting people just like the Devil likes hurting everyone. The Devil lived in him, and the second-born crucified him. The first-born deserved it, brought it on himself, and now the surviving brother has a cross to bear the rest of his life. You think I don't know the meaning of the crucifixion? And how about 'Thou shalt not kill'? I get that one loud and clear. That's why I'm staying out of the military."

"Your soul wants to be fed."

Now I was getting even more wound up.

"And you say I'm hungry? I *am* hungry! Hungry for life! Hungry for love! Isn't that the way to be a Christian without spouting it all over the countryside and annoying hitchhikers on a hot day in June? Sermon on the Mount? Man, I live it every time I mount my girlfriend and press up against her. At the moment of climax, I shout, 'Yes, Jesus! Thank you, Jesus! Heal me Jesus!' I tell you, Mr. George Reilly, if God made anything nicer than a woman, he kept it all to himself. Sex is my sacrament; loving others, my penance and my redemption; and, if that's not being a Christian, then screw you and the chariot you rode in on. I tell you, man, it's all happening here and now, and if we don't grab it, and run with it, it'll pass us all by while you stand on your little bully pulpit trying to convert people who don't want it, don't need it, and don't care!"

"Have you been baptized?"

"I just poured my heart out to you in confession, and you're not even listening! All I asked for was a ride. Now look at the mess we're in."

"I was only trying to help. The Bible tells me to help."

"Well, thank you and may the gods bless you, man, but I don't want to hear any more of your claptrap. Now, are you going to quit this bullshit, or do I have to jump out of the car?"

"Jesus says…."

"Jesus this, Jesus that! You're not listening, man! Stop the car! Let me out! I'll take my chances with the buzzards along the highway."

"I was only trying to do what …."

"Okay, that's it! I'm getting out of this car whether you stop it or not." I braced my right armpit on the bottom of the open window frame, and put my left hand on the door lever.

"I thank you for the ride thus far, but the devil is getting hold of me from head to toe, and I need to get out of this car. If you're really a Christian with a capital 'C', then do the Christian thing: give me the god-blessed ride for free— you know, Charity and all that—and, sorry for the expression, shut your pie hole, or let's talk about the weather or some superficial bullshit. Now, which is it going to be?"

"But Jesus says…."

"That's it, man, I'm outta here!" We were doing maybe fifty when I opened the door and swung my whole body out over the roadway.

I shouted, "I've jumped off of trains going faster than this. I can do this, man! If you don't stop, I'll just let go."

Gradually, he slowed down, not wanting to brake too suddenly. "Please," he implored, "get back in the car."

"Only if you promise to stop talking your Jesus bullshit. Promise now, or stop the car and let me off." I kept hold of the door, but I placed my feet on the ground like a hamster on a wheel, testing the speed to see if I could survive letting go. The car came to a slow halt, and I stood up.

"Please get back in. I'll take you where you want to go."

"Promise first, man. Promise!"

"Okay, just get back in the car."

We rode in silence the few more miles to the outskirts of Chico. A mile before the first exit, he asked me where I was going. By now, I didn't want him to know exactly, so I hemmed and hawed. What followed was a bit of a chess match, with him wanting to prove he would do right by me, and take me to my front door, and my not wanting him to know where I lived, so I asked where he lived, and I don't think he wanted me to know that, either. At least

I got him to tell me what part of town he lived in, the southeast side. It occurred to me that Gene's Tina and her sisters lived there. He could drop me off there, and I could get a ride the rest of the way. Having only been there once, I described the house and neighborhood and the girls to him, and he thought he knew who they were. In fact, he lived on their street.

"Is this it?" he asked, pulling up in front of Tina's house.

"I think so. Well, George Reilly, it's been fun. I'm sorry if I behaved badly, but the Devil made me do it! All I'm trying to say is don't impose your brand of spirituality on me, please. Thank you very much for the ride. I mean that. It was hell out there in that heat, and your ride was a godsend. And hey, if you ever want to come over to the house, we could have a lively philosophical discussion. I warn you, though, my roommate Jim is most persuasive. The last Mormons who came over there left wanting to live on a commune; and some Jehovah's Witnesses, well, I think they're now living on a Hopi reservation."

I didn't think the good reverend would be showing up anytime soon.

Getting out of the car and shutting the door firmly, I leaned against the windowsill. "See you in church," I said, and walked toward Tina's door. I rang the bell, and waited; knocked harder, and waited some more.

When I started humming the little song about Plastic Jesus, Tina's sister Lorna opened the door. Wrapped in a towel, she was dripping wet and gorgeous. She was happy to see me. Before stepping inside, I looked back to the street, and the reverend was gone.

32

Angel on my Shoulder

Sometimes a lack of preparation leads to adventure. It might not be an adventure one wants, but adventure nonetheless. One weekend in July of '71, I was looking forward to hosting a 48-hour party. My expectation of how it would turn out, and the way it did, were different things entirely.

In my mind, I had the weekend built up as a kind of coming together of my newly created family. Given that my father was seldom present, and my stepmother had for so long interposed herself between him and me while totally rejecting my brother, my thinking was that I could blend my stepsiblings with Tim and Janie into a family of choice. We were young adults now. We could choose.

For a couple of years I'd been building relationships with these people individually, but this would be the first time all of us got together. When I invited everyone, I billed the weekend as a bountiful harvest, the fruition of a dream, to create my own family on my own terms. Brother Tim, stepsister Elaine, and stepbrother Mark were all coming to town. Janie and I were "in tight." The house offered floor space only, so Janie and I yielded our bed to stepsister Elaine and stayed overnight with Steve and his girlfriend, Suzanne. In the morning, I remember awaking happy about the get-together, and horny. Just as we were warming up, Mark and his new fiancée, Gia, found us in bed in Suzanne's sunroom.

Janie, being a woman, suggested we get up and visit. I, being a guy, was thinking, "No way, we have business to attend to."

"I'm very happy to see you, brother…" (I had taken to calling Mark "brother" only recently) "but your timing is just a little off. Could we meet at the house in an hour?"

He obliged, and Janie and I took care of the biological imperative.

We showed up at the house in the late morning, an hour later than I had claimed. Gia, for reasons still unknown to me, had followed Mark in her own car and had already departed for the Bay Area. The rest of us looked at each other and asked the same two questions: What's for breakfast, and what are we going to do today? My fantasy breakfast of croissants, fruit and tea for everyone hadn't materialized, and it was almost lunchtime anyway. Tim, probably wise to my tricks, had been smart enough to have a big breakfast at some café between Davis and Chico.

Okay, we skipped breakfast, and brunch as well. I suggested an overnight camping trip to Butte Meadows, an area of pine forest and alpine meadows along the upper reaches of Butte Creek, an hour from Chico in the Sierras. It was really more like a fantasy camping trip, given that, between the five of us, we had only two sleeping bags and no other camping gear. We had it all planned out, except for the important parts.

"I have a plan," I said. "Share body heat. When it gets dark, we'll roast marshmallows. Then we'll huddle together on top of one sleeping bag, and watch the stars till we fall asleep. We can take turns sleeping near the fire and covering up with the down bag. As long as we have drugs, munchies, a campfire, and each other, who cares about camping gear?"

That seemed to be good enough for everyone, so off we went

in two cars, four of us in Tim's bulletproof Dodge Dart and Mark in his souped-up Austin Healey. On the way, we stopped at the market and pooled our money for munchies: two shopping bags full to the top with salami, cheese, crackers, sandwich fixings, sauerkraut, dill spears, apples, bananas, chocolate bars, and a box of Screaming Lemon Zingers. More than anything, I remember combining the Lemon Zingers (lemon snaps coated in powdered sugar), sauerkraut, and dill spears. Oh yes, and I remember the two bags of marshmallows.

We didn't know exactly what part of Butte Meadows we were going to. I had envisioned taking LSD, smoking pot, and "tripping" through the meadows all day with no one but our group around. A couple of years before, I'd spent a whole day in Butte Meadows wading in a marshy meadow on private property, ecstatically watching grass, dragonflies, flowers and running water turn into spinning mandalas. That was the way to do LSD, with no cops, cars, or strangers around, and no plate glass windows to walk through.

The memory of that day was where I thought we were going, but I couldn't remember exactly where the private property was, and it was too late to make other arrangements. Instead, we wound up at a public campground by Butte Creek. It was July 4, and the blazing sun directly overhead indicated the time was one o'clock.

"Good enough," we all said, not really meaning it. We passed around some joints and split some tabs of LSD.

"Shouldn't we make camp first?" someone suggested.

"What camp do we have to make?" I said. "We only have the two sleeping bags."

"Doesn't that sign over there say 'No Overnight Camping Allowed'?" someone asked.

"Yes," someone else added, "and 'Fire permits required. Fires only in fire rings.'"

"Does anybody see any firewood around here?" someone else asked.

"Maybe we'll go somewhere else," I countered. "What about supper?" someone asked.

"We have two bags of groceries," I said. "What about munchies?" someone protested.

Some discussion ensued during which we decided it was okay to snack on fruit and sweets, but leave all the other stuff alone, especially the marshmallows.

"We have to have marshmallows for this evening," I said, even though there was no firewood and no camping allowed.

"Yeah!" Elaine agreed. "It wouldn't be camping without marshmallows around the campfire."

I remember only two more things about that afternoon at Butte Meadows.

First, I remember Tim and I standing ankle deep in the creek, staring down at the water, feeling very hot and sorry we couldn't skinny dip in the family campground. Walking around in wet clothing didn't sound appealing, either. I was hoping the hallucinations would start, but we had split the LSD too many ways, so no one was getting off. I was hungry, though. Marijuana will do that to you.

Second, I remember the three children who kept staring at Tim and me. They must have thought we couldn't hear them or see them, because they kept pointing at us, loudly asking their father things such as, "Are they hippies? Are we safe? Are they on LSD? Are they going to take their clothes off?" and so on. They stood and stared, pointed, talked, and giggled among themselves. Then they ran away and came back with some other friends to stare and giggle some more.

I knew something was up when I heard two of the five kids saying, "No, I don't want to! I'm afraid!" When they tried to run away, the boy who was the apparent leader of the pack ran after them and pulled them back into formation fifty feet away from where Tim and I stood. Four kids formed a chorus line while their leader stood in front of them as their conductor. The boy waved his arms, and the chant began:

"Marijuana, LSD, love, peace, hippies, you and me!"

They repeated the chant several times until some of them broke and ran. The littlest girl ran away screaming.

The LSD wasn't working, my feet were cold, the rest of me was too hot, and the bags of groceries in the Austin Healey were calling me. None of us but Tim had eaten any breakfast or lunch. When I got to Mark's car, I discovered most of the food had been consumed.

"Don't blame me," Mark said. "Elaine and Janie came and started eating the stuff that we said we were saving for supper, so I joined in."

"Turnabout is fair play," I said while I rooted through the bags, looking for the makings of a Dagwood sandwich.

Tim came from the creek. Mark and I explained what had happened. "Don't blame me," I said. "Elaine and Janie started it, Mark joined in, and then I came along. Do you want half this Dagwood?"

"No, but I'm looking for something sweet. What do we have?"

I peered into the bags. "Screaming Lemon Zingers, a jar of sauerkraut, dill spears and two bags of marshmallows, but we're saving the marshmallows for tonight, remember?"

"Aren't there any sodas to go with the Zingers?" Tim asked. With their powdered sugar coating, Zingers had a way of forming an unswallowable blob of glop in your mouth if you didn't have something to wash them down.

"No. Remember, we spent the money on solid food and agreed to drink creek water."

"Zingers it is," Tim said.

We passed the Zingers around but Mark wasn't hungry anymore, and Tim chewed only a few before he wandered off toward the creek to get a drink.

Janie and Elaine appeared from somewhere and peered forlornly into the grocery bags. There was some discussion about the mysteriously disappearing foodstuff. By this time I'd finished the Dagwood.

"It's time for dessert," I said. "How about a Lemon Zinger?" I asked, proffering the box.

"Isn't there anything to drink with it?" they asked.

"Nope. Sorry." Looking for something moist to chase the cookies, my eyes landed on the jars of sauerkraut and dill spears.

"Who needs a beverage when you have sauerkraut and dill spears?" I chided. Then I told them about a guy named Cliff I used to work with. "Every day Cliff had a big hunk of chocolate cake that he chased with a huge deli dill pickle. Cliff couldn't stop talking about how great it tasted. 'Yummm,' Cliff would say. 'You get that sweet and that sour going together, there's nothing like it!' he would exclaim. I think I'll try Cliff's idea."

Janie and Elaine said "Yuck," and disappeared. While they were gone, Mark watched me eat Zingers with sauerkraut and dill chasers until he got disgusted and went for a walk.

By the time everyone came back to the Healey, half a box of

Zingers was gone and so were half a jar each of sauerkraut and pickles. My old supervisor's predilection for chocolate cake and deli dills wasn't working for me, but I was trying to believe it did, same as I was trying to believe we were all having a fun day in Butte Meadows. I was gagging on a huge sweet and sour ball of glop, pretending I was savoring it, but it lacked a certain *joie de saveur*. All of us stood there in the hot three o'clock sun looking at the nearly empty grocery bags and the undesirable combinations of foods, wondering what to eat next.

Everyone had a confession to make. "I ate three Dagwood sandwiches," said Mark, "because I was bored."

"Elaine and I ate the chocolate bars because they were just going to melt," explained Janie.

Spitting out a ball of glop into an empty grocery bag, I added, "I ate what was left of the sandwich stuff because I was afraid someone else would finish it all off before I got any," I added.

"I'm not that hungry," Tim said, "but I still want something sweet."

"What's left to eat?" someone asked. "Marshmallows," said Janie, looking in the grocery bag.

"No, not the marshmallows!" exclaimed Elaine. "Yeah, we're saving those for tonight!" I agreed. "Camping just wouldn't be camping without marshmallows," Elaine added.

"But," said Janie, "one marshmallow apiece wouldn't hurt."

"You're right," everyone agreed.

When we finished the two bags of marshmallows around three thirty, we were all thinking the same thing: it's a long time between now and breakfast, and camping without marshmallows just wouldn't be camping. With only two sleeping bags between the five of us, no air mattresses, and no marshmallows, and camping not permitted anyway, who wants to camp out? We can stargaze in the back yard at 2307 Mariposa.

"It's damned hot here," I said.

"Doesn't Sambo's restaurant have air conditioning?" queried Tim.

"Yes, air conditioning," I said, "and the biggest, best hot fudge sundaes on planet earth."

BACK IN TOWN, WE ALL sat in a semicircular booth under the air conditioning vent and ordered Paul Bunyan-sized hot fudge sundaes. Everyone ate in silence except for the clinking of spoons and occasional caveman oohs and aaahs. The cool air on my shoulders felt good.

"That main course was delicious," I said, when everyone was done.

"You mean it's time for dessert?" added Tim.

"We haven't tried Sambo's banana split," Elaine suggested.

"With a cherry on top," said Janie.

Between courses, Tim and I told the others about the chorus of kids at Butte Meadows who were chanting, "Marijuana, LSD, love, peace, hippies, you and me!

This day was not turning out the way I had expected. Waiting for the banana splits, I sat there mentally beating myself up. I was living in a fantasy world where planning was not required; where spontaneity was the highest virtue. And look where it had brought us—to a failed camping trip and a bummer day in a public campground on July 4. I had been so selfish that morning, wanting to get laid, that I had sent away my stepbrother and his new girlfriend. Then, while Janie and I were messing around, Gia had left in her own car and I hadn't had a chance to get acquainted, and everyone had sat around hungry, waiting for me and Janie to show up. When we finally got there, my hippie credo, "It'll all just come together, man," resulted in everyone skipping breakfast, and lunch hadn't been all that good.

I had been a lousy host, a poor planner. The day had gone off half-assed, and it was my fault. A bright red devil sat on my shoulder poking me with his trident. I could plainly hear him saying, "You idiot! You got everyone into this mess." I had expected some kind of cosmic group hug and instant bonding between the five of us. Instead, we were all sitting in Sambo's in sloppy, sugar-induced semi- comas. At the moment, though, nobody seemed to care.

I decided to forgive myself. Silently, I told the devil to get off my shoulder and quit bugging me. Only angels are allowed, I asserted. Once I forgave myself, I looked around the table and realized it didn't matter what we were doing, and I was just happy to have my people with me. Perhaps, I thought, one day I'd grow up and have the sense to get out of bed in the morning and serve croissants and coffee to my guests.

With the banana split dishes empty, everyone sat, sated and quiet.

"Life is truly good," I said out loud, and recited my definition of Heavenly Grace. "If all I ask for is a banana, I get three scoops of ice cream on top, in my three favorite flavors. If all I ask for is a banana and three scoops of ice cream, I get whipping cream on top. If all I ask for is a banana and three scoops of ice cream and whipping cream on top, I get nuts as well. If I only expect one cherry on top, I get three. How much better can life get? I can have my ice cream and eat it too. On a summer's day, I can enjoy all of you—the family of my choosing—all in the same place at the same time, just like three cherries on my banana split."

"The kid's getting mooshy on us," said Tim, but an appreciative silence followed.

Then Tim said, "Marijuana."

Taking the hint to continue the little ditty we had learned earlier, I said, "LSD."

"Love, peace, hippies," continued Elaine. "You and me," Janie said.

Softly we all chanted the chant together, not wanting to attract too much attention in Sambo's, especially since we were surreptitiously passing around a joint.

Then we came up with another version. "Marijuana," Tim said again.

"LSD," said Elaine.

"Hot fudge sundaes," I added. "You and me," everyone concluded.

BACK AT 2307, EVERYONE SPRAWLED on the living room floor and fell into sugar swoons, sleeping away the last heat of the afternoon. That was enough camping for one day.

Later we got up and played music and talked of this and that long into the night. Friends came and went throughout the evening, joining the jam session and contributing to the palaver.

We skipped supper, but around midnight Elaine joked, "Hey, who ate all the marshmallows?" And we repeated the little chant the children had taught us at Butte Meadows Family Campground.

In the wee hours, we all went out into the back yard of 2307 Mariposa Avenue and lay down on the cool ground, in a circle like spokes of a wheel, with our heads together at the hub. Holding hands, we watched the stars, feeling small, and naming the constellations.

Surely, an angel was sitting on my shoulder.

33

A Christmas Bizarre

I don't pretend to remember everything about Christmas 1971. As the saying goes, "If you remember it, you weren't there," but several salient memories ring clear as sleigh bells.

The previous Christmas had taken me to Lafayette cold and hungry and alone, with bronchitis that developed into full-blown pneumonia. This second Christmas was in stark contrast. I was healthy, and I was at choice: I could stay at the Mariposa house and have friends and family around, or I could go to Lafayette and enjoy the company of my brother and stepsisters and Janie all under one roof. This was an affirmation that everything happened for a reason. Even the stepfamily I deplored had brought me two stepsisters and a stepbrother I enjoyed, whom I could claim as my own. I had no call to dislike them just because their mother wasn't my favorite person. (It was during the Mariposa time that I stopped calling Elise and Elaine stepsisters and began calling them sisters; and stepbrother Mark became Brother Mark.)

Everyone I cared about was there: This was the realization of my Mariposa dream, to put together the Humpty Dumpty pieces of my broken family as best I could. The past could never be regained. Who would want that, anyway? If it meant I would have to relive the horrors of the past, it wouldn't be worth it. Or perhaps it would mean that I would be eternally stuck in childhood, never having the opportunity to grow up and make love with Janie. No, life was better this way, with an entirely new configuration.

MY FATHER'S GOLF PANTS

When I entered the Lafayette house, there was Tim, emerging from the hallway in red pants.

"Dad's golf pants," he said. The mere fact that he was there at all was a major triumph. Our father had been true to the words he had said on the day of our Two New Windows talk: "Bring Tim here." He and Dad had been in contact over the past year, and this was our first Christmas together—Tim's, Dad's, and mine—in twelve years.

Millie's interference in their relationship was taking a temporary hiatus. Her obstruction was far from over, but the years of estrangement were. For the next thirty years, until she died, Millie set herself up as the dragon at the gate. In her mind she was protecting my father from his black sheep son, Tim; but, by dribs and drabs, Tim and Dad cobbled together an ongoing relationship, and in the end, Tim returned triumphant as the prodigal son.

When I asked Tim how things were going, he said, "Been up all night on 'Dexies'. Can't sleep, so I just roam the house. Nothing much to do, and Millie doesn't like it, but it's pretty cool being here with Dad. Check out these threads."

Later in private, Millie confirmed this assessment: "Your poor brother; he's so restless. What's wrong with him? All he does is stay up all day and night, roaming the hall." She seemed more bewildered than angry. These words seemed out of place coming from her. They comprised the only compassionate thing I ever remember her saying about Tim.

LAFAYETTE BECOMES HAWAII

I think it must have been sometime Christmas Day that several of us hooked up with step-cousin Pat whose parents lived nearby.

She was visiting from Maui where she lived with her pot-grower husband. Something about the tropical climate creates potent pot. All I remember is standing at the top of the hill overlooking the reservoir behind our house. The reservoir became the bright blue Pacific; the oak chaparral, a lush tropical forest, palm trees and all. Lafayette never looked so much like Hawaii.

LOVE ON A CHAISE LONGUE

On Christmas Eve, when the time came to make sleeping arrangements, Millie played traditional mom. Janie and I were not married; therefore, we were not to sleep together. (I thought this was especially ironic considering Millie's own daughter, who had not yet come out of the closet, was sleeping under the same roof with her lesbian lover, but who was I to violate my sister's confidence?) We weathered the first night with Janie in the living room and me down the hall. All I can say is, on Christmas Day, where there's a will there's a way. Cousin Pat's pot must have acted as an aphrodisiac. Janie was wearing a mini skirt. A minor underwear adjustment was all it took. Dinner was rapidly approaching while we were *in flagrante delicto* on the chaise in the bedroom at the end of the hall. When my stepsister came to tell us we were late to supper, she wasn't any the wiser as to why we were late to dinner. Janie had her legs crossed. When we came to the dining room with Cheshire cat grins on our faces, everybody was waiting, fork in hand. Should I say it was a very relaxing meal, there among the white linen, Limoges and silver?

During dinner, on the wall behind me was a painting of a nude that my father and Millie had picked up in Bali. The exotic woman depicted was petite; she had dark skin, black hair, and small breasts. She was quite beautiful. During a lag in the conversation my father pointed at the nude and inquired, "Janie, that picture looks just like you. Were you the model?"

A very uncomfortable silence followed.

THE CASE OF THE DISAPPEARING PEN

Christmas night, when it was time for Dad and Millie to go to bed around eleven, Millie was still into her control thing. She was also three sheets to the wind. Tim and Janie and I, and Elise's love, Mary, and Elaine all crowded into the bedroom at the end of the hall. We thought we'd visit quietly and not bother anyone because none of us was ready to go to bed yet, and there were some joints to be smoked in private. We were happily talking and taking turns drawing pictures on the Etch A Sketch. Everyone was sitting on the floor, except I was sitting at a desk, calligraphy pen in hand, writing some swirly hippie calligraphy to my father on powder blue linen:

"I have a very good goblet.
I will share it with you."

I didn't have a goblet with me, but under the influence of *ganja*, I thought the message extremely profound, and I was sure my father would "grok" it. Just then the bedroom door burst open and Millie staggered in. She had to hold onto the doorjamb to stay upright. "All you kids GO TO BED NOW!" I knew she had two reasons for issuing this order. First, she thought we might keep her awake. Fair enough. Second, she thought Janie and I might sleep together. She was wrong on the first account and right on the second, but what business was it of hers? We were young adults.

After some attempts at negotiation, it was clear she wasn't giving up, drunk or not drunk. Suddenly, she fastened upon me as the ringleader. "Put that pen down now!" She was outnumbered, and now she was attempting to micromanage the situation. If she could break me down, the rest of the group might cave in.

She apparently didn't share the same sentiment we youngsters did, that this was the first Christmas any of us had ever spent together as a unit; that we were blending our two families and our friends and lovers into a preferred alliance. *We were stardust, we were golden*! All across the country, family reunions were being held on Christmas night. A series of paradigm shifts were occurring, one person, one family, and one interaction at a time. We were part of a much bigger picture in which a cultural cycle of uptightness was being broken. New human geometries were being formed every minute; yet, Millie wanted us "kids" to go to bed? The nerve of that woman!

I looked at the tall woman who had loomed so large in my upbringing, and suddenly she looked pathetic and weak and very small. While I was thinking of telling her how very much this gathering meant to me, I knew my words would fall on deaf ears. I murmured, "You just don't get it, do you?"

"Give me that pen NOW!"

"Okay," I said, "You want the pen, here it is," and I proffered it in her direction. She let go of the doorjamb, and stumbled across the room. She reached for the pen, but her hand was inscribing wobbly circles in the air. Extending the pen in her direction, I tried to catch up with her hand, but my motions only confused her and made her more uncoordinated. Finally, I stood up, grasped her right hand with my left, and willfully placed one end of the pen in the palm of her right hand. I'm sure she was thinking, 'Victory at last!' with the pen in her grasp, but I pulled it back into my possession, leaving her standing there with only the cap in hand. I sat down and continued writing.

She must have felt very foolish, not to mention too drunk to do battle. With a bewildered expression, she looked at her hand as she continued to bob and weave.

What happened next was even funnier. She tried to put the cap back on the pen! I even tried to "help". The more I aimed to insert the pen back in the cap's little hole, the more she weaved, and the more confused she got.

She gave up, put the cap back on the desk, and stumbled out of the room.

We stayed up late into the night, talking and signifying and passing the doobie. We were all very good and didn't make any loud noises to wake the dead or disturb anyone. At some point we were visited by Mr. Munchies, and I hatched a very rude idea. I'll tell you about that next, but first this footnote:

Janie and I obeyed the rules that night. We didn't sleep together. After love on the chaise, we didn't need to.

A VISIT FROM MR. MUNCHIES

Given that we were all smoking pot, it was only natural that at some point we would get a case of the munchies. We didn't want to clatter about in the kitchen eating leftovers. What could we do?

"Dad bought a five pound box of See's candy, and it's on top of the piano in the living room…." I trailed off, letting the profundity of five pounds of Sees soak in.

Elise had a conscience. "Yes, but he's saving it for company tomorrow."

A discussion ensued:

> *We could each take just one piece.*
> *Yes, but we're stoned, and it would be impossible to eat just one piece!*

We can wait until tomorrow. Are you kidding?

And so on. It was then that I came up with one of the best and dumbest ideas of my young lifetime.

"Well, guys, here's how I figure it. You know how everyone who ever eats Sees wants to know what's inside each piece? And then, you choose a piece, thinking it's your favorite vanilla caramel and it turns out to be yucky nougat? Well, we can do everyone a favor, guests included, if we eat half of each piece. Then everyone will know what they're getting."

Elise: "Well, I don't know. Your dad might get pretty pissed."

She was outvoted, and I volunteered to sneak down the hall and bring the box back to the bedroom.

We ate with guilty pleasure.

The next day when all the company had gathered, my father handed the box to his best friend. He set the box on his lap and removed the lid. Everything on the top layer was normal. The box went around to about fifteen people until the first layer was consumed. Then off came the corrugated whatchmacallum divider thing, and we were busted.

It would have been a little nicer had we used a knife to cut our samples. Every half piece had teeth marks. Now *that* was uncouth.

My father kept his composure, more or less. He collected the box, replaced the top, and put it back on the piano, and the party went on. "Kids always get into things," he said.

The chocolate didn't go to waste. Since none of the guests ate any of the half pieces we'd so kindly left, we finished off the box later that night.

I got around to apologizing to my father thirty-five years later.

WE TAKE A RIDE IN GYPSY MOTH

The day after Christmas, despite all our shenanigans, my father did something generous that I'll never forget. If I had only one memory to savor from that Christmas, this would be it. It seems especially poignant to me now, given that my father died two years ago.

When I suggested he take a ride with me in the Step Van (dubbed "Gypsy Moth"), he agreed, but took it one step better. He organized the whole clan—the same ones who had pilfered his box of Sees—to hop into Gypsy Moth and go to Baskin Robbins, his treat. Millie, of course, declined, but I derived cruel and callow pleasure from inviting her, knowing she would refuse. "Oh, gee, I'm sorry Millie. We'll miss you," I intoned insincerely, trying my best to say it straight and keep the sarcasm out of my voice, and savoring my duplicity.

Looking back now, it seems my father's willingness to take everyone out in my van made a statement. He loved and supported his sons, even though he didn't say so, despite his wife's disapproval. With John Whitcomb, actions spoke louder than words. As well, given Millie's intolerance of my brother and her disapproval of my lifestyle, it seems as if the trip to Baskin Robbins was almost an act of defiance on his part. A year earlier, he had grown his hair and beard long to make a statement to his coworkers. Now here he was, riding in the hippie van, treating the whole crew to some righteous munchies.

34

A Visit with Em

"Now here you go again
You say you want your freedom
Well who am I to keep you down
It's only right that you should
Play the way you feel it
But listen carefully to the sound
Of your loneliness
Like a heartbeat drives you mad
In the stillness of remembering
what you had and what you lost."
"Dreams" by Stevie Nicks,
Fleetwood Mac

One day in April of '72, Betsy came over and told me Em was back in town. She and her husband and baby were living in a house across the street from the entrance to Lower Bidwell Park, and Em was teaching English at the University. Ever generous, Betsy brokered a meeting. It took me a few days to work up my nerve, but I finally called. Em seemed abstracted, but agreed to meet me at her house the following day. I made the specific request that her husband not be there.

"I know that might sound inappropriate, but I want to see just you, not him." She agreed, and it was all set.

It all seemed so weird. Who was this person?

We'd met in our freshman year, and we were inseparable, except for our junior year when she went to Sweden and I to Spain, but even then we spent our Christmas vacation and summer together traveling around Europe. In our senior year, we started to come unraveled. She met Dennis, and one sad night in late May of '68 she handed me my walking papers. Dennis was a real straight arrow, a local Chico guy who came from an intact nuclear family that had never known tragedy. Dennis enlisted in the Air Force, and Em followed him to Del Rio, Texas. She gave birth to her daughter ten months after she and I split up, which obviously meant she was having sex with the interloper a scant month after she and I split up. It was a fact of life, but one that bothered me deeply. I felt so ripped off. Here I had spent four years with her "saving ourselves for each other" against the day when we would be married. We petted heavily, slept together, even got naked as time went on, but technically I was still a virgin when we separated. On our last night together, I begged to be inside her just once, but it was very brief, unsatisfying, and, given the circumstances, unbearably sad. No wonder I felt fundamentally ripped off and rejected on the deepest level when I heard she was pregnant so soon after we split up. It all seemed so unexpected, so sudden and confusing.

On the way across town, I retraced most of the route I had taken two years before on the day I found the house on Mariposa Avenue.

In the movie that was my life, an aerial shot captures the narrator riding his bicycle. The soundtrack plays "These Eyes" by Guess Who:

These eyes watched my world come to an end
These eyes could not accept and pretend

The hurtin's on me, and I can never be free....

As the narrator snaps down the kickstand of his bicycle in front of a lovely Craftsman-style house with a broad porch, the soundtrack fades on these lyrics:

These eyes have seen a lot of love
but they'll never see another one like I
had with you...

What the movie does not depict are the thoughts running through the narrator's mind.

I savored yet dreaded our meeting.

You might say I had an agenda. I was carrying both a torch and a grudge. Since Em and I had never fully consummated our sexual relationship, I wanted to set that straight. I knew it was senseless—with her and Dennis being married, and her being a mother—but I thought maybe she and Dennis were practitioners of Free Love and the Open Marriage. I could show her a thing or two. I thought the old magic could return, and then some. The voices in my head were having a debate.

Haven't you had enough sex in the last three years?

Yes, but I could always use some more. I just want this one time with her, to let her know how much I love her, to make up for lost time.

You fool! You bloody fool! Get over her. It's over. It's done.

Move on.

Yes, but I can't be held accountable for my actions when I see her. My love for her is overwhelming and all encompassing.

Give it up.

As I stepped up on the porch, adrenaline had my heart pumping fast, and I had to take some deep breaths to calm down. No one was home. Was she avoiding me? I sat on the porch and looked toward Bidwell Park in the direction of the tree where Em and I had "made out" one night in our sophomore year, and I had told her about my brother's death. Here in this compassionate young woman I was finally able to confide the deep dark secret my stepmother had so adamantly forbidden me to tell about the death of my brother. The confession brought catharsis in an hour-long crying jag. That night Em became everything and everybody to me. That must have been difficult for her, because those shoes were too much for one person to fill.

I was just about ready to give up and leave Em's place when I saw her approaching on the sidewalk. She still looked like Em, but her strawberry blonde hair was shorter and her glasses had been updated from the sixties cat's-eye look. She still had her slim, girlish figure. However, she did look somehow rounder and more mature, something I attributed to motherhood.

When she came up her walkway, three personae were observing her: The old me, the new me, and my ally, Hawk (more about him later). My old self cried out to run to her and press myself against her and nuzzle her neck and smell her hair and hold on forever. The new me somehow couldn't resolve the image of this seeming stranger with the load of grief I'd been carrying around. Hawk hovered and watched the scene with dispassionate interest. This triad continued throughout our visit.

She asked me how long I'd been waiting and told me she'd been visiting a neighbor, another English professor. Seeing her after all this time, I was nearly speechless, but somehow managed to engage in chit chat. We went inside, and the "surfacey" conversation continued. It all seemed so surreal, for two people who had been so intensely and intimately involved to be conversing like two people who had just met for the first time. Had the intensity of our four years together been merely a figment of my imagination?

She told me Dennis was at work and their girl was with the babysitter.

At that point I thought, *Alone at last. Now I can make my move.*

She told me she was on an assistantship, working on her Master's Degree in English, and she asked what I'd been up to.

I quipped, "While you've been working on your English degree, I've been getting my doctorate in Sexology."

"Oh? I didn't know you could get a degree in that. What kind of degree is that? Where are you getting it?" I wanted to wisecrack about "getting it" between the sheets. She was either playing it straight, or she didn't get what I was leading up to. I decided she really thought there might be such a degree.

Instead of cracking wise, I said, "It's not through any university. It involves direct personal research—you know, the Free Love thing and all that." I told her about finding the Mariposa house, and about Janie and the others. I refrained from saying I was still angst-ridden because of her departure, instead saying, "I needed some time to get my head straight, so I took it. I've been seeking God through direct mystical experience, and the senses are the pathway to that experience, chiefly through Tantric sex."

"What's that?" she asked.

Her question was my perfect lead-in. "That's where the man withholds orgasm. Instead, he and the woman concentrate on passing the energy back and forth in an infinite loop of ecstasy. This allows the sex to last for hours sometimes, and the woman can have her due with multiple orgasms. I can show you sometime if you like."

"Hmmm…."

"How about right now? Right there on your bed." I gestured toward the bed, which was visible from the living room where we stood.

For a few long beats, she seemed to be weighing the option. She held her gaze on the bed, then looked at her watch. "Well.... That would be nice, but I'm not so sure...."

"I know, the marriage thing and all that. Don't you and Dennis practice Free Love?"

"I know a lot of people are doing that nowadays. Dennis and I have discussed it. I was all for it, and we were going to do it until Dennis realized there were a lot more guys interested in me than women interested in him. He's not in favor of the idea anymore."

"Well, you like the idea, so c'mon, let's get down! I can give you more pleasure in an hour than...." I wanted to say, "....than that blockheaded, begoggled bastard who stole you away from me!" but instead I said, "....than Dennis ever has or will. C'mon, just this once. No cost, no obligation. We'll be good to each other, and you'll love it. How about it?"

Suddenly she changed tack. "Would you like some tea? Something to eat?"

I thought of oral pleasure that didn't involve food. "No, thanks."

"Are you sure? C'mon, have a snack."

"I was hoping for more than a snack."

"Well, fix yourself a sandwich, then. Go ahead, raid the refrigerator."

I got her drift, and changed gears as well. "Sure, what do you have?"

While I raided the fridge, we caught up on family news and happenings of recent times. It was easy and relaxed, but with the sex issue tabled, there was still the next item on my agenda, the unacknowledged elephant in the room. The old me wanted to cry out, "Why did you leave me?" But discussing that seemed like an exercise in futility. Maybe the question should have been, "We were together once, you and I, weren't we? And then you did leave me, right?" The present seemed disassociated from the past. It seemed so surreal. I could have been this woman's husband, hanging out in the kitchen of our home, waiting to pick up our daughter at the babysitter's, but I wasn't. Where had our dreams gone?

We finished in the kitchen and cleaned up and she escorted me to the door. Every cell of my being strained toward her, desiring to consummate a relationship that I now knew was finished.

I offered her a hug, and she accepted. It was somewhat formal, but it lasted a long time. I felt something settle in me. We had met as wounded children. We were adults now, in a different time and place. She seemed much more settled in her lifestyle than I, but that was the way of things. *She has a plan for her life, and I'm not in it.*

I nuzzled my face into her hair, and breathed in a thousand memories.

I whispered, "I miss you."

"I miss you, too," she said, and our visit was over.

As I mounted the bicycle, I had one bemused thought: *In the end I settled for half a block of Jack cheese, and a dozen Triscuits, and a hug that lasted a century.*

I rode the rest of the way home in the stillness of remembering what I had, and what I lost.

35

Down Butte Creek Without a Paddle

"I looked around and the waters flowing
had finally finally found me."
Fleetwood Mac

Geno the Scorpio flung himself into the flood-swollen river first. He mounted a tree overhanging Butte Creek and scaled the highest branches so that no single branch would hold him but collectively many twigs held him as he spread his own limbs like a spider in its web. He clung and weaved and swayed until you couldn't tell the difference between him and the wind-swung branches. Borrowing energy gathered from the tree, he let go, and the tree itself flung him in. Like an arrow shot from a bow, he flew out over Butte Creek, and he hung there in a Zen archer pose for a moment before dropping down the twenty-five feet to the rusty brown flood.

We chose this day on purpose, Geno and Jim and I. Perhaps it was the boredom of ten straight days of rain, huddling around the stove at 2307, running out of pot to smoke and stories to tell, that hatched the idea. (I had even recited the *Prologue to the Canterbury Tales* twice, for lack of anything better to do.) We decided to wait till the creek was cresting at fifteen feet, and go for a swim. We wanted to experience the power of the river. We got a little more than we bargained for, but we survived to tell the tale. We wore no helmets, no lifejackets, and common sense was missing as well.

We each chose our own way to enter the water, according to our nature. Geno's was the most spectacular. Mine was more mundane. I stood on the cut bank and jumped in. After Jim saw what happened to us, he went way upstream before entering the water.

It seemed that Geno didn't come up for a long time. When he did, he was already two hundred feet downstream. If he didn't make it to our goal, the opposite bank, he would be swept downstream around a dogleg and into a meat grinder of stones where any attempt to stand up might result in foot entrapment that would lead to certain drowning. At the least, one would be knocked off one's feet and beaten up on the rocks. Just before the dogleg, the choices weren't much better. About twenty feet out from the shoreline stood a giant sycamore with a wad of debris at its base. Between the tree and the shore, a series of serious strainers blocked passage. Anyone swept into those would be just another twig knitted into the growing web of debris.

When Geno hit the base of the tree, he flung himself high enough to avoid being pinned under the ball of flotsam. He climbed on top of the ball and puzzled out his course of action as Jim and I watched. He shinnied forty feet up the leaning sycamore and puzzled some more. Finally, he took a leap of faith, literally, throwing himself like a rhesus monkey to the awaiting branches of a tree on the shore. He climbed down and waited for us.

I knew the water was fast and cold, and I respected it, yet I wasn't prepared for how quickly I was swept downstream. In those few seconds before I became pinned on a root wad, I felt the adrenaline-filled ecstasy of daredevils everywhere. In some recess of my brain it occurred to me that I had almost died a year before, drowning in my own bodily fluids, but now every sense was on full alert and I was in the flow of life, taking a risk and loving it. Even my best collegiate strokes carried me only as far as the debris ball, and I crashed with an audible thump. I was pinned. Jim and Geno watched for half an hour while I pried first one limb, then the other off the debris like pulling a heavy-duty suction cup off a wall. Being naked didn't help. Hypothermia was setting in. If I made one wrong move, the river jerked me back down. Compounding the problem was the fact that the ball of debris was undercut. Every time I moved, the current tried to suck me under. At one point I was up to my eyes and slowly going under. The weirdest thought occurred to me. With only my nose above the surface, I was counting one, two, and three like the old joke of a drowning man holding his fingers above the water, counting off his last three seconds. Little by little I managed to inch my way back up the debris and climb on top.

Geno had climbed the tree, but I had a fear of heights, and this didn't seem like the time to try to overcome it. I spotted a partly submerged log lodged between the bank and my perch on top of the root wad. Ever so carefully I managed to climb down onto the log and cross its twenty-foot length on all fours. Had I slipped, I would have been fired like a torpedo into the strainer only twenty feet downstream.

Now Jim took a line of caution. He went 150 feet farther upstream and jumped in feet first. Just as Geno and I had traveled a great distance under water before surfacing, so did Jim. He was angling strongly for shore and making good progress, but he had miscalculated. Soon it became apparent that he was going to enter the dead man's zone between the sycamore and shore. I could see the recognition of his potential fate in his eyes as they got big and round. Miraculously, like the college halfback he was, all in one motion he purposely struck the log (which I had crossed) with his chest, and vaulted himself into a standing position on top. I can still see it in my mind's eye like a slow motion movie, running in reverse, of a Slinky climbing the stairs. From there, with his excellent balance he simply crossed to shore on the log.

We had each crossed the river and survived in a manner suited to our individual personalities and capabilities.

Now we were water-bound, naked and cold, while our clothing and transportation was on the opposite shore where we began. I was hoping no one had stolen our clothing or car. (I was thinking, *Hitchhiking home wouldn't be so bad, but try it naked!*)

The river had schooled us and now we were smarter. We went upstream about a quarter of a mile. There the water flowed in a deep channel between cut banks and overhanging trees. We had an entirely pleasant swim, riding a wave train through a tunnel of greenery, back to the point where we had originally thrown ourselves in but no farther. There we got out, safely.

Now hot baths in the clawfoot tub and dry clothing and bowls of brown rice awaited us back home at 2307. We had something new to talk about around the stove, and a memory that bonds us to this day.

36

Walkabout in Butte Creek Canyon

"My inner child is outward bound."
George Carlin

My days on Mariposa Avenue would soon be coming to an end. For three years since graduating from college (the last two on Mariposa Avenue), I had wandered in the dreamtime. Midway through those years, I survived a near death illness. Soon, I would complete my teaching credential, and 2307 Mariposa Avenue would recede in my rear view mirror. What better way to celebrate, and ponder upcoming changes, than a walkabout in Butte Creek Canyon? This would be my swan song

THERE WILL BE HAREMS, AND RUMORS OF HAREMS

Rumors had been going around about a man living in a treehouse in Butte Creek Canyon. Word was that he had his own private harem consisting of several beautiful young women. Jim must have been the one to tell me about this, because his old girlfriend Cher was one of the women in question.

One weekend shortly after my birthday in May of '72, I thought I'd ride my bicycle up the canyon for an overnight campout. Allegedly, I would be doing some firsthand research on the geology of the canyon, preparing a unit of study for my student teaching beginning the following Monday morning, but I was more interested in opportunities that might arise with women of the canyon.

First I'd drop by Butte Creek Family on the way, take a sweat bath, hang out on the soft sandy beach and hope to hook up with some lovely young lady. I fantasized spending the night in the arms of Marilyn in her hobbit house; or Goat Woman in her geodesic dome; or Carrot Woman in her cabin, if her sometime guy, Zig Zag Man, wasn't around. If a tryst wasn't happening at the commune, one of the Family would probably know about the treehouse and tell me how to find it. Maybe I'd get lucky with one (or more) of the treehouse women. The possibilities had me revved up like a randy pup.

If the treehouse harem weren't receptive, I'd heard another rumor, that an old girlfriend, Susan, (not to be confused with Sue of "Pretty Arms") was living somewhere in the canyon, but, with nothing more specific than that, I didn't expect to find her. One way or another, I thought, I ought to be able to get my horns trimmed this weekend. In another compartment of my brain, I was thinking,

Why this obsession with sex? Why not just go upcanyon like you did last year, take whatever comes, and enjoy yourself?

My focus on getting laid, and my plan to have a quiet walkabout, were at odds with each other.

A TEST OF ENDURANCE

Even seventeen months after collapsing with pneumonia on someone's front lawn, not all of my endurance had returned. This forty-mile roundtrip was to be a test of my stamina, so I left 2307 Mariposa at 7:00 a.m. on Saturday, May 20, hoping to have time to pace myself before the thermometer climbed too high for comfort.

The several miles ride to the south edge of town was flat, familiar, and easy. A slight elevation gain up Highway 32 to the Helltown turnoff presented no challenge, but I started to work up a sweat on the gradual climb to the covered bridge, four miles upcanyon. After that, the gradient increased along with the thermometer reading. When sweat started dripping off my nose, I started thinking how Albert Schweitzer, the missionary doctor in Africa, had said he never looked at the thermometer because then he'd know how hot he really was; I was thankful I didn't have a thermometer with me.

On the steep grade after the covered bridge, my still-recovering body just didn't have enough "oomph" to make the climb. Walking the bike was easier, so I did that, puffing hard and stopping often, until the downgrade to the steel bridge brought speed and relief. Then, more climbing to the dirt turnoff put me on an easy coast down toward Helltown, which was no town at all, but just a crossing over Butte Creek.

THE CASE OF THE DISAPPEARING COMMUNE

I thought I'd check in with Butte Creek Family.

The previous year, in May, a peaceful day of hanging out in the canyon had been enough. Before my herb hunt, I hung out on Butte Creek Family's sandy beach with other naked people, swam, and took a sweat bath. I played my flute, flirted with the ladies of the canyon, and they flirted back. After hanging out with the Family, I went to Helltown and gathered chamomile, yarrow, and golden seal to clear my still-congested lungs. (It worked!) On that previous walkabout, even though I fantasized about getting it on with the beautiful women of the Butte Creek Family commune, I had happily gone home to make love with Janie. This time would be different. Nominally, I was between girlfriends, not having broken with Janie (though I was weighing that choice), and not having taken up with Betsy. Wanting to wean myself from Janie, I was on a month-long sex fast, to see if I could stand it. The thought of a potential liaison with one of the nubile women of the canyon had me revved up like a horny teenager, obsessed with the notion that this year's walkabout might be a reprise of every Free Love moment I'd ever known since my stepsister's friend relieved me of my virginity at my belated age of 23.

Following the trail downhill, across the 80 acres, to the sandy beach by the creek, I found the beach empty. Something didn't feel right, not the same as before. The frame of the sweat lodge was still up, but nobody had draped it yet this year. The fire ring used to heat the rocks was filled with sand and cool to the touch. Maybe I got here too early; just sit and wait. Some hippie-looking guy I'd never seen before came down to the creek carrying a bucket. He eyed me suspiciously, not answering my greeting, filled his bucket, and went back the way he'd come.

The weather was getting hot and I wanted a cooling swim, but now I felt unwelcome and strangely inhibited.

Sitting in the shade, I meditated; but, too restless to sit, I stripped off my shorts and tank top and dipped in the creek. A dark-haired woman came to the creek carrying her water bucket, and filled it. Looking at me, she asked, "May I help you?" the way people do when they don't really want to help you; they just want to know what the hell you're doing there; they want you to leave.

Maybe she thinks I'm a redneck, with my newly cut hair. Other than the fact that I was naked, I wasn't wearing any beads or anything to identify me as one of the clan.

I told her I was just hanging out as usual. "Do you know somebody here?"

I got the game. "Sure, how about Carrot Woman?"

"She's with Richard now." She said frostily, in a tone that seemed to defend Carrot Woman's honor.

"Then, how 'bout Goat Woman?"

"She's in New Mexico on a vision quest."

"Marilyn?"

"She's with Michael now. They're getting *married*."

"I know Michael from the college dorm. I was his Resident Advisor."

"I think Michael and Marilyn are busy." Then she got to the point. "Do you know this is private property?"

I was getting irritated. "Private property? I've been coming up here for years, even before Butte Creek Family ever saw the place. You folks are newcomers. I used to come here when Old Man Snow owned the place. Raised goats, he did. I visited him in his house, way before all these different people came and built their rickety little shelters."

"This is private property," she repeated.

"I thought this was a commune. At least it used to be.

"We're not a *commune*," she sniffed. "We're a *community*, and this is private property."

"Who owns it now?"

"Some of us went in and bought it together. Others who live here are supposed to pay rent. We allow them to keep their structures and stay here, but some of them don't pay, so we have problems."

So much for my fantasy of skinny-dipping, sweat lodging, making love, and spending the night.

"Tell you what," I said. "Say hello to my friends for me." I told her my name and spelled it. "I'm going for one more quick swim to cool off. Then I'm going up the canyon. Have you heard about some folks living in a treehouse up there?"

"Yes, but I don't know them." She turned and walked up the bank with her bucket of water. As an afterthought, she turned and said, "Watch out for that old guy up there. He's been bothering some of us lately," and she left without supplying more details.

ZENCOUNTER AT THE SWIMMING HOLE

Disappointed and in disbelief, I rode my bike off the property and turned down the dirt road to Helltown, upstream of the commune that wasn't a commune anymore.

Rejecting the swinging bridge as too tricky with my bike, I lifted it over the barrier blocking the car bridge and crossed the creek. Upstream a short distance, shade and a refreshing swim awaited. Sitting in the cool overhang of a volcanic rock, I drank from the stream, ate a few nuts, and wondered what I'd find upstream and upcanyon besides worrying star thistles and chaparral. What harebrained idea brought me here, twenty miles from home, feeling weak, with no sleeping bag, little clothing, and a few handsful of nuts?

Weariness overtook me, the same kind of overpowering fatigue that had been affecting me ever since I had become gravely ill seventeen months before. I would run around feeling great for a few hours; then zap! I'd be down for the count. Perhaps a nap would restore my energy. Hunkered in a little cave, where there was just enough room to sit hunched over or lie down, I scrunched around until the bedrock of the cave best fitted my form. I was reminded of the inscription scratched on the ceiling of Gene's cave two Thanksgivings before: *Teach me*. Now, as I lay fatigued in my cool space, I said a prayer to Mother Nature and the spirits of the canyon: "Teach me," and I drifted into dreamland.

HAWK DREAM

I mentioned Hawk previously. He became my Ally during an out-of-body experience when I was ill. Through Hawk's eyes I found myself able to view any situation dispassionately, from a distance.

Now, in my little cave, I dreamed that I dwelt in the eyes of my Ally, Hawk, flying in the stratosphere with a view of the whole earth. Hawk took me on a journey, reviewing scenes from my past.

Hawk hovers over Spain. He sees a young, virgin man lying beside a lovely young blonde named Em in a pension in Barcelona. The young man's manhood is achingly erect and he is extremely frustrated. He wants to be inside her. They have been apart for five months, and this is their first time of being completely nude together. He thinks they have an understanding, but once inside her very briefly, his first time ever, she tells him to stop. Hawk sees that the young man feels extremely rejected, so near yet so far from the natural fulfillment that nature ought to provide. Hawk soars and sees many more unconsummated nights of sleeping together in Marseilles, Genoa, Naples, Rome, Munich, Vienna, Prague, West Berlin, London, and Paris.

Hawk speaks to the young man, and the dreamer residing in the eyes of Hawk comes to terms with the past: "You were both so young and inexperienced, but you loved well, and you did the best you could at the time. Do not fret. Your life has been good."

Now I'm in the eyes of Hawk flying west, and diving, diving until I've lost the curvature of the earth and we are falling over California, spiraling down to Chico until we hover over an apartment on Sacramento Avenue where Em and the young man lay on their last night together. Hawk sees the jilted young man walking out of the apartment, down the stairs, and out to the curb, at a total loss as to what to do, looking left, looking right, then shrugging and walking away.

Next Hawk hovers over the Captain America house on Second Street, and he sees the young man again, lying in bed with Susan, feeling the same sense of longing and lack of fulfillment he felt with Em in Barcelona, craving a deeper involvement with Susan which he knows will never occur, and feeling very unsatisfied despite his sexual activity with her because he still yearns for the lost Em. Hawk flies away to hover over 2307 Mariposa Avenue.

With Hawk's eyes, I can see through the roof as if it wasn't there. Through the dispassionate eyes of Hawk, I take in a slow montage of Mariposa scenes and seasons that seem to be a summary of my Mariposa years: People coming and going, eating in the kitchen, playing music; soft sweet voices of young women, laughter; smells of brown rice, bay leaves, frangipani, wet leaves, the scent of Dr. Bronner's peppermint soap; musky smells, and the sight of a young man writhing on the bed with a series of women.

Hawk's memory recalls an image of a young man lying gravely ill and remembers merging with the young man's spirit to become his Ally.

Despite the dispassionate point of view of Hawk, sex in the dream must have been getting to me. A painful bulge in my gym shorts awoke me. The urge got me to speculating. They were still out there, somewhere, all those women I'd gotten it on with in the Mariposa dreamtime, but where were they now? As my eyes started to flicker open, in a foggy state I pieced together where I was, lying semi-naked in a cave next to Butte Creek in the canyon, reliving the frustration of a horny virgin. Simultaneously, I missed Janie and realized we might not ever be together again. I thought about Betsy, and wondered why I would want to drop Janie for someone so sexually naïve. As well I remembered my disappointing visit, earlier in the day, to the disappearing commune.

What if I masturbated? Bad idea! I'd have nothing left for the women of my fantasy canyon weekend.

Then I thought about Susan (not to be confused with Sue of "Pretty Arms"). Three years earlier, she had left her fiancé in the lurch and come out from New Jersey in quest of the Haight-Ashbury experience. With her 4.0 grade average from Montclair University, she figured she was too smart for college, and dropped out of Chico State after a semester. She was a bright and beautiful cheerleader with a personality that attracted me instantly. When I met her, she was working at the natural foods store, a place called Etidorhpa (Aphrodite spelled backward).

Lying in my hidey hole, I remembered how we'd been together for a time; how she would pop out of some hiding place at 7:30 a.m. when I came home from graveyard shift at Continental Nut Company, and we'd spend the morning talking excitedly in the Captain America house, listening to Miles Davis, lying on the bed, and sometimes...well, you know, but our sex was still kind of naïve and inhibited, yet sweet, bringing up the feelings of loss and loneliness that came with Em's departure. But now in my little cave, I suddenly thought, *Susan must be somewhere in the canyon at this very moment! Oh my god!)*

The thought hit me like a jolt of electricity. My juices were flowing like mad. Suddenly, I wanted Susan badly.

My senses told me someone was approaching the swimming hole on the path. All I could see from my vantage point in my little cave was a pair of feet, calves, and the hem of a dress. The woman seemed to twist first right, then left, as if checking to see who was around. Figuring she was about to drop her clothing, I thought I'd hang loose and watch her swim. In case she saw me, I didn't want her to feel alarmed, so I did drape my tank top over me, to hide my concupiscence.

"Oh, you're there," a sweet voice said. Her feet approached me. "I didn't see you." She knelt down. Now I could see her face.

It was Susan.

Was I still dreaming or was this going to be a dream come true?

She didn't seem to recognize me; I don't know why, because her Italian-looking, cherubic face framed by wavy brown hair was unmistakable to me. Perhaps the weight I lost when I was ill threw her off, or the shave and haircut. "Hi, Susan, why don't you stretch out here next to me where it's cool, and we can talk."

"Do I know you?"

"Of course you do. Think." I held her gaze with my eyes, willing her to recognize me.

She might have been stoned. She had that goofy Susan smile that I had always loved since the first moment I saw her.

She said she was going for a swim. Would I join her?

"No, I'm cool, you go ahead."

It was disconcerting to me that my former girlfriend seemed not to recognize me, and acted self-conscious about disrobing in front of me, but she went behind a rock to remove her wraparound, and soon her lovely young body submerged in the creek and she swam around.

Equally disconcerting was the fact that she put her shift back on when she came out of the water.

She came over and knelt next to my little cave. We had a session of few words and much nonverbal communication—long silences, smiling, gazing, slowly nodding, LSD kind of talk.

I didn't tell her my name because I wanted her to recognize me.

Finally, she stretched out on the ground just outside the entrance to my cave.

Wanting to be close, I crawled out and lay beside her, resting my head on her shoulder and my hand on her belly. "Is this okay?"

I asked. I took her silence for assent. My manhood was definitely still at full attention. I was keeping my cool and taking it slow, and things progressed rather nicely, but I still wasn't sure if she knew who I was or if she thought I was just some guy she had run into at the swimming hole. She didn't seem to be resisting, but she wasn't helping either. Was this casual receptivity or passive disinterest? Given the dreams I'd been dreaming, and her apparent uncertainty as to whom I was, it was confusing; and, though I felt confused and hurt, I still didn't tell her my name. Maybe she would remember my kiss, my smell, something. Worse, if I told her who I was, she would waste time with chitter-chatter. Yada yada yada. Maybe if she thought I was just some handsome dude she had just met, she would want to get it on with *him*, whoever *he* was. It was all very confusing and titillating at the same time.

I started stroking her face and casually moved to other parts. I felt that the hot dreams of a half hour before were being relived. I was back in Barcelona, feeling utterly rejected and lonely; but wait—wake up! Here's Susan in the canyon; let's make a better dream come true!

We were kissing sweetly, getting intimately reacquainted. I was thinking, maybe there was a good reason why I rode all this way on my bike today. To heck with Butte Creek Family and the horse they rode in on! Private property indeed. Maybe I'll never see the treehouse or meet the harem, who cares? Susan and I will just hang out right here by the creek all weekend, and get it on repeatedly like mountain lions.

We were still semi-clothed, but getting pretty warmed up. I had just rolled over on top of her when we heard voices coming down the path.

At this point, I didn't care if they turned into voyeurs. Being a woman, however, Susan found the approaching strangers distracting. Women are funny that way. At a crucial moment, a guy will shut out any distraction while a woman will suddenly shift mood and answer the doorbell.

Two guys and two women arrived. Chatting away, they took off their clothes and started swimming. I fantasized: *orgy!* But Susan asked me to get off her, and she went out to visit. At this point, I still had something to hide that my gym trunks weren't going to conceal, so I crawled back into the cave, feeling very frustrated and hoping to relax.

The others left, but the mood was broken, and after a while Susan said she was going up the hill to the place where she was living in the woods overlooking the canyon. When I suggested I go with her to complete our business, she said, "I'm living there with a lot of guys, and they all want to have sex with me. One of them was my boyfriend for a while, but now he's not, but he still wants to have sex with me, and sometimes we do, but he bugs me. Actually, I started having sex with him because I thought it would keep the other guys off me, but it just made them jealous and they all started getting obnoxious." Suddenly, I was wondering if I was obnoxious too. Still, just in case, I got directions to her shelter for a future visit.

I watched her walking away and thought, "Damn, I guess I am going upcanyon to the treehouse after all."

Feeling rejected, I rode my bike through dry grass and stickers, up a rise, until I found a trace heading upcanyon.

I MEET A MAN NAMED CLIFF

It occurred to me I was having a day like a fairy tale in which the main character is met with three challenges: First, the disappearing commune; then, the frustrating encounter with Susan; and, *now what?* I was about to follow the trail into a thicket when a grizzled old man emerged. He was carrying a plastic gallon jug in his left hand, in the crook of his fingers. He was red-faced, wore ragged blue jeans and a chambray shirt.

He turned his right side toward me. "Where the hell you going?" he demanded gruffly.

That's when I saw the gun. It was nickel plated and slung low in a holster. His right hand hung loosely near the ivory handle.

Right away I decided I didn't like his attitude. My training kicked in, from so many martial arts sessions with Barney in the back yard at Mariposa. I covered the eight feet between us in a flash. He didn't know what hit him. Soon I had him face down on the ground with his pistol hand twisted up behind his back. With my free hand, I unholstered his pistol, flipped the cylinder open, shook out the bullets, and tossed the gun into the poison oak.

Now, if you believe that, I have a very good gold brick I can sell you. Actually, the gun scared me, and his gruff manner didn't help; but, something told me I'd better go on the offensive, so I got right in his face. "None of your damned business, old man."

We circled each other like prizefighters. First he was uphill and I was down. Then I was uphill and he was down. Round and round we went, clockwise, jockeying for position. Finally I took a step counterclockwise and that threw him off balance. He stopped on the downhill side with the sun in his eyes.

"What the hell are *you* doing here, redneck? *That's* the question."

"Walkin' around with my jug. Here, drink some." He proffered the jug.

"Well, mister, that looks an awful lot like the 'lemonade' my brothers fooled me into drinking one hot summer's day. What you got there?"

"Can't say rightly. Panther piss, some call it."

"What's in it?"

"I don't tell no one, but it's got honey in it."

"Mead? You're making your own mead?"

"Go on. Have some."

I thought if I didn't take some, he might shoot me.

"Thanks, but I'm a Mormon."

While he took a tug on the jug, I pressed on.

"Didn't your mother ever tell you alcohol and guns don't mix? Why you carrying that peashooter?"

"For troublemakers." He wiped his mouth on his sleeve.

"Do you think I'm a troublemaker? Do you want toshoot me?"

"Not unless you make trouble."

"No trouble from me. I'm a peace-loving guy. Here, shake on it."

We shook hands and began to relax and have a conversation. I learned that his name was Cliff; he grew up on a farm in Oklahoma; he was dishonorably discharged from the Army during WWII for being drunk and AWOL; he didn't hate hippies or draft dodgers; and, he didn't give a damn about Vietnam. The whole time we were talking, I could sense my Ally, Hawk, nearby.

I felt more trusting, but not so trusting that I wanted to turn my back on Cliff. "Well, Cliff, I guess we're about done here. You worry me, my friend, walkin' around with that peashooter and gettin' drunk up here in the canyon. You know, my brother was killed with his own gun by a family member. I've got no use for guns. Next time, you oughta think about leaving the gun or the jug at home, one or t'other."

I still wanted him to be the first one to leave, but he wasn't budging. I had to improvise. "Hey Cliff, do you know Marilyn?"

"Can't say I do."

"Well, Cliff, she's young and real good lookin' and I just saw her and some of her beautiful women friends at the swimming hole by the bridge. They usually swim naked. You oughta go check them out."

As quickly as he had emerged from the bushes earlier, Cliff turned tail and started down the hill. I watched him till he was out of pistol range. He wobbled a little as he walked. I spoke aloud to myself: "Drunk old fucker couldn't hit the side of a barn with that .22."

I kept watching until Cliff was almost to the Helltown Bridge. Just then a red tail hawk swooped directly over Cliff's head and hovered as if getting ready to stoop. Then Hawk extended his wings and glided to alight on an oak tree. Hawk and I watched until Cliff ambled out of sight into the woods, carrying his jug of panther piss. Hawk took off again in Cliff's direction, as if leading the way.

A YELP FOR HELP

I walked my bike into the overgrown stretch of trail where Cliff had emerged earlier. After fifty feet of being rudely scratched by brush, and watching out for poison oak, I heard loud yelping that sounded like someone had stepped on a dog's foot. Slowing down so as not to alarm anyone or any wildlife, I crawled to the end of the brush tunnel where it gave into a clearing, and I peered through the branches in the direction of the noise. What looked like a domestic puppy was flattened on the ground, pawing its snout. It pawed and yelped, and pawed and yelped. When I approached to see if I could help, it got up and took off running into the woods and disappeared. It moved so fast, at first I wasn't sure if it was a dog or a coyote or a fox, but its bushy red tail told me it was a fox.

Stepping out into the clearing, I scanned the woods for an explanation of what I'd just seen. A hundred feet away, near where I'd seen the canine, I saw an unusual looking salt and pepper colored mound slightly larger than a rugby ball. It was so well camouflaged, I thought it might be an oak branch, but that afforded no explanation of the canine's behavior. The ball was twitching, so I walked slowly in its direction. The closer I got, the more it twitched.

Thinking to look at this object from the viewpoint of the yelping critter, I swung wide and examined the ground where the canine had been pawing its snout. The ground was scuffed, and I saw several long, thin, sharp objects whose color matched that of the twitching ball: porcupine quills!

I approached the porcupine again. The closer I got to it, the more it twitched and hissed, and it made several bluff charges in my direction. Each time it charged, it would stop and back up before repeating the gesture. This porcupine was not happy to see me, especially after a young, inexperienced fox had tried to attack it, bringing a discharge of quills into the hapless creature's snout. On the porcupine's back, a small bald spot revealed a number of quills missing. I tried talking sweet nothings to the agitated pin cushion, as one would to calm an aggressive dog, but it wanted no more of my attention than the fox pup's, so I walked back to the bike and started riding thetrace.

The porcupine and fox incident should have served as a warning that I shouldn't stick my nose where it didn't belong.

FINDING THE TREEHOUSE IN A BALL OF LIGHT

Before long, it became evident that two-wheeled travel was not going to be practical, so I locked the bike to a tree and continued bushwhacking on foot, setting cairns along the way to lead me back to the bike the next day.

The farther I went, the more the canyon narrowed, the steeper the terrain I was trying to traverse, and the more I slipped and slid and got scratched up in the chaparral. It was getting hot; I'd had no liquid to drink other than miming a pull on Cliff's jug, and just a handful of nuts and creek water since supper the night before. About to give up, I thought of going downhill to walk up the creek, but a steep, brushy draw separated me from its cooling water; nothing to do but forge ahead and look for a chance to attain the creek.

Before long, I came upon a game trail and followed it till it hooked up with a wider, apparently human-trod piece of trail that clung to the forty-five degree side of the canyon. I walked about twenty paces on this and stopped to look around. I could see the creek a few hundred feet downslope. A hundred feet up the trail, I could see a sort of notch into a relatively clear draw that might take me to the creek. Walking the hundred feet, and turning right at the notch, I found the treehouse almost by mistake. The trail forked right, down the notch. Starting down, I had to keep my eyes just in front of my feet to avoid slipping, but, reaching a level spot, I raised my eyes and there, in front of me, a narrow boardwalk seemed to stretch into a glowing ball of afternoon sun. Shading my eyes, I could see the boardwalk led straight into the silhouette of a stout oak.

After all the earlier difficulties, I was thinking, women in a treehouse: highway to heaven. I was also thinking, I wonder if a troll lives under this bridge, and if his name is Cliff.

By now the sun had passed the northwest rim of the canyon. I'd been bushwhacking for a couple of hours, and I guessed the time:

about five o'clock. When I stepped onto the boardwalk, I seemed to be walking in midair toward the heart of the tree in the heart of the sun. So bright was the heart that the treehouse structures were not clearly visible.

Approaching the center of the tree, I entered the golden ball and shielded my eyes with one hand until the boardwalk branched in two. One branch veered left in a long curve. Turning my back to the sun, I could drop my hand and look along a piece of boardwalk that went to my left. Twenty feet along, a very well constructed treehouse seemed to hover in its roost. Borrowing an expression from the mountain men I had read about in *Give Your Heart to the Hawks*, I shouted, "Helloooo the campfire!" Nobody replied, so I approached the door and listened, then gently knocked. Nobody home. Turning around and shielding my eyes again, I retraced my steps back to the other branch of the boardwalk. I walked until I almost bumped into another treehouse.

This one had its door open. I saw the interior of a very well-constructed and well-furnished cabin in the sky. Plainly, no one was home.

Returning to the first treehouse, I opened the door. Like Goldilocks, I went in and saw three palettes on the floor, and I tried each one for comfort. They all smelled good, but they were all too firm. *This must be where the women sleep*. I smoothed the covers when I was through. The twelve by twelve room was bare absent the palettes; no Three Bears trio of chairs, no bowls of porridge to sample.

Stepping outside, I was in a quandary. With dark less than four hours away, I could possibly make it back home, but would I have the energy? If I left, would I be missing an opportunity? *What if the occupants arrive and don't want me here?* I decided to wait. If no one arrived, I had shelter for the night, and I could leave at first light. If someone did arrive, so much the better; or, so I thought.

Descending to the creek, I stripped and lay in a shallow eddy. Parched, I drank some water. Back at the compound, I sat cross legged in a patch of sunlight at the end of the boardwalk, to dry off. An hour's meditation passed the time until someone arrived.

HELLO, ANGELINA!

Angelina was five feet ten with wavy chestnut hair past her shoulders. Like many of the canyon women, she wore the simplest shift that draped loosely over her shapely figure. Without makeup or adornment of any kind, she was nice looking in a wholesome way, late teens or early twenties.

Some initial suspicion on her part gave way to casual banter. Here's what I found out about Angelina and the treehouse harem. Lewis built the two tree houses and the boardwalk. Jim's old girlfriend, Cher, knew Lewis because she and Lewis's daughter grew up together in the Bay Area. When Lewis built the first tree house, Cher went with Lewis's daughter to visit him, then Cher and Lewis became an item. Angelina had been living with Butte Creek Family but they wanted to start charging her rent to stay on the property. At some point she ran into Cher during a sweat ceremony with Butte Creek Family, and Cher invited Angelina to join her in the tree house.

Angelina said, "For a while, Cher and I were living with Lewis in his tree house. Lewis invited me to make love with him, and Cher didn't mind. For a while we tried three, but that didn't work so well, so Lewis built the second tree house, and now we take turns."

While we were talking, another young woman showed up. I

can't remember her name; let's call her Anne. She breezed right past me and Angelina, ignoring us. "That's my friend, Anne. We've been friends since we were children. She came to visit a few months ago, and stayed. Even though she's my friend, I didn't want her to stay because I didn't want to share Lewis with her. I don't even like sharing Lewis with Cher, but it's his place. When Anne first came to visit, Lewis said she could stay, and I have to go along with that if I want to be with Lewis, but Anne has a new boyfriend in town. That's where she just came from, so mostly it's Cher and me with Lewis."

Since Angelina was so free with information, I thought I'd return the favor. I told her I had heard a rumor about some guy up in the canyon who had a harem, living in a tree house.

Angelina interrupted, "We're not a harem. We're three women who love Lewis." What she said suddenly reminded me of something I'd heard earlier in the day on the Butte Creek Family property: "We're not a commune. We're a community."

"Well," I said, making my lame move, "Lewis must be quite a guy…." (I refrained from calling him a stud) "...and I'm quite a guy too. That's why so many women have enjoyed making love with me. I'm athletic and sensuous and considerate and I take my time. Like I said, I heard about this place, and I thought I'd come up to the canyon on a vision quest. I'm fasting from food this weekend, and I've been on a sex fast for a month, for spiritual reasons, but this morning…"

Now I really started bullshitting. "…I fell asleep in a cave by the swimming hole at Swinging Bridge, and Hawk came to me in a dream, saying, 'follow me up the canyon, and you will find what you are looking for.' Hawk told me I would find a roost among the trees, and make love with one or more beautiful women, so that's why I'm here. Do you think you would like to help me fulfill my vision quest, Angelina?"

Her reply was, "Well, I'm waiting for Lewis to show up here tonight, and if Cher's not here, I'm hoping to be with him, but maybe....If it's not my turn tonight, we'll see." Here was a woman who liked to keep her options open.

I tried to close the sale. "Lewis can't accommodate both of you at the same time, and I'm here now. Like the song says, 'Love the one you're with.' How about it?"

"Let's see if Cher shows up."

"Well, cool then. If you're with Lewis, I'll see what Cher's up to." I omitted any reference to Cher's former relationship with my best friend and roommate.

Of course, I knew this was a long shot, but sometimes it pays to advertise. At least it was a better possibility than the disappearing commune, or the frustrated tryst with Susan, or bushwhacking my way back down the trail and riding my bike twenty miles home.

DISCLAIMER: DON'T BLAME ME

Testosterone can make a guy do strange things. Walk around in a daze. Run panting around the block. Prison sex. Political coups. Wear a sport coat. Walk up to a woman in a bar, throw down a book of matches on her table, and say, "Got a light?" Acts of desperate inanity. Parts of what happened that Saturday night in the tree house, and the following morning, are just too embarrassing to admit, and shall be disclaimed. Film directors and parents of young children, keep the camera angles above our main character's waist. The author forgives himself for once having been young and hormonally driven.

SLEEPING WITH TWO WOMEN

I slept with two women that night: Angelina and Anne.

More accurately, they slept on their palettes while I lay there, wishful and agitated, on Cher's. Making matters worse, around eleven p.m., Lewis and Cher arrived—I recognized Cher's voice—and they clomped along the boardwalk to Lewis's tree house; it wasn't long before the lovemaking noises began and lasted well into the night.

Once it got quiet in Lewis's annex, sleep still evaded me, so I lay there thinking, *Might as well use the largest sex organ known to humankind: my brain!*

First I went through the Thesaurus of Shame and Blame, calling myself all sorts of names: shallow, callow, juvenile, arrogant, presumptuous, puerile and so on. Then I translated the words into Spanish, and gave myself another working over. I started on French, but didn't do so well because my vocabulary is limited.

I'm not sure if anyone else does this, but when I'm being self-critical, I often refer to myself as "you". For example, on the night in question, I lay there asking myself, *How can you be so arrogant as to assume that you could just waltz up the canyon expecting any woman you meet to jump your bones? What have these past three years been about, anyway? Haven't you had plenty of sex already? Haven't you learned to go with the flow? Have these years been about spiritual growth, or merely a protracted, illusory excursion into promiscuity? Sexual pleasure is just like money. No matter how much you have, it doesn't make you any happier. It's transitory. I thought you knew that!*

After a while, I got tired of beating myself up, and switched gears. Trying to see the big picture as Hawk had taught me to do, the self-critical voice gave way to revelations.

As I lay there reviewing the past, it made a lot of sense that my virginal years of high school and my college years of horribly frustrating petting sessions had built up a strong desire in me.

No wonder I wanted to make up for lost time! Given the license to roam, I did so, but I wasn't really very good at promiscuity because it wasn't all it was cracked up to be. It was like a sugar high when I really needed protein. I was just trying to be loved, but I've been trying to play it both ways—be promiscuous and monogamous. No wonder I'm confused. Maybe I'm just undergoing a temporary regression. Could it be I just don't know how to act around women unless seduction is involved? Has free love taught me about letting go or made me into a sex addict?

And what about the spiritual lessons of the Mariposa years? Recalling my narrow escape from death, I reminded myself what I had learned:

1) Hope for the best, and let go of the outcome.

2) Maintain an attitude of gratitude.

3) If the moment sucks, change the moment.

So I lay there choosing to improve the moment by using my intelligence while ignoring the horrible throbbing somewhere below my waist.

What other spiritual lessons have I learned? How about Kerouac, Ginsberg, Snyder, and that crew? What did I learn by reading their work? What sort of bodhisattva am I?

I lay there thinking about Buddha's Four Noble Truths as I understood them:

1) Life contains suffering.

2) We cause suffering when we do not understand our own true nature.

3) We experience suffering when we do not understand the true nature of the world.

4) When we do understand the true nature of ourselves and the world, we get into the flow, and experience happiness beyond description, a kind of bliss called Nirvana.

In regard to the first and second Noble Truths, it occurred to me that all my angst was bullshit. *The Mariposa years have been about separating the wheat from the chaff, and watching the chaff blow away on the breeze. Psychology can take us only so far. The real goal is bliss. Thank the gods that I've had this time to grow and mature.*

In regard to the third Noble Truth, lying there next to Angelina, I asked, *What is the nature of the world with regard to womankind? Look around at the animal kingdom. The female always selects the male, not the other way around. Angelina hasn't chosen me, so I should just relax.*

The Sex Monster in me still hoped Angelina would wake up ravenous and devour me, but the part of me that understood the Noble Truths let go of the outcome. Starting to relax, I reminisced about all the beautiful young women who had chosen me for their pleasure, and I began to feel extremely grateful for the women I'd known, especially Em and Janie, and womankind in general. Sexual thoughts subsided, replaced by joy. But Sex Monster's niggling voice chimed in: If woman is the decider, why not give Angelina the chance to decide on me?

Around four a.m, I scooted over next to Angelina and stroked the lovely contours of her body. After a few minutes, she clasped my hand, rolled on her side with her back to me, and held my hand snugly against her waist, letting me know she was more interested in sleep than sex. Good enough. I nuzzled my face into the nape of her neck, but I avoided spooning tightly. Instead,

I smelled her hair, enjoying its fluffiness, and felt her feminine energy flowing into me. Accepting defeat, my emotions oozed into happy contentment upon contact with the lovely Angelina, and tension flowed out of my body. I just wanted contact; I wanted to be loved. After a time, feeling both blissful and exhausted, I drifted off to sleep.

I dreamed about upsetting a hornet's nest while plucking forbidden fruit in the Garden of Eden.

At some point in my dreams, I could hear my mother's voice as if speaking right in my ear: *Why do you always go for these sex goddesses? Didn't you know sex can lead you down the garden path?*

MORNING HAS BROKEN

It seems the revelations of the wee hours were for naught.

When I woke up at the break of dawn, Angelina and Anne were not in the room. Outside, they weren't in plain sight, either. Back inside, I got some real rest for an hour or two.

When I got up, I found Cher sitting cross-legged on a small level spot atop the steep decline that gave way to the creek, a hundred feet below. She must have been facing southwest because the morning sun met her face directly. Judging by the angle, I figured the time to be about 7:00 a.m.

Cher didn't seem in a mood to talk. Meditating, I guessed. Two can play that game. Cher had the best, most level spot. I tried to make do with a place on the slope twenty feet to her right, but it was too steep and chafed my bum. After trying two or three more places, and still feeling agitated from the events of the past twenty-four hours, I couldn't sit still.

Why not get up and stretch? Why not impress Cher with my magnificent body? Maybe she'll get excited and have me for breakfast. Off came the gym shorts as I positioned myself directly in front of her, about ten to fifteen feet down the bank. The terrain was difficult and awkward, but I started stretching.

Cher tucked her shift between her legs.

Stretching became karate moves. Karate moves became dancing. Fertility dancing, I hoped. Dancing became frenzied gyrations with hip thrusts. If strutting was good enough for a peacock, it was good enough for me. This must have looked especially absurd as my manhood arose to greet the sunrise and salute Cher. Even though I knew I was acting the fool, desperate imagining had Cher inviting me to get it on with her right there, in the dirt, on her little ledge in the morning sun. Periodically, Cher opened her eyes. I thought, *to admire my form.*

CHANNELING ELVIS

With my mating dance in full swing, I entertained a fantasy. I was channeling Elvis (who was still alive) and doing him proud. In my ever-active imagination, I saw myself on stage as a naked, gyrating Elvis, with a crowd of screaming female groupies going wild and reaching for me. In the back of the crowd, like still, silent witnesses, I saw Pretty Arms Sue and Helen and Susan from the canyon and all the other women who'd given me their favors in the three years since graduating from college. Among them, in the far left corner, stood Janie, looking angry. In the far right corner, shaking her head, and mouthing the words, "Poor, pathetic man," stood a primly clothed Betsy. Front and center in the crowd sat Cher, with her eyes closed. She was naked, save pink underwear, but upon flickering her eyes open she calmly removed her undies and threw them on stage; then pointing at me she mouthed, "You and me, after the show, big boy."

Meanwhile, the sober, sensible part of me was thinking, *this is ridiculous!*

UNEXPECTED RESULTS

The real Cher was not impressed. After my stage act had been going on for a few minutes, her eyes popped open suddenly, and her jaw thrust forward. With the intensity of a hissing panther, she commanded me, "RELAX!"

I couldn't take it anymore. First the month of celibacy, trying to break free from Janie. Then the ill-conceived notion that I'd come up to the canyon to get laid by some stranger. Then the tortured, hot dream in the hidey-hole by the creek. Then the almost-coitus with Susan, the scary incident with Cliff, and the restless night in the treehouse next to Angelina while Lewis and Cher tripped the light fantastic, and now Cher wanted me to "RELAX!"

I got the point. I walked up the slope past Cher, and went behind an oak tree.

IT WAS TIME FOR MY morning bath, so I went to the creek to get cleaned up and calm down.

Wading in, I lay in a shallow eddy, soaking up the morning goodness of earth, air, water and stone. Picturing my Elvis act, I had a good laugh at my own expense.

Gazing at the clear blue sky, I looked for my Ally, noble Hawk, but only buzzards wheeled in thermals above the canyon rim. Feeling stupid and ashamed of my behavior, I said an ecumenical prayer to all gods and all saints: "Forgive me for being a randy young fool. Guide me on the path of moderation. Help me gain control of my aberrant impulses."

Then I apologized to Hawk for falsely invoking his name in

my "sales pitch" to Angelina. Then I thought, *what a story this will make someday when I retire and write a book,* whereupon I chuckled, and fell asleep right there in the eddy beneath the hot morning sun.

Having made up for sleep missed the night before, and with a head less clouded by testosterone poisoning, I thought clearly, *You've got to make something good of this walkabout yet. Maybe Susan....No, forget about that. You have no control over that outcome. Tomorrow morning at 8:00 a.m., you're on stage, taking over the classroom for your first time, and you haven't even begun to prepare. What are you going to do?*

Regrouping, I devised a plan for the day that would incorporate enjoyment of the surroundings, preparation for teaching, and maybe even a tryst with Susan. The latter would require at least four hours for my body to return to performance level before engaging with her, so the plan incorporated the required time as well.

1) Finish bathing.
2) Meditate, and dry off in the sun.
3) Get dressed.
4) Skip breakfast (there isn't any).
5) Very important: Find Cher, and apologize.
6) Meet Lewis and talk. See what he thinks about sharing his harem.
7) Make one last run at Angelina. If no go, be a gentleman and thank her.
8) Say goodbye, and find China Wall to research my science unit for student teaching.
9) Try to find Susan. Hope for the best, but let go of the outcome.
10) Go home and get ready for tomorrow's starting bell.

A VISIT WITH LEWIS

Back at the tree house, Anne was gone and Cher was nowhere to be found. I heard voices, so I knocked on Lewis's door. "Come in," said Lewis. Opening the door, I saw Angelina and Lewis lying on his bed. Angelina got up immediately and left. Lewis was wiry, about 145 pounds, with dark salt and pepper hair and facial stubble. "Come in, come in," he said. It's ironic that the best interaction I had all weekend was with Lewis, without the overlay of sex.

Here's what I learned about Lewis and his mysterious tree houses. The reason the boardwalk and tree houses were so well constructed was that Lewis was an engineer. He had been a married man working for twenty years in San Jose when his marriage went on the fritz. The difficulties brought him to the brink of a nervous breakdown. He had some savings, enough for two or three years, and he figured out that, if he made little or no money, his alimony payments would be a lot less, so he took the option. The tree house was a solution to his housing and mental health issues. This way, he didn't have to pay rent as well as a mortgage, he could reside in nature, and he could be near his daughter at Chico State. His daughter brought her childhood friend, Cher, to visit and the rest was history. The whole setup didn't seem so magical after all.

At some point, I asked Lewis if he'd like to share "his" women with me.

"Up to them," was his reply, and the end of the issue.

BIDDING FAREWELL TO THE TREEHOUSE HAREM

I thanked Lewis for his kindness and went to the annex to find Angelina. After some formal chitchat, I said Lewis was a very nice man, but I couldn't resist asking, "What do you see in Lewis? Isn't he a little old for you, like your father's age?"

She replied, "I could have a boyfriend my own age, but I'd rather be with Lewis. I really like making love with him. I like talking with him. He listens and has interesting things to say. He's wise. He invites me in and we talk, then after awhile, we start massaging each other, and…." She paused. "….Oh, it's soooo good!"

"Angelina," I said, "thank you for explaining that to me. You know, I'm a good listener, and I give a good massage, too, and if you were with me, you wouldn't have to share."

"That's different," she said.

"Okay, I hear you. Well, Angelina, it's about time for me to go now. Thank you for your hospitality and…." I hesitated. "….for sleeping with me last night."

"Í didn't sleep with you!"

"Sorry, I don't mean in a sexual way. I hope I'm not sorry for saying this, but were you aware that I moved next to you, about four a.m., and we were snuggling the rest of the night?"

A shadow of resentment crossed her face. "I thought you were Lewis," she said.

"I'm sorry you were disappointed," I said. "And thank you again for sharing your tree house and *sleeping* with me. You're a lovely young woman, and I enjoyed soaking up your feminine energy and nuzzling your fluffy hair."

"You're not Lewis!" she said angrily.

I suppressed an urge to ask her, "What happened between you and your father that you're trying to work out with Lewis?" Instead, I felt sorry for her. Suddenly, at twenty-six, I felt so much older and wiser than her nineteen years. I said, "Thank you for your hospitality. You're a lovely young woman."

Just then, sunlight broke through the treetop and bathed my face. Angelina stood in shadow. Making a stage exit, I walked backward on the boardwalk, waving goodbye to Angelina, and singing some Bob Dylan lines:

Farewell, Angelina,
The sky is on fire,
And I must go.

Turning upcanyon, I headed toward China Wall. I never got to apologize to Cher. I never saw any of the treehouse harem or Lewis again.

REVELATIONS AT CHINA WALL

The canyon sides got narrower and steeper, but a bench trail made fair passage. Where the trail dropped down near the creek, I could hear the sound of cascading water. I scrambled my way to the edge of a jade green swimming hole twenty-five yards in circumference. On the other side, a volcanic cliff twenty-five feet high, rising out of the creek, revealed the source of the cascading sound as a fairly small amount of water dropping into the pool. The sound was lovely, mysterious, and soothing.

I sat on the bank and chided myself once more for acting the fool, but forgave myself, chuckled at my Elvis impersonation, and soon turned to inquiries about the future.

What about Betsy versus Janie? Just as I wasn't sure I was ready to leave Janie and Mariposa behind, so was I unsure if I was ready to be monogamous without the occasional side trip. *Maybe*, I thought, *some day I'll be wise and mature and sex won't matter so much, but for now, it's only natural that lust has its home in me.*

Reflecting upon the second Noble Truth, I just knew things weren't going to work with my prim and proper friend Betsy, but just as I'd cut my hair and changed clothing styles and traded my beloved Step Van for a station wagon, I was trying to act on the "as if" principle: Act as if you're settled and straight and responsible and maybe you will get used to it. Act as if you're in love with Betsy and maybe things will work out. But my heart wasn't into it.

Enough introspection already. Tomorrow comes too soon; better get to work on that geology unit.

RESEARCH AT CHINA WALL

The cliff face had been dubbed China Wall by the few locals who knew it as a remote swimming hole. The Wall, or cliff face, was composed of the same kind of volcanic basalt that formed Gene's cave, where I'd spent a Thanksgiving two years before. On the ceiling, he had incised, "Teach me." Looking at the Wall for the first time, I pleaded out loud, "Teach me."

A couple of hours there made me no more a geologist than I'd ever been, but a revelation occurred to me: It's not about the rock, it's about developing one's power of observation. The Jim Beattie Doctrine of Unlearning: That's what I want to teach! Use your senses, children. Look, and tell me what you see. *Teach me.* With that in mind, I spent the time there swimming under the cascade, and listening to the story the rock told me about how it became, and how it got where it was, and why it looked the way it did.

TO SUSAN OR NOT TO SUSAN?

It's strange how one can know something yet not actualize it. In my case, I knew my behavior was addictive, but, like a true addict, I was unwilling to give up the objects of my sex/love addiction. Therefore, as soon as I finished my swim, and geological observations, at China Wall, the two of me— the smart, sensible me, and the hormonally driven addict—went back down the trail, having an argument: to look up Susan or not, and for what reason?

Both of us won—the part of me that wanted a friend to talk to about the strangely disappointing weekend, and the self-absorbed "horndog".

On the way back down the canyon, I breezed right past Lewis's boardwalk, followed the cairns I'd set the day before, and found my bicycle; back past the porcupine and fox clearing and the scene of my visit with the tipsy gun toter, Cliff; downhill I sailed like Hawk toward the swinging bridge. Locking the bike again, I followed the directions Susan had given me to a lean-to shelter next to a burned-down cabin, arriving as the sun angled toward two o'clock.

FINDING SUSAN

I found Susan, the only woman among several guys, at her lean-to on a knob half a mile above the Helltown Bridge. This time she seemed to remember who I was, if only from the day before. I begged for privacy, and we went back downhill to an unoccupied cabin near the swinging bridge. I told her the whole story about my disappointment at the disappearing commune; about my frustrating dream at the swimming hole and how strange and lonely I felt when she didn't seem to recognize me. She offered no explanation and I didn't press for one. Then I told her all about the scary encounter with Cliff and the frustrating time at the treehouse, and my revelations at China Wall; and I thanked her for listening and being a sweetheart and a good friend, as ever.

Then it was the sex monster's turn. "After all I've told you about, I'm not sure I have any sex to give you, but if you want, we can try."

Her reply was, "Sometimes you can get too much sex just like you can have too much food or drink. You might want it and enjoy it but it's not necessarily good for you. I've had a visitor inside recently. That's enough for me."

I don't know how we got from there to getting it on atop the dusty old cot in the cabin, but we did. Maybe it was pity or the line of least resistance for her, because she seemed blasé and, to tell the truth, I was just going through the motions. But when someone banged on the door, I wasn't ready to quit yet.

She said, "I'll bet that's Bruce," the jealous, jilted guy she had talked about the day before at the swimming hole.

She started to get up. "Wait," I whispered, and we lay quiet, pretending we weren't there until he pounded on the door again, yelling, "Susan, I know you're in there!"

"Carry on without me," I said. "I'll be right back."

I jumped off the cot, crossed the room, slid the bolt and flung the door open. A portion of my anatomy made it pretty obvious what we'd been doing. Pissed off, I said, "Can't you see we're busy, *asshole*?"

Susan wasn't helping. "Oh, hell, let him in," she said.

"No *fucking* way!" I shouted. (Even as pissed as I was, I enjoyed the double entendre.)

Undeterred, Bruce was like a bloodhound after the scent. Nothing I said seemed to faze him, until I got in his face and threatened to kick his ass; then he left.

Once again the mood was broken, but Susan let me finish. It was such a waste and so sad. I felt like just one more obnoxious dude in Susan's lean-to. Just then it occurred to me I was getting some of my own medicine, the kind I had taken with me to the treehouse harem. I was no better than the horny asshole Bruce who banged on the door.

I felt I'd disrespected Susan and myself. I'd aimed for the lowest common denominator and got what I asked for. The sweetness we'd known a few years earlier was buried beneath the burden of my obsession. Like the hippie movement, the spontaneity of Free Love lay in Gothic ruin.

"Oh well," I thought ruefully as I left Susan and wheeled down Butte Creek Canyon. "At least I got the consolation prize."

37

In The Classroom

"Education is not the filling of a pail,
but the lighting of a fire."
W.B. Yeats

Something good came from my walkabout in Butte Creek Canyon after all, but it wasn't sex.

I got home around six p.m. Sitting on the edge of the bed, I tried to get philosophical about what I'd learned from my strange excursion, but panic hit me when I realized I had no activities planned for the following morning at school. Given that the next two weeks were going to be my first time in complete charge of a classroom, my performance was going to make or break my career. This was the point at which, however reluctantly, like a magi slouching toward Bethlehem, I came to accept the responsibilities of teaching. Incrementally, at least, I was putting 2307 Mariposa Avenue behind me. The future would take care of itself, but what was I going to do Monday morning?

I went to bed with scant idea what I was going to do in the classroom, but five points I wrote down gave me hope:

1) I probably have a lot more prior knowledge of geology than most nine or ten year olds.
2) Students probably have more prior knowledge of geology than they realize. Draw on their prior knowledge as well as my own.

3) Find out what they want to know, and go from there.

4) Write down their questions, and help them look up the answers.

5) If need be, I can bullshit my way through.

STUDENT TEACHER

On Monday morning I get up, shower, shave, and brush my hair two hundred strokes. *Dress like you mean it*, I tell myself. Like a mild-mannered Clark Kent, I step into the closet and come out Super Teacher, wearing shirt and tie, slacks and sport coat, and shiny shoes.

After roll call, the Master Teacher hands the class over to me, and I begin telling the story of my weekend, omitting any references to sexual matters or guns, but emphasizing my exploration in nature. I tell them, "I went on a journey of discovery in Butte Creek Canyon. Now I want you to go on one with me, to learn about the formation of our planet."

Every day for two weeks, I start the day by telling the class a story. Bit by bit I unroll the scroll of my walkabout in the canyon. The students get to hear of my visit with Porcupine and Fox. My description of the treehouse and the people living there fascinates them. You can hear a pin drop. Conveniently, I mention that the man and the women were living in separate dwellings in the treetops, and I emphasized how well made the structures were, and how storybook and magical was the boardwalk which led me into the bright heart of the tree. The thought of unusual dwellings leads me to a sidebar synopsis of *The Boxcar Children*, and a comparison of that children's adventure to my living in a caboose of a house at 2307 Mariposa Avenue for the past two years. Later, we check *The Boxcar Children* out of the school library and I read enough of it aloud to tease the children's interest. The book makes the rounds among the children for the next several weeks.

Relating my love of gardening leads to sprouting lima beans between moist paper towels, hardly a geology lesson, but a simple science lesson nonetheless, and the students get to hear how the garden saved my life.

My encounter with Cliff becomes a fascinating conversation with an old man who comes out from under the swinging bridge like a troll, and tries to tempt me into drinking his magic potion that he makes himself. I tell the students, "The magic potion is something called mead which people hundreds of years ago in Ireland used to drink when they worshiped trees. I told the troll no thanks, I can worship a tree without getting drunk."

The homebrew-making leads to an account of "the time in junior high school when my science teacher harnessed my desire to make my own wine by allowing me to ferment grape juice with yeast. When we distilled it in front of the class, the teacher allowed me to try a drop, but it came out undrinkable because it was about 200 proof, burning all the way down. Do not try this at home without your parents' permission." At this point, one boy raises his hand and tells us that his father makes his own beer in the garage at home—one of hundreds of such delightful interjections I'm treated to in my career.

Another day I tell them about hiking the John Muir trail from one end to the other and back, a distance of hundreds of miles, when I was thirteen years old, and how that experience in the mountains cemented forever my love of nature and being in the outdoors, and taught me to use my senses to sharpen my powers of observation.

Talk of mountains segues to geology, the subject I'm supposed to be teaching, and takes me back to more details of my walkabout. My visit to Butte Creek Family highlights my observations of composite rock in the eroded bank across from the sandy beach. I ask the children to imagine a pile of all sorts of different kinds of rocks mooshed together with mud layers and sand, placed under the tremendous pressure of subduction, which cooks the mud and sand into a kind of Krazy Glue that holds the many rocks together. The result is later exposed by erosion. To teach about volcanic rock, I talk about finding arrowheads in the desert when I was a kid on family vacations, with a sidebar on how arrowheads are made. One day we make "volcanoes" of newspaper strips and laundry starch. When the hollow mounds dry, we load them with baking soda. Pouring vinegar over the baking soda, we watch the resulting acid "erupt".

Talk of volcanoes and obsidian leads to an account of my visit to China Wall. A description of China Wall caps the sequence when I roll back Time to the beginning of our planet, including a balanced view of Evolution versus Creationism: "Was the earth made in seven days or did it evolve?" We learn about the continents and how the jigsaw pieces of Africa and South America at one time were one vast continent called Pangaea. Vividly, I describe erupting volcanoes and how they oozed and cooled to create Mount Shasta, Mount Lassen, and the bedrock of Big Chico and Butte Creek canyons, and the volcanic rock of China Wall with its cooling cascade that I swam in.

Each day after my story, the class gets to ask questions. I answer the ones I know, and challenge the students to find their own answers in the library. We check out dozens of books and students work together, finding answers and writing new questions. Long before the buzzwords, "Cooperative Learning," come about, I have the students working in teams to do research and write down the most interesting facts they find. Each day they share their results. At the end of two weeks, they have a written report and illustrations that they present to the class.

On the final day of the two-week unit, I share my revelation, that it's important to use your senses and ask questions. "Sometimes the answers don't come for years. You carry the questions around with you and, one day, pop goes the weasel, there's the answer, and it makes life interesting. Or you might have a question that leads to a new invention or a better mousetrap. It's more important to want to learn, and to teach yourself how to learn, than it is to know everything. You'll never know everything because once you find the answer to one question, another arises. That's the beauty of learning. It's a lifelong experience. Teaching yourself how to learn; that's what matters most."

The unit was a great success. Maybe I would succeed as a teacher after all. My Master Teacher's evaluation, which I still have decades later, says, "Mr. Whitcomb has real talent in preparing new units of study. He shows great promise." It seemed too easy. I thought I was bullshitting the whole time.

It seemed I was on my way. Little did I know how rocky the road would become. I would succeed in some measures, and fail in others. Living in the dreamtime of 2307 Mariposa Avenue hadn't prepared me for the pressures and realities of full-time elementary school teaching. Despite my native talents, a journey into madness would derail my long sought career. But that's another memoir altogether, the one I call *Later Days*.

One thing certain: I'm a better teacher than seducer of women.

38

Approaching Perfection

After my first-ever two weeks taking over the classroom, I needed a break. My sojourn to the tree house harem had been a failure as spiritual walkabouts go, heavily laden as it was with ambiguity and sexual frustration. This weekend I would do one better: a walkabout in the Upper Park by myself. Soon my student teaching would end. Along with it, my Mariposa days would end as well.

Scrambling up steep switchbacks, I climbed the short trail from the flats to the north rim of the park. Once on the plateau at the canyon's edge, a trace of tire tracks led through stunted oaks and dry grass along the canyon's serrated edge. After a mile or so, I needed to rest in the shade, but I decided not to pick just any tree. It had to be a tree that spoke to me. Emptying my mind of all thought, I scanned the scattered trees for a sign. Clearly, I heard a male voice whisper my name, and my eyes fastened on one tree among many. It was saying, "Come; sit here; rest awhile."

I hugged that tree for several minutes. Something about the tree reminded me of the goodness and strength of my brother Tim. A profound sense of gratitude reached into my bones that we had been reunited these last few years; we had come to know each other; and, he and our father were at least talking to each other again.

I sat down in a shaft of shade. Leaning against the trunk, I opened my senses to the surroundings: The feel of rough bark through my tank top; the rustling of leaves and ticking of branches; the smell of bay leaves and river water wafting up from the canyon. Soon I was overtaken by a meditative trance where I stayed long enough for the sun to progress from straight overhead to halfway down the sky. The shaft of shade swept like a sundial, but I remained where I was, sometimes superheated like a happy reptile, sometimes shaded as bits of shadow from nearby trees swept over me. All cares, all desires vacated my body. Time stood still. Past, present and future melded into a single sense of timelessness. All that marked the passage of time was my deep, slow breathing and my heartbeat, which seemed to have slowed to about twenty beats per minute. I was an empty mirror, a happy Buddha under the bodhi tree.

The temperature must have topped one hundred degrees, but heat and thirst were of no concern.

After what must have been a few hours, I arose and thanked the tree, naming it Brother Tree. I followed my feet to the canyon rim. Cicadas buzzed. Upcanyon, I watched buzzards wheeling on thermals above the opposite rim. Surely, I could walk on air.

Just as I had imagined leaping off the hundred-foot pole nearly two years before, on the day I called Mrs. Whitlow and found 2307 Mariposa, now without a thought, I stepped off the edge of the cliff and dropped six feet, where I landed lightly on my right heel on a grassy slope eroded from the canyon rim. My heel made a divot, and I remained there in the crane position, scanning the canyon. Then I began to walk down-slope. My feet of their own accord skirted obstacles and found the right contours to lead me safely to another cliff above a draw, a thirty-foot drop. There my feet chose to follow the left edge of the draw until they found their way to the bottom and began climbing the draw.

A cool breath seemed to exhale from a cave at the base of the cliff where I had stood moments before. Drawing closer to the mouth of the cave, I could hear and smell water. My feet found the seep that led from the cave, and soon I was standing ankle deep in cool water amid a patch of miner's lettuce bearing a spray of small white blossoms. Squatting on my heels, I picked some miner's lettuce and placed its coolness on my tongue. For dessert, I savored a sprig of mint.

Standing up, I asked the cave if it would allow me to enter. It breathed a cool, "Yes," and I climbed over exposed basalt into the cave's cool womb.

"Lie here," it said, and my body conformed to its curves on a ledge above a pool.

Surely the Yahi who occupied this place before the white man must have known this spring. My earlier sense of timelessness shifted. I was taken from a place where time didn't exist and re-inserted into a time before Columbus's arrival. I didn't have to imagine it. I was there.

Drifting in this visit to the past, I remained in the cave's coolness for some time, shedding body heat like a reptile. Stirring from my rock ledge, I eased into the waist-deep spring and submerged neck deep. After my meditation in the baking heat of the north rim, the sensation of cool water was delicious. Taking some deep breaths, I lowered myself to the bottom and my hair floated on the surface.

I drank deeply of the fresh water; emerged for another breath and floated face down like a rag doll. With my ears under the surface, water trickling into the pool sounded like an echo of itself.

I thought of Jesus and Saint John. *This is what baptism is all about. I am Jesus and I am John. I find my God in nature.*

Just short of shivering, I crawled out of the spring like the first creature to ever emerge from the sea. I felt like a new person. I felt reborn.

I left the cave, and each slow step had me walking a little more erect, like a stop-action film of First Man taking centuries to learn to walk upright.

Again my feet led me out of the draw and down the side of the canyon until reaching the dirt road. Stepping onto the road seemed to bring me back to time-bound awareness. I walked along the road till it became asphalt and I found my bike. I unlocked it from a tree and rode home to 2307 Mariposa Avenue.

As I rode, I tried to imagine what a future in the teaching profession might be. What bearing, if any, would my walkabout, my visit to the Brother Tree, and my spiritual renewal in a spring-fed cave have to do with my prospective teaching profession? I could sense a big disconnect, and that worried me. Had my time on Mariposa been a complete waste, an irresponsible dawdle in La La Land?

Then, putting aside these thoughts, I recalled the glorious events of the day. I had found a Brother Tree where I could return in the future to calm my spirit. My spirit was refreshed in the spring of living water. I found a sense of peace that surpasses all understanding. My soul was washed clean. Surely, the ability to remain calm in the midst of a storm would stand me in good stead in the stressful times to come.

Then I remembered what Jim said on the day of Fried Green Tomato Blues: "I don't know what we're doing, but we're getting ready for something!"

As uncertain as I was of the future, I knew one thing: I had done right, living on Mariposa. At the time, it was the only thing to do, to keep my sanity. Mariposa was a place of *anamnesis*, a place to overcome spiritual amnesia.

Riding along on my bike, I thought, *whatever the future holds, whether I succeed or fail at my chosen profession is too scary to think about right now. I only have this day, this moment, in which to live. Meanwhile, I know I will always have my Brother Tree to return to. I will always return to water for spiritual renewal.*

39

Last Concert in San Francisco

In early June, about a week after I played a tune for a lizard on my leg, and after Calhoun got bitten a hundred times by red ants, word went all over town about a Leon Russell concert in San Francisco. Jim and Steve and his girlfriend Roxanne and Janie and I hopped into Jim's white '65 Dodge van and blasted down to San Francisco. I couldn't help but visualize the thousands of others like us who were also hopping into vans and caravaning to the concert even as we drove down Old Highway 99. On the way down, I was especially happy that Calhoun wasn't with us.

Remembering other concerts I'd attended at Fillmore West and Winterland, and recalling the day I'd met Janis Joplin in the summer of '68, I was looking forward to an evening of freestyle dancing in strobe lights amid a crowd of stoners moving together as one throbbing mass of flesh, but I wondered out loud if something would be different because of what happened at the Stones' Altamont concert in December of '69 when an eighteen year old was stabbed to death by Hells Angel Alan Passaro. This was fresh in my mind because Passaro's trial was due to start soon. I thought it was odd that a Leon Russell concert was going to take place at Civic Auditorium, a sit-down venue.

Sure enough, when the concert began and people started jumping out of their seats to dance in the aisles, a troop of big buff black dudes in white jumpsuits began aggressively stuffing everyone back down into their seats.

Lit "doobies" were summarily confiscated and ground into the floor. There would be no Altamont here.

Despite not dancing, it felt awfully good to be sitting there soaking up Leon's wall of sound and holding hands with Janie without the corrosive presence of that snake-in-the-grass, Calhoun; but, upon exiting the concert, who should we run into but the infamous Calhoun himself. The erstwhile Janet, of "Three Days in a Loft" fame, was in tow, apparently having re-entered Calhoun's life.

In lieu of driving home that night, we decided everyone would go to Roxanne's parents' house in the East Bay and crash. (Her parents were out of town.) Needless to say, I wasn't too happy about Janie and Calhoun being in proximity, even though Calhoun was with Janet. Sure enough, as everyone was settling down and I was cozying up to Janie, I could tell by sounds from the living room that Calhoun was trying to get it on with Janet, but she wasn't in the mood. He got mad and called her a bitch and I heard thumping as if he was hitting her. Cussing, she went to another room to sleep. Like a big dummy, I quipped to Janie, "Gee, Calhoun's all alone. Maybe you and he should get together," at which point I instantly thought better of what I'd said, as Janie bolted out of bed and started toward the living room.

It was then and there I decided to split up with Janie for good. No more ambivalent bullshit; well, almost none. We were through, but not that night. I would break up with her later, at a time and place of my choosing; not this way, not on Calhoun's and her terms; not tonight. I wasn't about to give her the perfect excuse to move to the other room. The thought of listening to her and Calhoun get it on in the first few hours of grieving the end of a relationship was not the way I wanted to spend the rest of the night. First we had some business to attend to.

I jumped up and physically put her back in bed. I declared my undying love for her and we got it on, but it was bittersweet and reminded me too much of another night, the night Em and I split up four years earlier. Though it seemed I had come a long way in that time, suddenly it felt like I was back where I started, alone in the world.

Calhoun must have been stirred up, because he was still awake in the living room and singing B.B. King, probably for Janet's benefit:

"The thrill is gone,
Oh yeah, baby, the thrill is gone."

Meanwhile I went to sleep holding Janie's hand while one of Leon's songs ran through my mind:

"I'm up on the tightrope,
One side's hate and the other's hope...."

All in one night, we had reached a nadir: the death of psychedelic, free-for-all dancing at concerts, and the death of a relationship.

40

Love and....What Did You Say?

With my credential under my belt and a need to plan for moving into new digs, I went to a phone booth for privacy, took a deep breath, and tried to call my father.

Millie answered. I was blown away by her cheerfulness. Words I'd never heard from her came out in unfamiliar happy tones. "How are you? And what have you been doing? I'm so happy to hear from you!" she exclaimed. "You finished your student teaching? Oh, wonderful. You are magnificent!"

Was this behavior an answer to my prayers?

I was guarded at first, but she was gushing with affection. Like a fool, I thought the door to a healing dialogue with her had opened. I bared my soul to her, telling her I'd been trying to shake off the demons of the past. For each revelation I made, she had positive words in response.

I felt so encouraged; I even told her why I had called, to ask for financial help with my upcoming relocation.

"No problem!" she exclaimed. "I'll buy you a whole houseful of furniture! Anything you want! You deserve it."

Her friendliness was hard to believe, but I wanted very much to do so. In fact, I became so emboldened that I opened up to her even more. I shared how living with friends on Mariposa had surrounded me with the love and affection I'd always missed while living in Lafayette.

"Oh, no," she interrupted, "your father and I had so much love for you kids!"

"What do you mean? You and Dad were affectionate to each other, and to your little girls, but not to me."

"Oh, no, your father and I had such love and *a-fuck-tion* for you kids!"

I began to realize she was drunk, and my confessional had been for naught. I was more pissed off than amused, but I picked up her lead and ran with it.

"A-*fuck*-tion, indeed. That's really what it was all about with you two, wasn't it? Isn't that how you reeled my father in, with a-*fuck*-tion?"

"Oh, yessh, un-blee-bubble!" she rhapsodized.

This conversation was going nowhere. Why not amuse myself with some word play of my own?

"Oh yes, oh yes, Millie…" I panted as if I were approaching orgasm. "Oh yes, your love and affucktion were un-be-lee-*vulva*!"

"Oh, yessh…." she continued to gush.

I was fed up with this bullshit. "Millie, let's see if you remember this conversation later."

She was still talking to herself when I hung up.

On the way home, two opposing sentiments pulled at me. One was to ridicule her—to rush home and repeat the conversation to anyone who would listen, in hopes of amusing them. The other sentiment was pity. I felt sorry for her in much the same way as I did a decade before, the day she made her Nuts and Kooks speech and I found out she had been jealous of my mother since high school because my father had thrown Millie over for my future mother; but, this time things were different. I was no longer her victim, and I viewed our so-called conversation with a sense of detachment. I was my own person now, and in that knowledge I sensed release and freedom. I could see that Millie was insecure and a bully, same as ever, but now I added to that: She's a drunk.

Her love and affection were unbelievable indeed.

In the short time it took to get home, the urge to repeat the conversation died. Feeling sorry for her was my best revenge. I felt sorry for my father as well, but there was no revenge in that, only sadness, and a question: Why does he put up with her shit? Amusement had turned to somber reflection.

I decided not to retell the conversation to friends at the house. It wasn't interesting or amusing. It was, after all, pathetic and sad.

41

In My Father's Garden

On my way to Betsy's in late June, I stopped at the Lafayette house. I had traded my Step Van for a beat-up station wagon, got a haircut, shaved clean, and broke up with Janie. I was wearing polyester slacks, a dress shirt and tie, a sport coat, and the shiny new loafers my brother had bought me.

As usual, I found Millie sitting in the den, smoking and watching golf. She didn't recognize me at first. Dressed as I was, she took me for one of Dad's business associates, but after I reminded her who I was, she said automatically, "Your father's not here."

"Where is he?"

"He'll be along any minute."

Just then I saw some movement on the hillside. I thought I saw my father out there, but I couldn't tell what he was doing.

To Millie I said, "I think I saw a deer outside. Have the deer been eating your daisies?"

"No." She took a slow drag on her cig. "Then what's moving out there?"

"Well, if you must know, it's your father, but wait. He doesn't want to be bothered."

Quickly I bolted from the room, out the back door, around the back corner of the house and up the hillside.

There on a relatively level spot I saw my father, hoe in hand, bent to his work. My father was tending a vegetable garden, something he hadn't done since he was a youngster. (In retrospect it occurs to me that Millie didn't want me to see what my father was doing. She must have thought gardening was a seditious activity that put him in league with hippies.)

I stood a body length apart from him. "I see you're getting back to your roots, Papa."

He said nothing and kept hoeing weeds. My father had a way of concentrating with intensity; he could shut everything out.

I let well enough alone and watched. "Go, Pop!" I thought, and remembered his long hair and scruffy beard two Christmases before; and, the most recent Christmas when he organized everyone to take a ride to Baskin Robbins in my hippie Step Van. I flashed back to Santa Monica where I was born, and our ranchette in Van Nuys; back to my grandmother's cooking and her stories of milking the cows at three a.m. on snowy Wisconsin mornings; back to three towheaded boys running and sliding across Grandma's linoleum floor to the cookie cabinet where her freshly baked tollhouse and sugar cookies awaited; and even farther back to our farming ancestors in ancient Bavaria; back to First Man, the first planted seed, and the seeds of my father that made Jon and Tim and me.

I continued watching my father hoeing weeds, and my thoughts slid forward to more recent times at 2307 Mariposa Avenue; to the many communal meals made with fresh produce from my garden; to a memory of homemade vanilla ice cream hand-cranked and plopped on top of fresh peaches on a hot summer day; to the first day of spring a year earlier when I arose in the peachy glow of dawn and saw the first seeds sprout and I knew I would live again.

And here was my father hoeing weeds to make room for new life. I thought my stepmother must be looking out the window saying, "Tsk, tsk, your father's gone nutty— first the hair and beard; now, the garden!" But here was something she could neither stop nor ever change: who my father and mother were, and where my brothers and I came from.

Careful not to soil my new clothing, I squatted down next to my father and clasped a handful of soil. Rubbing my hands together, I broke the clods down to powder just as I had done so many times in my garden on Mariposa Avenue. I kept working for a full minute till my father noticed I was there.

He stopped only briefly. "Oh," he said. "You're here." And without further words he went on hoeing.

42
Closing Thoughts

"If my life weren't funny,
it would just be true.
And that's unacceptable!"
Carrie Fisher in her
one-woman show,
"Wishful Drinking"

I sometimes ask myself what those times on Mariposa Avenue were all about. Indeed, the question has arisen many times during the three years I spent writing this book. From time to time a clear thought leaped out wholly formed, seeming pithy and profound: a quotation from a famous author, some verses from a poem or popular song, words that awoke me from a dream and had me leaping out of bed in the middle of the night to write on a note card. Yes, that's it! The meaning of it all in one cogent statement! The Pulitzer Prize of pontification!

Perhaps the meaning of it all is this: it all means nothing. When I think of it that way, it's wonderfully absurd and even hilarious.

If there's any meaning in life, it's this: the meaning of life is to live it. And live it I did, in glorious fullness, on Mariposa Avenue. I do know this: the Mariposa time was necessary for my survival and my sanity. I took the time when I needed it. The Mariposa days were the best of times and the worst of times, and I have no regrets, only stories to tell.

I visited the property at 2307 Mariposa Avenue many times in the two decades following my departure, before the place burned down. Sometimes I went alone, sometimes accompanied by Jim or Barney; other times, with the wife or girlfriend *du jour*. On occasion, I visited the then-current occupants, and related the history of the old place in tales that seemed to get better with each telling. On two of those visits, I met beautiful young women who became friends and loves—the place still hadn't lost its sexual energy.

In the summer of 1990 I found the place abandoned, boarded up. The front porch awning had collapsed. The back door swung open to my touch, but I was afraid to go in. Later in the day I went back with Jim, and we used a handsaw to cut a section of the fascia from the front porch where, twenty years before, we had tacked the store-bought digits 2-3-0-7. (I stashed the board in the trunk of my Lincoln, and it hangs over the workbench in my garage today, to remind me to be resilient and creative.)

Then we went inside. It was pitch black and our eyes took time to adjust. Even then we walked very carefully. We found the old Wedgwood still in place, but the orange and green refrigerators were gone. Not a stick of furniture was left. In my old bedroom we found a chest-high pile of wet, moldy carpet. Barely discernible on the walls in the dark was graffiti: hate messages and swastikas. The scene was one of Gothic ruin. Fearing respiratory disease, we got out of there fast.

Our old neighbor across the street told us that the last residents had been members of a band, probably punk. At least they were musicians. They got that part right. Later that year, Jim and I had a reunion with Barney during the holidays. On New Year's Day, 1991, I suggested we visit the old place. Barney was too busy with his family to come with us, and Jim said to me, "You don't want to go there." He knew something I didn't, but he wasn't going to tell me what it was. He agreed to go with me, but he warned me, "You're not going to like what you see." Then he temporized, "Well, maybe you'll like it. I don't know. You'll have to experience it for yourself." I thought nothing of this, having seen the place in ruins already. That was the day we found the house had gone missing.

A year or two after Jim and I discovered the old place burned to the ground, I took an old friend, Auril, to see the vacant lot. On a wet and gloomy day, I positioned her between the two redwood trees that guarded the front of the house that was no more. The trees rather nicely framed the shot. That's all I was thinking about at the time, but when I got the pictures from the developer, behind Auril I could see the land narrow to the vanishing point. "Vanished, into infinity!" I thought. Then I noticed how nicely the redwood trees created the impression of a portal, and a sudden flash of insight occurred. Excitedly I called Auril and described the picture: "The Portals to Narnia!" I exclaimed. "No one will ever know—much less believe—what went on behind those doors, except for those who lived there. And what if it all never happened? What if it all was just a figment of our imagination? What if it all took place inside the glove compartment of a Volkswagen bus? We were all children then—young adults, really, but still children. Maybe I made the whole thing up!"

Even with the house gone, I couldn't help but feel that for me the place would forever be haunted by the ghost of a young spiritual warrior struggling to heal his wounds, finding order amid chaos, and sanctuary among friends in a humble little shack on the edge of town.

No matter what, I'll always have Mariposa.

Acknowledgments

Gratitude and thanks go to my cheerful and talented editor, Marnie Sperry, who kept me motivated and on task; to my partner, Wendy, who listened to my stories on long walks and gave me honest feedback every step of the way; to Cheri Miller, who near the beginning of this project asked the poignant question, "How did you get to be the person you are today?"; to Bud Miller and Jim Lohr and my other buddies, who listened to bits and pieces over long lunches after surf sessions; Meade Fischer for constructive criticism of the opening chapters; Suzanne Freeborn of Pacific Coast Church, whose article on anamnesis helped me identify my overarching theme; and to Susan Sutherland for final proofreading.

Made in the USA
San Bernardino, CA
08 March 2020